The Hals

The Power of Animals

An Ethnography

Brian Morris

Oxford • New York

First published in 1998 by
Berg
Editorial offices:
150 Cowley Road, Oxford, OX4 1JJ, UK
838 Broadway, Third Floor, New York, NY 10003-4812, USA

Berg is the imprint of Oxford International Publishers Ltd.

Library of Congress Cataloging-in-Publication Data

A catalogue record for this book is available from the Library of Congress

British Library Cataloguing-in-Publication Date

A catalogue record for this book is available from the British Library

ISBN 1 85973 220 8 (Cloth)
1 85973 225 9

Typeset by JS Typesetting, Wellingborough, Northants.
Printed in the United Kingdom by Biddles Ltd, Guildford and King's Lynn.

**To the Memory of
a Friend,
Andreé Lefevre (1945–1997)**

Contents

Preface ix

Introduction 1

1   Matrilineal Kinship and Subsistence Agriculture   17

2   Hunting Traditions   61

3   Folk Classifications   120

4   Attitudes to Nature   168

Glossary   235

Appendix: Some Common Malawian Proverbs   237

Bibliography   242

Index   261

Preface

I first came to Malawi in February 1958, sitting with my rucksack on the back of a pick-up truck as it passed through the Fort Manning (Mchinji) customs post. I had spent the previous four months hitch-hiking around south and central Africa, mostly sleeping rough. During that time I encountered no other hitch-hiker and very few tarred roads, and the only place I met tourists was at the Victoria Falls. I was, however, so attracted to Malawi and its people that I decided to give up my nomadic existence. I was fortunate to find a job working as a tea planter for Blantyre and East Africa Ltd., an old company founded by Hynde and Stark around the turn of the century. I spent over seven years as a tea planter working in the Thyolo (Zoa) and Mulanje (Limbuli) districts, spending much of my spare time engaged in natural history pursuits, my primary interests being small mammals (especially mice) and epiphytic orchids. The first article I ever published was based on my spare-time activities in Zoa, where I spent many hours with local people digging up mice. It was entitled 'Denizen of the Evergreen Forest' (1962), and recorded the ecology and behaviour of the rather rare pouched mouse (*Beamys hindei*).

Since those days I have regularly returned to Malawi to undertake ethnobiological studies. I thus have a lifelong interest in the country and its history, the culture of its people and its fauna and flora. Some of my most memorable life experiences have been in Malawi, and many of my closest and cherished friendships have been with Malawians or with 'expatriates' who have spent their lives in the country. Altogether, I have spent over ten years of my life in Malawi, and apart from Chitipa and Karonga, I have visited and spent time in every part of the country, having climbed or explored almost every hill or mountain – usually with a Malawian as a companion, and looking for birds, mammals, medicines, epiphytic orchids or fungi, whichever was my current interest.

The present study is specifically based on ethnozoological researches undertaken in 1990-1991, which were supported with a grant from the Nuffield Foundation. For this support I am grateful.

With respect to this present study, I should also like to thank many friends and colleagues who have given me valuable data, encouragement, support and hospitality over the past thirty years, in particular, Derrick

Preface

Arnall, Father Claude Boucher, Wyson Bowa, Carl Bruessow and Gillian Knox, Shaya Busman, Salimu Chinyangala, Janet and Les Doran, Jafali Dzomba, Efe Ncherawata, Cornell Dudley, the late Cynthia and Eric Emtage, Peter and Suzie Forster, Jillian Hugo, Revd Peter and Vera Garland, the late Paul Kotokwa, Frank and Iona Kippax, John and Anne Killick, Heronimo Luke, Useni Lifa, Kitty Kunamano and her daughters, John Kajalwiche and his sister Evenesi Muluwa, Catherine Mandelumbe, the late Ganda Makalani, Late Malemia and her family, Bob and Claire Medland, Davison Potani, Kings Phiri, Lackson Ndalama, Hassam Patel and his family, Pritam Rattan, Pat Royle, Lady Margaret Roseveare, Brian and Anne Sherry, Chenita Suleman and her family, Patrick and Poppit Rogers, Francis and Annabel Shaxson, Chijonjazi 'Muzimu' Shumbe, Lance Tickell, Catherine and Stephen Temple, the late Samson Waiti, George and Helen Welsh, Brian and June Walker, John and Fumiyo Wilson, and the late Jessie Williamson.

I should also like to thank those who generously gave me institutional support: the Centre for Social Research, University of Malawi (Wycliffe Chilowa); the National Archives of Malawi (Frances Kachala); Matthew Matemba and many members of the Department of National Parks and Wildlife; and M.G. Kumwenda and George Sembereka of the National Museums of Malawi.

Finally, I should like to thank my family and colleagues at Goldsmiths College for their continuing support, and particularly Pat Caplan, who helped me to structure my English, and Irene Goes, who typed my manuscript.

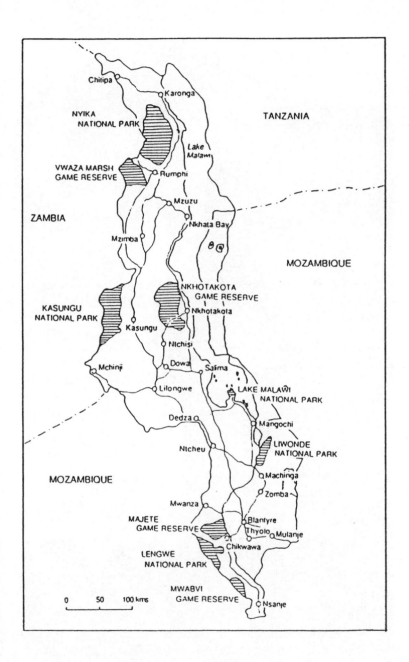

Map of Malawi's Wildlife Reserves

Introduction

This book is about Malawi culture and the relationship of Malawian people to the animal world, with a specific focus on mammals. The core of the study hinges around a dialectic between subsistence agriculture, focussed around a group of matrilineally-related women – and in the context of which mammals are seen as opposed to human well-being – and hunting, which is centred around men, or more precisely, around men as affinal males. Thus, while women are closely identified with agriculture, the matrilineal kin group and the village community, men are identified with the woodland and wild mammals, hunting and masculinity being intrinsically linked. The organizing principle of the study, then, focusses on hunting and agriculture (matriliny) as two complementary domains that have historically constituted Malawian social life.

Over the past two decades, within the context of an emerging ecological crisis, anthropologists, philosophers and historians have become increasingly concerned with exploring the relationship of humans to the natural world. We have thus seen a plethora, indeed a deluge, of books on ecological thought, on people's conceptions of nature or landscape, on animal rights and on green political issues. This interest is comparatively recent. When in 1980 I gave a talk on 'Changing Conceptions of Nature' to the Wildlife Society of Malawi, the number of books then available that dealt specifically with people's conceptions of nature (and wildlife) could almost be counted on the fingers of one hand (but see Collingwood 1945, Glacken 1967, Nash 1967, Barbour 1973, Worster 1985). As far as most philosophers, anthropologists and historians were concerned, nature was simply an existential background that could safely be ignored, and mammals hardly existed apart from the role they played in rituals and symbolism (in relation to Africa see the pioneering studies of Willis 1974 and Douglas 1975). Since then the 'environment', 'ecology', 'nature', 'landscape', 'hunting' and 'animals' have all become major research topics among academics, although some philosophers seem quite unaware that students of natural history and biologists (for instance, Charles Darwin) have for more than a century expressed a sustained interest in the natural world (cf. Merchant 1992, Soper 1995). But most of these recent texts describe cultures, even whole epochs, in rather monolithic terms, and a contrast is made, usually in the most stark and simplistic fashion, between such cultures or contexts, and Western culture – which, in turn, is also interpreted in monolithic fashion, Western thought being conflated with mechanistic science and Cartesian philosophy.

Contrasts have thus been made between the 'Promethean' (anthropocentric) and 'Sacramental' (ecological) visions of the world, between the 'Western' world view, which is said to entail an attitude of 'domination' towards nature, and almost every other religious or cultural tradition, which are eclectically lumped together by the deep ecologists as 'ecocentric' or 'organismic' (Merchant 1980, 1992, Devall and Sessions 1985, W. Fox 1990). Among anthropologists we have the radical contrast between Western 'dualism' and the attitude of 'domination' towards the world, and the 'benign' attitude of hunter-gatherers, who perceive nature only in terms of 'trust' or 'giving' or as 'sacramental'. Hunter-gathers' perception of the natural world has even been described in terms of a single metaphor, which is interpretative reductionism taken to extreme (Bird-David 1990, Ingold 1991a, 1996). It is also of interest that these various explorations of 'ecological thought' – seen as almost a pan-human phenomena – tend to completely ignore African people who are not hunter-gatherers (cf. Spretnak 1991, Marshall 1992, Holm 1994).

Such stark dichotomies, and the tendency to conceive of cultural traditions, including those of 'Western' philosophy and culture, in the most monolithic fashion, although having an element of truth, are nevertheless highly misleading. For they hide the fact that religious traditions are theocentric rather than ecocentric and tend to assume that in Europe little has changed since the seventeenth century. Such texts ignore the fundamental re-orientation of thought that was initiated in the nineteenth century by Hegel and Darwin, by the rise of the biological sciences and by the development of historical understanding, anthropology and the social sciences more generally – quite apart from theoretical developments within physics itself. The writings of Jonas (1966) and Mayr (1982, 1988) present a much more balanced view of the history of Western thought than do many contemporary writers on ecology.

These stark dichotomies and monolithic interpretations also obscure the fact that all human societies have diverse, multifaceted, often contradictary attitudes towards the natural world, especially towards mammals (Benton 1993: 62–9).

In this study, then, I do not describe *the* Malawian perception of nature or animal life, certainly not in terms of a single metaphor, but rather outline some of the *diverse* and contrasting ways in which Malawians relate to mammals – how they perceive mammals as competitors in relation to their livelihood as subsistence cultivators, the complex attitudes they express in their hunting rituals, how they classify animals, the role that animals play in oral traditions, and the way they utilize mammals as food (meat) and medicine.

What, however, is of particular interest in recent writings on the 'animal estate' is a growing recognition that cultural attitudes towards animals contrast markedly between hunter-gatherers and agricultural societies. Having undertaken anthropological research in both social contexts, this contrast has been confirmed by my own studies.

The Hill Pandaram of South India are a foraging community, though they have long-established trading contacts with wider Indian society. They are entirely nomadic, living in small forest camps of never more than twenty people, and have no domestic animals apart from the dog. But importantly the Hill Pandaram do not make a stark contrast between themselves and the environment in which they live, being themselves a forest people. They are largely hunters of small game – bats, flying squirrels and tortoises – and as I described in my study of their socio-economic life (Morris 1982: 79), they do not hunt but rather gather animals from the forest, in the same way that they collect nuts and yams. An egalitarian ethos pervades their culture, and they do not make a stark contrast between themselves and the animal world. Like other hunter-gatherers they often keep pets, and I have recorded how one young woman breast-fed and cared very affectionately for a young chevrotain deer, only to put it in the pot later (Morris 1978: 15; cf. Serpell 1986: 156; Katcher and Beck 1991: 265–7). Like other hunter-gatherers, therefore, the Hill Pandaram attitude towards animals is both empathetic and pragmatic (cf. Guenther 1988).

The sharing and generally egalitarian attitude towards animals expressed by the Hill Pandaram is consonant with that described elsewhere among hunter-gatherers. Animals are seen essentially as social and spiritual equals, with thoughts and feelings analogous to those of humans. Keeping pets, as Serpell remarks (1986: 142), is popular among them, and the hunting of animals is hedged with ritual, the focus of ambivalent feelings. As James Frazer long ago maintained (1922: 679–98), an attitude of respect towards animal life was characteristic of many tribal people, and a hunter might expose himself to vengeance 'magic' on the part of the animal's spirit if he did not show proper ritual respect towards the slain animals. (For discussions of hunter-gather attitudes towards animals, see A.Tanner 1979, Morris 1981: 130–1, Nelson 1983, Campbell 1984: 81–122, Serpell 1986: 142–9 and Ingold 1986: 243–73.)

Such beliefs, however, implying an essential 'kinship' between humans and animals and an emotional involvement between the hunter and the animal, such that, as Serpell writes (1986: 144), the act of killing has the flavour of homicide, are not confined to hunter-gatherers. They have a resonance throughout the world and are widespread in Africa, where beliefs relating to the 'vengeance' power of the blood of a slain mammal, if the killing is not done without appropriate ritual respect, have been widely documented (Baumann 1950). Nevertheless, it has to be recognized that the advent of farming has had a profound effect on the way humans relate to the natural world, especially towards animal life. F.D.Goodman (1992: 19) speaks of the change in culture ushered in by the advent of horticulture as being a profound one, and the working of the soil as representing a 'fundamental break' with hunter-gatherer attitudes, though she has little to say on people's attitudes towards animal life *per se*. In his lucid study of human-animal relationships, Serpell (1986: 174–6) is equally explicit in contrasting hunter-gatherer attitudes towards animals – predominantly one of respect and egalitarianism – with those of farming communities. The neolithic revolution is seen as a 'journey of no return' and a 'fall from grace', for farmers have no choice but to set themselves up 'in opposition to nature' in keeping the fields clear of weeds, protecting themselves and their crops from wild animals and controlling and confining domestic livestock. The entire system, Serpell writes, 'depends on the subjugation of nature' and on the 'domination and manipulation of living creatures' (1986: 175; cf. also Kent 1989). Thus the 'ethic of domination' towards animal life does not begin, it seems, with the rise of mechanistic philosophy in the sixteenth and seventeenth century, but much earlier, with the advent of agriculture.

Thus two attitudes towards the natural world and specifically towards mammals may be discerned: one, the sacramental egalitarian, associated with hunter-gatherers, the other, implying an ethic of opposition and control (rather than domination), associated with agriculturists. What is of interest about the Malawian context being explored in this study is that these two contrasting attitudes do in fact co-exist. As agriculturists, protecting their crops and livestock from the depredations of wild mammals, Malawians are fundamentally in 'opposition' to animals. Yet in their hunting rituals, as described in Chapter Two, a profound identity and sympathy is expressed towards the hunted mammal. They form together a pervasive attitude towards mammals in Malawi which may be described as one of dialectical opposition. This 'unity in opposition' does, however, have gender implications. While men, as affines, are identified wild animals and the woodland, women are closely identified with the village environs and are seen as being in opposition to wildlife. The village in essence consists of a core of matrilineally related women, and agricultural production in Malawi is also closely identified with women. We thus have a complementary symbolic opposition between two contrasting domains that permeates much of Malawian social life.

Hunting	**Agriculture**
Men as affines (Semen)	Women and the matrilineal kin group (blood)
Woodland	Village
Phiri Clan	Banda Clan
Dry season	Wet season
Activating medicines (*Chizimba*)	Medicinal herbs *(Mitengo)*
Ancestral spirits}	Living people
Mammals}	

These contrasting themes, and the dialectic it embodies, are explored throughout the study and in a companion volume which explores the role of animals in Malawian religious culture and rituals.

It must be recognized, of course, that mammals have been a central fact of existence for Malawian people over the centuries and that people and animals have always lived in close proximity, sharing the same life-world and thus being closely involved and interrelated. In terms of the deep ecologists, Malawians have neither expressed a Promethean attitude towards mammals, nor are mammals seen as part of a pristine nature, completely divorced from humans. Rather, between humans and wild animals there has always been, historically, a close interrelationship. For Malawians, as subsistence agriculturists, wild mammals have always been a threat to their livelihood, their depredations a constant menace to human existence. On the other hand, mammals have been a source of meat, medicines and skins for clothing and receptacles, and they play a significant role in folk traditions, mythology, divination and ritual. Equally important has been the role of mammals in long-distance trade, for the rise of political chiefdoms from the seventeenth century onwards was intimately connected with the hunting of mammals and the ivory trade.

Besides exploring the diverse and contrasting attitudes towards nature, and more specifically towards mammals, that are expressed in Malawian culture, two other themes are explored in this study. The first is that Malawians, like Aristotle, view the natural world, including mammals, in terms of a realist ontology. Complementing their idealist beliefs about the deity (*mulungu*) and the spirits (*mizimu*) of the dead, Malawians thus also conceive the natural world as having intrinsic powers and agency. They may, therefore, be said to have a nature-based cosmology. This interpretation runs completely counter to much contemporary anthropology, which tends to put a focal emphasis on discourses or culture and, in the tradition of Plato, tends to oblate or downplay the intrinsic value, even the existence, of the natural world. But Malawians do not make a categorical distinction between the spiritual (unseen) and material aspects of life, and the natural world is viewed as consisting of real entities, with inherent powers and potentialities, not simply as pegs for symbolic forms or hierophanies of the spirit (though the spiritual and symbolic dimensions of the world are not without significance, as I explore in the companion volume on Malawi religious culture). I emphasize this realist ontology and perspective in my discussion of animal medicine in Chapter Four.

Secondly, and this is fully discussed in Chapter Three on folk classifications, Malawians express a consistent anthropocentric or pragmatic attitude towards the natural world, but this, it is important to stress, does not imply an ethic of domination.

This present study is focussed on the matrilineal people of Malawi, who form the majority of the population and belong to four ethnic communities, namely the Maravi cluster (Chewa-Chipeta-Nyanja-Mang'anja), Yao, Lomwe and Tumbuka. I provide a brief account of these four ethnic communities below, but two points may first be made about ethnicity in East Central Africa, as is evident from the historiography. One is the existence, from the very earliest period for which we have historical records, of distinct ethnic communities in the region. Early Portuguese travellers write of such people as the Chewa, Nsenga, Lolo, Mang'anja and Makua. These ethnic communities were clearly distinct from the political structures or chiefdoms that were collectively described as Maravi – Lundu, Kalonga and Undi – and they were evidently associated with particularly localities. Indeed, their names usually referred to landscape features such as Chipeta (a place with high grass), Nyanja (of the lake), Mbo (of the termite hills), Mang'anja (associated with iron-smelting), Nsenga (of the sand country, i.e. the Luangwa Valley), Makua (Likuwa, valley or grassland) and Kokhola (woodland). Alternatively, the specific community derived its name from its hill of origin, such as Yao or Lomwe (Nguru), from *Nlomwe*, the black soil on Namuli hill (Rangeley Papers Society of Malawi Library,1/1/3, Young and Banda 1946: 10, Bandawe 1971).

The other important point is that although these ethnic communities spoke Bantu languages (or dialects) that were distinctive, though often mutually intelligible, they did in fact share a common cultural heritage. This has been commented upon by both Malawians and Europeans alike. Antonio Gamitto while describing the various ethnic communities of the North Zambezia region – Chewa (Cheva), Lolo (Bororo), Mang'anja (Maganja), Makua (Makwa), Nsenga (Senga) and Yao (or Nguru) – all of which he saw as belonging to the 'Maravi Race', nevertheless recognized their cultural affinities in terms of 'habits, customs, languages, etc.' (1960: 63). Cullen Young, Levi Mumba and, more recently, Edward Alpers all affirm that the people of East Central Africa share a common culture. Thus Cullen Young, discussing the religious culture of the Chewa, Nsenga, Mbo, Makua, Nyanja and Mang'anja, suggests that they are for practical purposes 'one people' and – though this is a contentious issue – sharers of a common name, Maravi (1950: 37). Alpers, in similar fashion, writes of the 'cultural unity' of all the three major peoples – Makua-Lomwe, Yao and Maravi – of East Central Africa (1975: 7), a sentiment that had earlier been expressed by Clyde Mitchell when he wrote that the 'tribes' of the Southern region – Yao, Nguru (Lomwe) and Nyanja – were culturally 'all very similar' (1956: 14).

In an important sense, then, the matrilineal people of Malawi share a common cultural heritage. The four ethnic communities with which my study is concerned are the following:

The Maravi Cluster

All members of the Maravi cluster claim to be descendants of groups of people who moved into the North Zambezia region in or around the fourteenth and fifteenth centuries. Coming from the Luba country, these people were under the authority of the Kalonga chief, according to Chewa oral traditions, and are intimately associated with the Kaphirintiwa Shrine. In Malawi four groups are generally recognized: the Chipeta in the highland regions south of Lilongwe and on the Kirk Range – those Chipeta taken by the Ngoni being described as Ntumba (Ntara 1973: 18); the Chewa, the largest group, who settled on the Kasungu – Lilongwe Plain and who, as an ethnic community, extend into Zambia, now numbering well over one million people; the Nyanja, who reside on the southern and south-western lakeshores and have long been noted as a fishing community; and the Mang'anja, who frequent the Shire Highlands and the Lower Shire Valley.

Historically, the Maravi peoples were agricultural people, combining shifting cultivation focussed around a group of matrilineally related women with hunting traditions important for men. Around the lakeshore, near Lake Chilwa, and in the Lower Shire Valley, fishing was important. Apart from some goats, sheep, pigs and chickens, the Maravi had few livestock, and there was no developed pastoral economy. From the earliest times there was a developed handicraft industry, focussed around the manufacture of salt, cloth and iron goods. When Livingstone journeyed through the Shire Highlands in 1859, he noted that the Mang'anja (and Chewa) were 'industrious' people, that almost every village had its smelting house and blacksmiths, and that the weaving of cotton was widespread (1887: 79–82). Despite the developed cash economy, the basis of the Maravi social system was and still is matrilineal kinship, and uxorilocal residence is still widely practiced in rural areas. It was among the Chewa and Mang'anja people that powerful kingdoms emerged around the seventeenth century, the most important being those of Kalonga, Undi and Lundu.

Towards the end of the nineteenth century, a number of immigrant ethnic communities moved into the Maravi country, Ngoni into the Dedza highlands, Yao into the South lakeshore and Shire Highlands, Lomwe into the Mulanje and Thyolo districts, and the patrilineal Sena from the Zambezi into the Nsanje district. In all these areas complex interethnic relationships developed, such that Malawi has been described as having 'no strong tribal organization' (Pike and Rimmingtom 1965: 124). In fact throughout Malawi, but especially in the south, the social context is essentially multiethnic.

At the present time the Maravi cluster – the Mang'anja, Chewa, Nyanja and Chipeta ethnic communities – constitute about 43 percent of Malawi's population – around 3.8 million people. The majority are peasant farmers or engaged in small-scale business or wage labour. (For studies of the history and culture of the Mang'anja and Chewa, see Chafulumira 1948, Rangeley 1948, Marwick 1963, Schoffeleers 1968, Ntara 1973, Mandala 1990.)

The Yao

The Yao came into Malawi at the end of the nineteenth century, although Mitchell (1956: 2) describes them as 'invaders' rather than immigrants. While hunting was important for the Maravi, their men seemed to have been more actively involved in the local subsistence economy than were Yao men, who had a wide reputation as itinerant hunters and traders. Like the Bisa, they were actively involved in the ivory and slave trades from the end of the eighteenth century. But agriculture was important for the Yao. Abdallah (1973), calls it their 'principal industry', sorghum and millet being the staple crops, and cassava and maize becoming established during the nineteenth century. As with the Maravi people, iron-working was important in the past. Like the Nyanja, with whom they intermarried, the Yao are a matrilineal people, and uxorilocal residence is still common in rural areas. Today the Yao are mainly peasant farmers, tobacco, maize and cotton being important cash crops in suitable areas, while many people are engaged in a variety of occupations, as petty traders, herbalists and mechanics, as well as in government and commercial employment. As the new president Bakili Muluzi is a Yao Muslim from Chiradzulu, it is probable that there will be a reaffirmation of Yao identity, with the publication of many texts in Yao – until recently marginalized as a language. There are about one million Yao in Malawi, representing about 11 percent of the population. (For studies of the history and culture of the Yao, see MacDonald 1882, Stannus 1922, Mitchell 1956, Rangeley 1963, Abdallah 1973, Alpers 1969, 1975, Thorold 1995.)

The Lomwe

Rangeley was of the opinion that the Yao were originally 'Ngulu' (Lomwe) people, who became separated from the parent group when they became successful traders and took their name from a local hill in northern Mozambique. This was not the opinion of the Yao historian Abdallah, who associated the Nguru with a hill south of Blantyre, possibly Mt. Mulanje, and he stressed the distinctiveness of the Yao (1973: 8). Nguru, in fact, is said to be a Yao term for a neighbouring people who could not speak fluent Yao, in the same way as Mpotola was a Nyanja term for Yao who could not speak Njanja correctly (-*potola*, to twist, make crooked). Throughout the colonial period, Nguru was the common name for the Lomwe people, but the Lomwe themselves resented this term because of its negative and derogatory connotations. In 1943 Lewis Bandawe formed the 'Lomwe Tribal Association' and petitioned the government to abolish the name Nguru. However, some Lomwe still identify themselves as Nguru. They are closely allied linguistically with the Lolo, who are settled around Quelimane, and the Makua of northern Mozambique. The Lomwe, as an ethnic group – this 'great tribe' as Bandawe described it – is itself divided into a number of dialects or 'sub-tribes', such as Thakwani, Kokhola, Mihavani and Meeto. As already noted, the term Lomwe itself refers to the black soil or *nlomwe* that abounds on the plateau of Namuli Mountain (2419m), which is considered the Lomwe homeland and lies some 130 km due east of Lake Chilwa (Bandawe 1971: 31).

Archaeological evidence suggests that there may have been Lomwe in the Mulanje district prior to the emergence of the Maravi chiefdoms (Robinson 1977: 42–3), but it was essentially from the middle of the nineteenth century that Lomwe groups began moving into the Shire Highlands and into the Upper Shire Valley. With the opening up of the European plantations in the Shire Highlands and the need for labour, many Lomwe moved into the region, encouraged to do so by the planters, who sent labour-recruiting officers into Mozambique. Showing a similar cultural heritage and clan system, the Lomwe either attached themselves to local Yao or Mang'anja chiefs or established their own village communities. Having large tracts of land available for settlement and needing the labour of the Lomwe immigrants, the planters, through the colonial government, established the *thangata* system, essentially a form of bonded labour (see Pachai 1978, Kandawire 1979). This exploitative system was the cause of much political unrest during the colonial period, and Lomwe people were the main supporters of the Chilembe rebellion in the Chiradzulu district in 1915, for many Lomwe had established themselves as small but successful tobacco farmers. One of the leaders of the rebellion, John Gray Kufa, came from Kongoni, at the mouth of the Zambezi, and may have been a Lomwe. Like Chilembwe himself, Kufa was a keen hunter (on the Chilembwe rising, see Shepperson and Price 1958, White 1984).

In the 1920s and 1930s, with the opening up of the tea estates, there was a further influx of Lomwe migrants into the Shire Highlands, especially into the main tea-growing areas of Thyolo and Mulanje. In these districts they now constitute the majority of the population, although they have intermarried extensively with the local Yao and Mang'anja. The Lomwe number perhaps about a million people in Malawi, representing around 12 percent of the population.

In terms of their kinship organization, general customs and religious beliefs, the Lomwe are very similar to the Yao and the Mang'anja. Although essentially subsistence agriculturists, in the past hunting seems to have played an even more fundamental role among the Lomwe than it did among the Yao, Chewa or Mang'anja. One writer suggests – with some exaggeration, although the remark is significant – that the Lomwe formerly subsisted 'almost entirely on hunting' (Whiteley) or the proceeds from it. They had established hunting fraternities associated with the hunting of buffalo and elephant. Bandawe notes that it was the 'custom' among the Lomwe that 'every male adult in every village should possess a gun' – usually an old 'tower' musket – in the nineteenth and early twentieth centuries. (Bandawe 1971: 33, Alpers 1975: 8–11; for other important studies of Lomwe, see Soka 1953, Boeder 1984, White 1987.)

The Tumbuka

Like the Maravi peoples and the Yao, the Tumbuka have myths of origin which suggest that they came into Malawi from the Luba country sometime in the eighteenth century. They came as a cluster of clans, with no centralized authority, and settled in the area between the Nyika plateau and the Dwangwa river. These communities, Cullen Young suggests, 'had not yet developed any organized tribal form' (1932: 27). Travellers like Rebmann and Livingstone made references to the Tumbuka in the middle of the nineteenth century, but it is a little unclear whether this was originally a clan name (as Pike 1965: 42 suggests), signified an ethnic community or was what Young describes as a 'locality name'. Nonetheless, in time the Tumbuka-Khamanga peoples came to be recognized as a linguistic and ethnic category that covered several related communities such as the Henga, Phoka, Hewe, Chimaliro, Munthali, Senga and Nyika. These terms refer either to the 'type of country' that the people inhabit, or to a geographical location (Young 1932: 28).

As Vail writes, the Tumbuka are situated between two distinct cultural zones. To the north are people like the Nyakyusa, Lambiya and Ngonde, for whom cattle is important and who have a patrilineal/virilocal kinship system. To the south are the matrilineal peoples we have described above, the Chewa, Mang'anja, Yao and Lomwe. Prior to the Ngoni invasion, the southern Tumbuka were a matrilineal people practising uxorilocal residence, and their cultural traditions were very similar to those of the Chewa and the other matrilineal peoples. In the pre-colonial period they were skilled iron-workers, and the writings of all the early missionaries suggest that hunting was an important occupation for Tumbuka men.

During the post-colonial period under President Hastings Banda, the Tumbuka, who number perhaps around 700,000 people (7.4 per cent of the population), were politically marginalized. When, in 1968, Chewa was imposed as the national language, Tumbuka, along with Yao and the other languages, ceased to be used in schools or even on local radio. All this caused much resentment among the Tumbuka, who had a strong presence in education and the civil service (Lwanda 1993: 191–6). (For important studies of the history and culture of the Tumbuka, see Cullen Young 1931, 1932, Vail 1979, Vail and White 1989, Forster 1989.)

To conclude this introduction, I will discuss my research methods and outline the content of the book.

Introduction

This book is essentially an ethnographic study and is primarily based on one year's anthropological fieldwork, undertaken in 1990–1. But it differs from other ethnographic texts in a number of ways.

The first is that the empirical data on which much of this text is based is essentially derived from *my own* fieldwork experiences in Malawi, that is, from my own active participation in social activities and rituals, from conversations in Chewa that I have had with numerous Malawians – mostly informally and in an outdoor setting – and from my own observations of Malawi social life. The latter was an *engaged*, not a detached form of activity, as many scholars falsely suppose in their rather belated critiques of moribund positivism. There is, then, in the study much more than simply a record of 'dialogical' encounters that I have had with my friends and informants (cf. Marcus 1995). Dialogical anthropology has much in common with Durkheimian sociology and post-modernism in divorcing humans from the natural world. With Malawians digging up mice, participating in initiation rites, collecting mushrooms or medicines or out searching for mammals in the woods, I have been engaged with my companions *and* the world, observing, not simply looking at, both.

Much of my understanding of Malawian social life, however, has been gained from discussions with informants who are close friends of mine, some of whom I have known for over two decades. I have particularly drawn on their knowledge as local hunters, herbalists or ritual participants. I have used such friends to enquire into specific aspects of Malawian cultural life. However, unlike, it seems, most anthropologists, I have not employed a full-time (or graduate) research assistant, still less a team of undergraduates, to go out equipped with tape-recorders, interview schedules and questionnaires to gather empirical data on my behalf. In fact, given the welter of literature now being published on 'research methods', I have to admit that I have never myself utilised any questionnaire or formal research schedule. I simply participated in those social activities relevant to my purposes or chatted (*ku-cheza*) with people, making enquiries about Malawian cultural life as these emerged spontaneously from the activities or from my encounters. Nor, I must also admit, have I gone around interviewing important local chiefs or famous spirit mediums or healers, nor – like many anthropologists – have I sponsored some ritual in order that I may freely record its details, although I could easily have done all of these things. I have been content with simply sharing their activities – from beer drinking to hunting – and chatting with ordinary Malawians and friends. All the data I gathered was jotted down as notes on bits of paper carried in my pocket and then written up in a journal, data which would make sense to nobody but myself. I thus have no typed field notes or interview schedules that I could bequeath to prosperity or deposit in some library – just personal journals, full of notes, maps and sketches, which all serve only as memory aids to my experiences.

Secondly, although I was based at Makwawa in the Domasi Valley, with a house bordering Mponda village, so that all my neighbours were local Malawians with whom I had close and intimate relations, this study is not rooted in a particular community, as is the custom with ethnographic texts. In fact I have travelled widely in Malawi and have lived and gathered empirical data in every region of the country. I have visited all the forest reserves (except Tuma) and all the wildlife sanctuaries, camping for several days in each. Apart from the Misuku Hills, I have climbed and explored – usually with a Malawian companion – almost every hill and mountain in Malawi. The focus of my study is therefore neither on a particular locality nor a specific ethnic community, but rather on Malawi as a whole as both a geographical and a social unit, the subject of my study being the matrilineal peoples of Malawi and their relationship to mammals.

Thirdly, as I am particularly concerned not only to describe and inter- pret Malawian cultural life but also to explicate it by situating it in a socio-historical context, I have incorporated into my study not only data derived from my own fieldwork experiences but also historical and ethnographic data from a wide range of sources – newspaper reports, archival material, school essays, unpublished articles, earlier ethnographic studies (the perceptive and pioneering writings of Cullen Young, Stannus, Rangeley, Ntara, Sanderson, Marwick, Mitchell and Schoffeleers have a presence throughout the text), as well as the historical and ethnographic studies of many Malawians, much of which is in the vernacular (in this regard I pay tribute to the writings of Soka, Gwengwe, Makumbi and Chafulamira). The notion that ethnography should 'break' with the 'trope' of history and social structure and be simply a kind of autobiography (Marcus 1995) seems to me to be both limiting and unnecessary, a reductive form of 'textualism'. To assume that ethnographic 'realism' implies a rejection of hermeneutics, an unmediated relationship between the text and the world, and is a kind of 'salvage' operation seems to me to caricature the valuable and insightful work of an earlier generation of realist ethnographers. Autobiographic writing – and the recording of life-histories – is an important and worthy genre within anthropology (see Okely and Callaway 1992), but there are no grounds for making it synonymous with ethnography, nor for the repudiation of realist texts. Although I admit that this study is a work of literature, and I trust it is readable, lucid and interesting, I do not myself conceive of it as a form of 'fiction', though this term is now indiscriminately bandied about by post-modernist anthropologists (Strathern 1990). By 'fiction', it seems, literary anthropologists simply intend the idea that ethnographic texts are human artefacts and do not convey absolute truths (Clifford and Marcus 1986: 5). As no anthropologist, as far as I am aware, has ever suggested that their writings are divinely inspired or convey 'absolute' truths, this suggestion seems to me somewhat banal, though frequently offered as a profound insight. Good ethnography would then be 'true fictions'!

I have, therefore, given my realist aspirations, declined to make this study into a post-modernist text. Of course, my personal proclivities and experiences, my anthropological background and the theory I espouse, all implicate what I observe and how I interpret Malawian culture. The social mediation of knowledge has long been recognized and acknowledged by philosophers of science, and this is as true for botany and physics as it is for anthropology. Thus I have been reluctant to make my study a record of my own fieldwork experiences, to enliven the text with personal vignettes and anecdotes about my friends and informants, or to make it semi-autobiographical; nor have I filled it with reports of 'dialogical' encounters, which would, I suppose, have had to have been transcribed from tape-recorded interviews – something which I rarely indulge in!

I trust that in this study, Malawian people are allowed some textual space where their 'voice' may be heard – after all, I see myself as a kind of 'medium' describing and interpreting Malawian culture for a wider audience. Yet I have not engaged in cultural poetics, nor explicitly attempted to give my Malawian friends, colleagues and informants a 'voice'. Such an explicit endeavour seems to me somewhat patronizing: Malawian people are quite able to speak for themselves, and Malawian scholars have done so in their ethnographic and historical writings, much of it in the vernacular.

But while in this study I have tried to avoid the fashionable temptations of textualism and autobiography, I have been equally reluctant to engage in what Hegel, in his *Phenomenology*, described as 'monochromatic formalism', that is the imposition of abstract ahistorical and somewhat abtruse concepts, such as 'modernity' (Giddens), power and knowledge (Foucault), zone (Bakhtin) or the other (Levinas) upon the empirical data. Equally, I have not followed the common trend of many social scientists in being obsessed with the creation of analytical jargon, transforming everyday ideas and concepts into abtruse conceptual abstractions and then using these abstractions to explicate the empirical data. Thus, you will not find me describing the Malawian love of roots as 'rhizomatic affect-ivity' and then employing, in erudite fashion, the latter concept to explain their love of roots! I have deliberately tried to refrain from such academic mystification. What I have tried to do instead in this study, throughout its many pages, is to combine phenomenological understanding and hermeneutics with empirical science, explicating Malawian social life, as it relates to mammals, in terms of the socio-historical context. In addition, I have situated my ethnographic reflections within some of the current theoretical debates in anthropology.

I thus intend my study to be a contribution to African ethnography in the realist tradition of such fine scholars as Junod, Fortes, Richards, Marwick, Berglund and Turner. The notion that such anthropology is 'racist', portraying African people as an 'inferior race' (Meena 1992), seems to me quite mistaken (see S.F. Moore 1994 for a useful, much more engaged and scholarly assessment of anthropology in Africa).

The study is in four chapters, each focussed around a particular domain of Malawian social life. Chapter 1 provides background material to the study, focussing on matrilineal kinship, gender and agriculture. It empha-sizes that the Malawian economy was historically based on an explicit gender division, subsistence agriculture being mainly in the hands of a group of matrilineally related women, the men (as affines) being actively engaged in hunting and trade, especially in the dry season.

Chapter 2 deals with hunting traditions in Malawi. After a preliminary discussion of hunting from a historical perspective, I outline the nature of trapping small mammals and hunting. Each section deals with hunting in its various aspects – as both an individual and a community activity, its ritual component and as a rite of transformation, and its relationship with masculinity and the politics of trade.

Chapter 3 deals with Malawian folk classifications, the basic cognitive categories that structure their understanding of the environment. I outline the crucial empirical and symbolic demarcation that Malawians make between the village domain, which is associated with subsistence agri-culture and the matrilineal group and therefore focussed around women, and the woodland, which is associated with hunting, men (as affines), mammals and the spirits of the dead. I then go on to discuss the recent debates surrounding ethnobiological classification and outline Malawian life-form categories and their classification of mammals.

In the final chapter, Chapter 4, I discuss explicitly the diverse attitudes to nature that Malawian people exhibit, especially as this relates to mammals. I then discuss the role that animals play in oral tradition and the pragmatic use of animals as food (meat) and medicine. Throughout the chapter I emphasize the realist and pragmatic outlook of Malawian people.

In conclusion, I note two things. The first is that although this is self-consciously an anthropological text, I have to admit that my outlook on the world is very much that of a natural historian. In my youth my 'hero' figures were all naturalists – W. H. Hudson, Frances Pitt, H. Mortimer Batten, Richard Jefferies and Ernest Thompson Seton. Even now the scholars I tend to admire all have 'naturalistic' leanings, combining history, philosophy and biology – Aristotle, Mayr, Dubos, Jonas and Bookchin. You will therefore find in this text echoes that may remind you of a rather old-fashioned natural history essay: here, I plead forgiveness.

Secondly, although this study is focussed on the matrilineal peoples of Malawi, I have used Chewa terms in the text for two reasons. First, this is the language I used in my conversations with Malawians, and secondly, Chewa (or Nyanja) has long been regarded as the national language, being spoken and understood throughout Malawi, although one may occasionally encounter an elderly Yao or Lomwe woman who speaks little Chewa. The principal Chewa terms used in the text are included in the glossary.

–1–

Matrilineal Kinship and Subsistence Agriculture

Introduction

In this chapter I present some background material to the study, outlining the importance of matrilineal kinship and the close association of the local kin group, largely focussed around women, with subsistence agriculture. In fact, social life in Malawi is largely structured around an explicit gender division, with women being the main agriculturists, the men, in rural areas at least, focussing their activities on fishing, hunting or trade, or in employment outside the village community.

The chapter is divided into four sections. In the first section, I outline the three main forms of kin group in Malawi, the matriclan (*pfuko*), the sororate group (*mbumba*), based on a group of matrilineally-related women which forms the core of many villages, and the family or household (*banja*). I emphasize that historically matrilineal kinship is typical of a situation where hoe agriculture, largely under the control of women, is combined with the importance of hunting and trade focussed around men and where there was an incipient development of state systems, in the form of chiefdoms, as in Malawi.

In the second section, I describe kinship categories in Malawi, specifically focusing on those of the Nyanja/Chewa, and outline patterns of marriage. I emphasize the importance of affinal ties between village communities and the fact that the in-marrying male affine is essentially seen as an outsider, uxorilocal residence being the norm.

In the third section, I discuss historically the impact of those social factors that have profoundly influenced matrilineal kinship in Malawi, namely, the slave trade and the intrusion of the patrilineal Ngoni in the nineteenth century, the influence of the Christian missionaries and the socio-economic changes that have accompanied the development of capitalism.

In the fourth section, I focus more specifically on gender and after a brief theoretical preamble – in which I question the cultural idealism of much contemporary post-modernist anthropology – I outline agricultural production in Malawi as this relates to subsistence, emphasizing that such production is still largely in the hands of women. I discuss specifically the notion that such agriculture is being 'feminized' and undermined by recent socio-political developments, as well as issues relating to gender equality.

Matriliny and Matrifocality

In his classic study of Chewa witchcraft, Marwick suggested that a 'fundamental social group among the Chewa is the matrilineage' (1965: 121). And in an important sense all the people of Central and Southern Malawi – Tonga, Mtumba, Chewa, Chipeta, Mang'anja, Nsenga, Yao, Lomwe – are by theory, tradition and custom matrilineal people, for matrilineal descent is an important organizing principle of their social life. Village communities are invariably focussed around a group of matrilineally related women under the guardianship of a senior relative, usually an elder brother (*mwini mbumba*), and residence is uxorilocal.

Over the past fifty years or so, Islam and Christian missionaries, government and development agencies, and such economic changes as cash crop production, have had a fundamental impact on Malawian kinship patterns, particularly by placing a crucial emphasis on the family household. Nevertheless, as Poewe has described among the Luapula of Zambia (1981), matrilineal ideology and practices still have a strong salience in the rural areas of Malawi.

Among the matrilineal peoples of Malawi, kinship organization essentially relates to three levels, consisting of the clan system (*pfuko*), the local matrilineage or sororate group (*mbumba*) and the family household (*banja*). I shall consider each of these kin groups in turn.

Pfuko (Clan System)

In pre-colonial times the many African countries living north of the Zambezi essentially constituted a clan-based society. Social identity focussed less on local politics – the various Maravi chiefdoms or states – or on ethnic categories than on clan membership.

In the early period, ethnicity was related primarily to language and to bioregional criteria and had little political or even cultural significance. The area was, as many early writers have hinted, characterized by an underlying cultural unity. Antonio Gamitto, who accompanied the 1831–32 expedition from Tete to Chief Kazembe, recorded in his narrative the names of the various people living north of the Zambezi (Chewa, Mang'anja, Makua, Bororo, Nsenga, Yao), but suggested that 'it is beyond dispute' that they belong essentially to the same Marave people in having the same habits, customs, and language (1960: 64). Linden's essay on Nyau societies in the Mua area, which specifically emphasizes 'Chewa' identity, nonetheless quoted a local headman named Njoro, who, when asked his tribal affiliation, identified himself not as a Chewa but as belonging to the Banda clan (1975: 36). Cullen Young (1950) emphasized the 'essential identity' of the various ethnic communities of Malawi, stressing their linguistic affinities and their common historical and cultural traditions. He noted the widespread occurrence of four basic clans, Phiri, Banda, Nkhoma and Mwale.

In Malawi the term *mtundu* is a general category meaning variety, kind or tribe and is akin to the concept of *gulu*, which means grouping, assembly or type. These terms are used to refer to different kinds of plants and animals. When people are asked what *mtundu* they belong to, they will often respond with an ethnic category such as Nyanja, Chipeta, Yao or Chewa. These terms have an essentially geographical connotation or refer to place of origin; they often have pejorative associations and tend to be used more by neighbouring people (Nurse 1978: 16). In the past, however, clan affiliation was of more social significance. Although many people still recognize clan membership and clan names serve as surnames, it is nowadays socially less important. The matrilineal people of Malawi inherit clan membership through the mother. The terms usually employed to describe clan affiliations are *pfuko* (pl. *mafuko*) or *mfunda* (Yao *lukosyo*); this clan name is distinguished from the praise-name (*chiwongo*), which is inherited patrilineally (Mwale 1948: 33–4, Nurse 1978: 25).

The matriclans play an important role in historical traditions, as well as in the politics of the various pre-colonial chiefdoms, for the inheritance of the chiefdomship was matrilineal, passing to the sister's son, and the various chiefdoms which emerged at specific historical periods – Kalonga, Undi, Lundu, Mwase Kasungu, Kaphwiti – were all linked by kinship ties. According to tradition, the Malawi peoples migrated from the Luba country and initially had no clan system. The first clan that became predominant and assumed political control of the country was the Phiri clan, to which the majority of the territorial chiefs belonged. The nominal mother/sister of the Phiri chief was known as Nyangu, who was married, like her brother/son, to a member of the Banda clan. Whereas the Phiri clan is associated with hills (*phiri* = hill or mountain), with fire and with being outsiders, the Banda clan is seen in oral tradition as the original inhabitants of the country. Associated with the country at the foot of the hill, their name is said to derive from the fact that they had to level the grass (*ku-wanda* 'to beat down grass'; Ntara 1973: 6, Hodgson 1933: 144). The Banda clan is closely associated with the land and is credited with rain-making powers (Marwick 1963: 378). The nominal mother/ sister of the Banda clan was known as Mangadzi. She was especially recognized in Central Malawi, where she had important rain-making powers as Makewana (the mother of the children), and her sister was the principal wife (*mwali*) of the territorial chief (*kalonga*). The Phiri and Banda matriclans were thus related to each other as cross cousins (*usu-wani*), and together they constituted an implicit moiety system that is intrinsic to Maravi culture and to contemporary Malawian kinship. Other important clans such as Mwale, Mbewe, Kwenda, Nkhoma, Dzimbiri, Chulu and many others, are seen as essentially derived from these two original clans (Ntara 1973, Nurse 1978). The moiety system by which the individual clans are linked intrinsically forms a part of a wider cos-mological system, a complementary system of polarities that permeates many aspects of Malawian cultural life.

Phiri	Banda
outsiders	autochthones
hunting	agriculture
fire	water
hill woodland	cultivated land

The terms *pfuko* and *mfunda* (*ku-funda*, to warm) are often used inter-changeably in the central regions, but Nurse suggests that whereas the latter term signifies a blood relationship, *pfuko* denotes actually clan membership, matriclans being dispersed over a wide area (1978: 25). The term *chiwongo*, a term of address or surname, is derived from the clan (*pfuko*) of a person's father. There has been some discussion as to the exact nature of the distinction between *pfuko* and *chiwongo* and as to whether it constitutes a double-descent system (Rita-Ferreira 1968; Nurse 1978; 25–9). But what is important in the Malawian context is the implicit moiety system of intermarrying kin groups and the close association, even identification, of alternate generations, one's FF being in fact of the same clan (*mfunda*) as oneself. Thus, as Nurse indicates, many of the men he questioned gave the same name for *chiwongo* as for *pfuko*, stating that the reason for this was *chisuwani* (cross cousinship) (ibid.: 29).

Clans in Malawi do not have any corporate functions, either eco-nomic or ritual, nor do they carry out communal tasks. In the past they were strictly exogamous units, and a person was not allowed to marry (*saloledwa kukwatira*) anyone of the same clan, since clan members were viewed as kin (*mbale wake*). Clan exogamy these days seems to be less strictly observed. As one woman said, *Masiku ano anthu amangokwatira mfunda uliwonse*, 'These days people may marry [someone] from any clan'. What was important about clan membership in the past was that it enabled people to establish substantive relationships, interpreted as kinship, with people in distant places. It thus facilitated the movement of populations: over a wide area, either clan names are the same or else the clan names of the different ethnic groups are identified or considered to have the same meaning (Soka 1953: 35–6).

Many clans have totemic associations, in the sense of being associated with specific mammalian species, after which they are named, and which entail dietary restrictions. I discuss these prohibitions below.

Generally speaking, a person's name (*dzina*) consists of three parts: a personal first name, a second name derived from the father's first name, and an address or surname, the *pfuko* of one's father or one's clan name. In terms of the moiety system, one's FF and MM are siblings and belong to one's own matriclan (*pfuko*). There is no evidence to suggest that the 'clan system' in Malawi had any political significance or that it constituted a 'lineage model' of political organization – which Adam Kuper has suggested is a 'myth' or 'phantom' that must be exorcized from anthropological theory (1982: 43–58). Kinship was important: but in the past it functioned mainly with respect to the ruling Phiri dynasty, and at the present time functions mainly at the local level with respect to the sororate group, to which we now turn.

Mbumba (Local matrilineage or sororate group)

Among rural people in Malawi the basic local unit, in terms of both residence and social organization, is the village community (*mudzi*). Mitchell described the village as the 'key concept in Yao thought' and as the fundamental unit in their social structure (1956: 2–3). The term *mudzi* refers both to the village as a physical entity, consisting of usually between fifteen and sixty huts (households), and as a human community, with a strong sense of social identity. In the past there were elaborate communal rituals which symbolized the unity of the village community; such rituals are now focussed mainly around initiation rites and commemorative ceremonies for the dead. The village headman (*mfumu*) is a key figure in the community, having both ritual and political authority: ideally he should, as a personality, be a male mother, striving to keep peace and harmony within the village setting. A woman, however, may also be a village headman, and Mitchell remarks that the *singwa* (the grass ring that women place on their heads when carrying water) symbolically represents the village headman in divination rites (*maula*) (1956: 113). The headman also represents the village community to external authorities. Large complex villages associated with the territorial chiefs, who have authority over a wide area, are called *mzinda*.

The nucleus of each village is made up of a group of matrilineally related women, a sibling group of married women and their daughters with their young children. When Lawson suggests (1949: 181) that the 'relationship of blood' formed the basis of village life, this is essentially true, for 'blood' is the substance which a person inherits from his or her mother, although kin links are usually expressed in terms of the imagery of the breast (*bere*). Members of a local matrilineage are thus seen as belonging to the same breast. The bearing of children, or fruit, is described by the cognate term *ku-bereka*.

The sororate group(s), which forms the basis of the village, is under the guardianship of the eldest brother, who may or may not be the village headman. He is described as a *mwini* (Yao *asyene*) *mbumba* (owner, or more correctly guardian, of the sororate group). As marriage is uxorilocal, all married men in the village are outsiders or 'foreigners', as Mandala describes them (1990: 22), although the headman usually has his wife residing with him. Polygamous husbands often move between villages in order to visit their wives in their natal communities. Mandala describes the *mwini-mbumba* as a senior woman (1990: 33), and this may be the case, but in all the communities that I knew well – those in the Zomba and Mulanje districts – this role was assumed by the elder brother. In a sense every man is a potential village headman, for the *mbumba* consists of his sisters and their dependents, while he himself is part of his mother's brothers' *mbumba*. When a young boy is born people may exclaim *kwabadwa mfumu* ('a headman is born'), for if of good character and disposition (*makhalidwe*) he has the potential to be publicly recognized as a headman (Marwick 1965: 118). In essence, however, authority within the village community is shared between the *mwini mbumba* and one of the older women, usually a grandmother (*ambuye*), and perhaps the headman's sister. This person will often play a crucial role, as *namkhungwi*, in the initiation rites (*chinamwali*) of both boys and girls.

The social unity of the village and its underlying matrilineage (sorority group) is premised on the notion that they belong to one breast or one womb (*chibaliro*). The verb *ku-bala* also means 'to bear children or fruit', and *chibale* (sing. *mbale*) is a general term for kinship, or a kin relationship in its widest sense. The founding ancestors of the group are known as *makolo* (sing. *kholo*; Yao, *likolo*). Although *makolo* includes males and females from both lineages and, as Bruwer writes, no differentiation is made as far as gender is concerned (it was always stressed to me that makolo includes both men and women) in fact *kholo* in the Malawian context always has connotations of 'mother of the village' or founding ancestress (Bruwer 1948: 185). But such an ancestress is never named, and the *makolo* are always conceived of as collective ancestors, as the dead (*amanda*, of the grave) or as spirits of the ancestors (*mizimu ya makolo*). Such ancestors are associated with the graveyards (*manda*) and with the earth, being spoken of as *anthaka* (*nthaka* earth, soil). Through sacrifices and offerings, the spirits of the ancestors are kept quiet and content, but they make their presence known especially in dreams and through possession rites. Importantly, there is a reciprocal and on-going relationship between the living community in the village and the dead ancestors (*makolo*).

The symbolic potency of the *mbumba* concept was utilized by the President, Hastings Kamuzu Banda, himself a Chewa from Kasungu. He organized women in Malawi as his *mbumba*, and large contingents of women always attended his political rallies, dressed in gaily coloured skirts that carried his picture. Malawi was thus conceptualized as a village community, all the women being his sisters, and he the guardian of the people. He frequently referred to himself as Nkhoswe Number One (Lwanda 1993: 21, Forster 1994: 491).

The Malawian context has always been seen as an example of what Audrey Richards (1950) referred to as the 'matrilineal puzzle', involving a tension or conflict between marriage and matrilineal kinship. A structured contradiction is seen as expressing itself, according to both Richards (1950) and Schneider (1961), in the problematic nature of male authority as discussed above. Both Schoffeleers (1968) and Boucher (1976) interpret Nyau rituals among the Mang'anja and Chewa as a way of resolving the 'matrilineal puzzle'. All these writers assume the universality of male dominance, in the sense of male authority over women and children, and thus assume that men have divided loyalties and allegiance as brothers or husbands. If this authority is not assumed, the 'matrilineal puzzle' ceases to be a puzzle, as Leach (1961) implied.

Many have stressed the authority of the males within Malawian society. J.P. Bruwer, for example, writes of the Chewa that although matrilineal descent is important, their pattern of social organization entails that men are the dominant sex in all practical matters, differing very little, he suggests, from the patrilineal context. He writes:

Men are the rulers and councillors of State. They are the judges in court and the settlers of disputes within the village unit. For all practical purposes they dominate in the various avenues of everyday life . . . The dominant position of males is an inherited factor functioning within the matrilineage as a unit. They act as guardians over the interests of their matrilineages which they themselves cannot perpetuate' (1955: 116).

It is important, however, to distinguish between the political level of the territorial chief (chiefdom), where men have dominion, and the local village community, where authority is to a large degree shared by senior men and women and where women often take on the role of chief – that is, have authority over, and are responsible for, village affairs. Gamitto long ago noted a few instances of women chiefs among the Maravi and Chewa (1960: 416, 425), and both Marwick (1965: 144) and Mitchell (1962: 33) mention meeting village 'headmen' who were women (cf. Mandala 1990: 23).I knew several village chiefs who were women. Mitchell notes that there is 'necessarily' a conflict between a man's duties as guardian of the *mbumba* sorority group and his duties as husband, for men customarily live in the village of their spouses. But this conflict is to some extent lessened if authority in the village setting is to a large degree shared between the *mwini mbumba* and his sister, and it does not exist if authority is in the hands of a woman chief. Though mentioning the conflicting loyalties that a Chewa man often experiences towards his own and his sister's children, Marwick notes that among these people there is a tendency 'for the conjugal link frequently to be sacrificed on the altar of the consanguineal matrilineage'. And he mentions too, but does not develop, the fact that cross-cousin marriage between closely related matrilineal kin groups may to a large degree alleviate this conflict (1965: 180–1).

Both Marwick on the Chewa and Mitchell on the Yao emphasize the segmentation of the *mbumba*, the matrilineal group, one in relation to sorcery accusations, the other in relation to the succession to the village headmanship. The tensions and conflicts within the matrilineage are, however, primarily seen in terms of male rivals, frequently mother's brother and sister's son contending for authority within the kin group. Marwick writes on this issue:

So long as the matrilineage remains united, subsequent leaders compete for its overall control; and accusations of sorcery have the function of discrediting rivals. Once division has started, subsequent leaders may abandon hope of ever achieving overall control; and accusations of sorcery then have the function of accelerating and justifying the incipient separation (1965: 147).

Women seem to be largely bystanders in this process. But as Mitchell recognized, or implied, women are intrinsically involved in the process of village segmentation, for a woman has close ties with her mother and her mother's mother – with whom she is 'identified' – and these links have predominance over those with her collateral siblings (mother's sister daughters) (1956: 175).

Land, among the matrilineal people of Malawi, essentially belonged to the community as a whole; in essence it belonged to no one and to everyone. No person had individual property rights over land, trees, animals, or even termite mounds, and there was generally free access to all the necessities of life. But territorial chiefs claimed authority, in the sense of ownership or guardianship, over the land and were known as *mwini dziko* (guardians of the country). Territorial chiefs were also described as *mwini mzinda* or guardians of the capital village, which entailed specific rights with regard to the ritual burning of the bush, the hunting of large mammals and the organization of initiation rites. Village headman were nominally under the authority of the *mwini dziko* and formerly made gifts or paid tribute (*mtulo*) to the territorial chiefs. But essentially the village headmen had a good deal of freedom in selecting the site of the village and in alloting the garden sites for members of the village community in the matrilineage. The family household only held usufruct rights to the land for cultivating purposes. These rights did not extend to the trees, grass or mammals on the site. When a person or family ceased to cultivate the land, the site reverted back to the community, usually becoming regenerated woodland (Rangeley 1948: 51–2).

In an important sense, then, the *mbumba* or matrilineage was not a corporate group and did not collectively hold property rights in land. Both Vaughan (1983) and Mandala (1990) stress that the *mbumba* did not constitute an economic unit, the latter writer indeed suggesting that 'kinship never formed a regular channel for mobilizing agricultural labour' (1990: 51). He stresses instead the importance of the family or household (*banja*). Vaughan is more ambiguous, although she does write of the 'near invisibility' of the economic role of the matrilineage in southern Malawi, in contrast with its formal role as a ritual and political unit. Vaughan's essay focusses on the 'history of the family' as an economic and social unit in Malawi. Her discussion seeks to problematize many of the concepts utilized by anthropologists and historians, such as household, lineage, and specifically the family. She considers writers like Mitchell to be 'trapped' within their 'preconceptions' of the formal workings of the matrilineal system. Although sensitive to the contrast between ideology and social realities, unlike Mitchell she does not explore indigenous conceptions of kinship – *banja, mbumba, pfuko* – and describes the clan, which is a descent group, as 'the widest 'family' group to which the individual belonged' (1983: 27). But what is important about her analysis is the emphasis she puts on labour co-operation between women. A great deal more labour co-operation between women takes place, she writes, than is generally articulated:

> Women, especially those without husbands, help each other at all stages of the cropping cycle, as well as in harvesting, storing food, pounding grain, fetching water and firewood. As with food-sharing, labour co-operation between them has always taken place, but it assumes a more crucial role in the absence of so many adult men (1983: 278).

Vaughan writes that subsistence production is 'increasingly' becoming the responsibility of women working without men, implying that female-headed households are a new phenomenon, as if the conjugal family was the past norm. But women in Malawi have always been centrally concerned with subsistence agriculture, and matrilineal kinship has never been 'invisible', inscribed as it is in the layout of the village, where a group of matrilineally related women always live in close proximity around their mother, and where kinship ties are expressed in beer-making, the collection of mushrooms and other wild foods and local rituals – particularly those focussed around *chinamwali* ceremonies – as well as the various tasks that Vaughan notes. Labour co-operation between kin and neighbours was mentioned frequently by early writers on Malawi. For example, Buchanan wrote that 'The custom of helping each other to hoe the garden . . . is very common and widespread', the task usually ending with a beer feast (Yao, *chijao*) (1885: 140–1; cf. also Marwick 1965: 45 on the Chewa working parties).

The important point is that matrilineal kinship is strongly associated with a socioeconomic context in which women are the main cultivators and men are away for long periods, engaged in hunting, trading activities or migrant labour elsewhere. As Mandala writes, 'Male mobility was an integral feature of the Mang'anja matrilineal system', as it was for the Chewa, Yao, Lomwe and Nyanja (1990: 22).

Within the village community, focussed as it is on agriculture and matrilineal kinship, there was generally an egalitarian ethos, with an important emphasis on peace (*ntendere*) and harmony (*cholingana*), even though age senority was always recognized and affirmed. Malawian peoples place an important stress on being tranquil, gentle and warm-hearted (*ofatsa ntima*), on not being angry or aggressive, and the disposition to visit others and engage in conversation (*ku cheza*) is greatly esteemed. There is a Chewa saying: *chibale n'kuyenderana mowa m'kumwerana*, 'Kinship is to visit each other to drink beer together'. All this is related to the deep sentiment that is attached to the mother and to the fact that should members of the matrilineage fail to maintain peaceful relations between themselves, then misfortune may be inflicted upon them by the spirits of their ancestors. The *mbumba*, therefore, though not a corporate group, functions as an important social and ritual unit, even in a context where the family or household has been increasingly isolated from the wider ties of matriliny. Formal incorporation into the matrilineage takes place when the child is still an infant, through a ceremony described as *ku-tenga mwana*, which I describe in a companion volume.

The strong emphasis that Malawian people place on cooperation, friendliness and peaceful and polite social relationships is apt to be completely misconstrued. In a travel report on Malawi, for example, entitled 'African Dream' Nettel (1995) describes the country as still living in an 'age of innocence'. Its people, she writes, exhibit a 'sweet-natured friendliness' such that one is 'accosted' (her words!) in the market place only with 'smiles'. This she interprets as an expression of people's 'timidity' and 'submissiveness'. The characterization is hardly new. E.D. Young, who led the Livingstone Search Expedition in 1867, described the people of the Shire Valley as a 'shy and timid' race (1877: 36). Coming from a political culture that emphasizes competitiveness, greed, egoism and aggression, both Nettel and Young mistake an emphasis on friendliness and harmonious relationships, rooted in matriliny, for timidity and submissiveness.

In contexts where matrilineal ties become difficult to maintain, such as on tea estates, where company housing takes the form of 'lines' (*chithando*), quasi-kinship ties may be established between women. Thus among the Lomwe on the Thyolo tea estates, informal relationships between women known as *chinjira* (*njira*, path) are formed, whereby mutual support and the exchange of grain for household commodities (like soap and sugar) is made between two women. One is usually living independently on *thangata* (estate) land, the other in the *chithando* and thus dependent on the wages of herself and her husband. Significantly, though, the women are not usually related: although they knew each other intimately before establishing a *chinjira* partnership, their children and husbands address each other as siblings (Vaughan 1983: 282–3, Boeder 1984: 54–5).

Banja (Family-Household)

The basic production unit of Malawian matrilineal peoples is the *banja*, the family household focussed around a woman, her husband and children. The term refers to both the residential unit, the homestead enclosing the family house (*nyumba*) and the family grouping itself. Mandala describes the *banja* family-household as 'socially incoherent and impermanent' (1990: 50), but it has at its core the matricentric family of a women and her children. Husbands are not necessarily permanent members. The *banja* is a commensal unit with the women normally having her own kitchen and fire, as well as control of her own granary. It was customary for the in-marrying affine to build the house in his wife's village, the woman having rights to the land there. Men were expected to clear the land initially if under woodland, but although women were mainly responsible for domestic work – pounding the maize, collecting wood and water, preparing the food and cooking – and for caring for the children, agricultural tasks were to a large degree shared. Nevertheless, to an important degree women were 'the real owners and chief cultivators of the soil', as an early observer put it (Mandala 1990: 52), and this is still the case in many rural areas. Vaughan noted that in the Zomba district 'female-headed households' were the norm, some 40 percent of women working entirely without a husband, and a further 20 percent in fact cultivating the land entirely by themselves, though their absent husbands may send them remittances. She notes that in recent years women have come to assume more and more responsibility for subsistence production, but this seems to have been a common pattern over a long period, certainly in colonial times, when a large proportion of adult men worked as migrant labourers in Rhodesia and South Africa. She also estimated that 70 percent of households surveyed were unable to meet their subsistence needs (1983: 277).

In pre-colonial times, the household or lineage (*mbumba*) of the chief was often enhanced and strengthened by the incorporation of slaves or *akapolo* (sing. *kapolo*). These were people, often taken in various inter-village conflicts, who were considered to be the property of the *mbumba* and were used as a subsidiary labour force. They were conceived as lacking in freedom (*ufulu*) (Rangeley 1948: 63–4, Mandala 1990: 32–6).

Kinship Categories and Marriage

The kinship system of the Chewa, Yao and Mang'anja communities is essentially a variant of the 'bifurcate merging' pattern, there being a clear distinction between cross and parallel cousins, the latter being equated with one's siblings.

An idiom of kinship permeates Malawi's cultural life, and people addressing one another, even if strangers, will invariably use kin terms, the most familiar of which being mother (*mai*), father (*bambo*), elder brother (*achimwene*) and elder sister (*chemwali*). The various kin terms and relationships can be considered under a number of headings.

Grandparents

The combination or equation of alternate generations was one of the three principles, along with the unity of the sibling group and the assumption of cross-cousin marriage, that Marwick considered to constitute the basic framework of the Chewa kinship system (1965: 126). Kinship among the matrilineal people of Malawi's is premised essentially on three generations, for great grandparents, still living, have no specific kin term and are usually referred to as *amai* (mother or *bambo* (father). Boucher (1991) referred to the situation of great grandparents as 'anomalous', although it fits in with the alternating generation scheme.

Mbuye (pl. ambuye, Yao mbuje) FF, FM, MF, MM. Grandparents, both female and male, are referred to as *ambuye*, though gender distinctions may be expressed using the suffixes *wamkazi* (female) and *wamwamuna* (male). All the brothers and sisters of a person's grandparents, whatever their matrilineage, are addressed as *ambuye*, or alternatively *agogo* or *anganga*.

Mdzukulu (pl. adzukulu, Yao chisukulu) SS, SD, DS, DD (grandchild), ZS, ZD, SDH, SSW. Relationships between grandparent and grandchild are extremely close, and they are virtually identified with one another. A young child will spend the early years of its life under the care of the grandmother for long periods, and grandchildren will often take the name of their *ambuye* of the same sex. A special ceremony, *manyumba*, will cement this relationship, after the death of the grandparent. An informal joking relationship exists between grandchildren and grandparents, and they will address each other as if they were affines: a man may call his grandmother (*mzaki wanga* or *mkazanga*, 'my wife'), while a woman may address her grandfather as *mwamuna wanga* or *mwamunganga*, 'my husband'). Grandparents will address their grandchildren in a reciprocal manner. Grandmothers and granddaughters will likewise refer to each other as co-wives (*mkazimnzanga*, 'my woman'). Importantly, however, distinctions are made between grandparents who belong to one's own matrikin and those of one's father's matrilineage. Thus a woman will call her father's mother *alamu* (relative by marriage) or *asuwani* (cross-cousin), and her fathers' father *achimwene* (elder brother), describing him as *mlongo* (opposite-sex sibling). An implicit moiety system is thus evident in how people address and refer to each other. To differentiate between the two groups of grandparents, people use the suffixes *akuch-ikazi* (on the female side) and *akuchimuna* (on the male side). But the terms *mdzukulu* and *ambuye* are also frequently used to describe the relationship between the mother's brother (*ambuye*) and his sister's children (*mdzulukulu*). Finally, *mduzukulu* is used to describe those of the younger generation whose duty it is to bury the dead, who are usually affinal neighbours of the deceased (cf. Stefaniszyn 1954).

Parents

Although the biological mother and father are recognized with reference to the term '*wobadwa*', 'birth, natural', both *mai* (mother) and *bambo* (father) have a wide spectrum of reference. As already noted, both terms are widely used as a term of address, the plural *amai* and *abambo*, being used as a mark of respect. Also, each term has strong connotations with the two matrilineages with which one is associated, one's own (*mbumba*) and one's father's.

Bambo (tate, Yao atati) F, FB, FZ, MZH, MH.   All 'affinal' males of a person's father's generation belong to this category, and it includes also the father's sister, who is described as *bambo/tate wa mkazi*, female father (Yao, *atati wakongwe*). A person's own father may be described as *bambo wanga* (my father), while paternal uncles are referred to as *bambo wathu* (our father).

Mai (Yao, amao) M, MZ, FW, FBW.   Besides being used as a general term of address, *mai* (mother) essentially refers to women of the matrikin who belong to a person's mother's generation. As already noted, throughout Malawi the notion of mother carries with it a strong resonance, particularly in the plural, *amai*, with reference to a group of senior matrilineal women who constitute the core and central focus of the village community. As a collectivity, women or 'mothers' (*amai*) play a funda-mental role in all communal rituals, even the *nyau* and the boy's initiation rites. The sense that 'mothers' form the 'core' of the village was rightly emphasized by Mitchell (1956: 135). This is confirmed by Lawson, who writes that the care of one's mother is 'the deepest and most lasting affection in the life of most Nyanja' (1949: 185). With both parents, in the classificatory sense, a distinction is made between senior (*mkulu, waukulu*) and junior (*ng'ono, wang'ono*) members, relative to the age of one's own parents.

Malume (Yao akwelume) MB, WMH.   Scott (1929: 265) writes that *malume* may refer to the grandfather (*agogo*) as well as to the maternal uncle, and the term may indeed be so used in addressing a persons father's father, who belongs to one's own matrikin. But *malume* specifically refers to the mother's brother, who is a key figure in the matrilineage, often taking on the role of guardian of the sororate group (*mwini mbumba*) or of marriage advocate (*nkhoswe*). In the central region the MB is called *mtsibweni* (pl. *atsibweni*), and occasionally the term *mai wamwamuna* (male mother) may be used to describe the mother's brother (Pretorius 1949).

Siblings

The relationship between siblings, especially siblings of the opposite sex (*alongo*), is very close among all the matrilineal communities of Malawi. Lawson indeed suggests that the relationship between a brother and sister is deep and lasting, a 'far deeper affection' than that between husband and wife (1949: 186). But the gender distinction between siblings is a crucial one, and like that between affines is essentially an egalitarian one, contrasting with the seniority expressed in relations between siblings of the same sex.

Mbale (pl. abale) FBS, MZS, FZDH, MBDH (male ego); Z, FBD, MZD, FZSW, MBSW (female ego).   This is often translated as 'brother', but the term essentially refers to classificatory siblings of the same sex as oneself, i.e. members of the matrilineage belonging to the same sex. But, as already noted, the kin term is widely extended to cover all kin relationships.

Mlongo (Yao mbako) Z, FBD, MZD FZSW, MBSW (male ego); B, FBS, MZS, FZDH, MBDH (female ego).   In contrast to *mbale*, this term applies to opposite-sex siblings (members of the matrilineage), and has a much more restricted meaning. Among the Yao it specifically refers to members of a matriclan or local matrilineage (*ulongo*), and Sanderson suggests that the term is a corruption of *mu-ulongo* ('in the clan') (1920: 374).

Chemwali. A term of Yao derivation widely used, by both men and women, to refer to an elder sister, in a classificatory sense.

Achimwene. Also of Yao derivation, this term is correspondingly used to address an elder brother. Both these terms are widely used in addressing people of the same age category as oneself – even though no kin relationship may pertain. In addressing siblings of the same sex – in classificatory terms i.e. *abale* – distinctions according to seniority are always made, by both men and women.

Mkulu. (plural *akulu*, *mnjira* refers to the senior or older sibling, of the same sex, while *Mphwanga* [*mpwanga* Yao, *mng'ono* (small)] for the younger sibling in the relationship. Whether or not a man or woman is speaking it thus refers to a father's younger brothers' son or a younger brother, or (for a woman) a mother's younger sister's daughter, or a younger sister. All *mkulu/mphwanga* relationship are gender-specific and refer to matrikin. Mphwanga means '*my*' younger sibling of the same sex, for all Malawian kin terms may take various suffixes e.g. *mpwao*, their . . . *mpwanu*, your . . . *mpwache* his . . . or her . . . *mpwako* that . . . *mpwathu* our . . . younger same-sex sibling.

Cross-Cousins

In the Malawian context, a clear and unambiguous demarcation is made between one's siblings and matrikin (*chirongo* or *alongo*) of one's own generation and one's cross-cousins (*chisuwani*). Between siblings and matrikin, all sexual relationships are prohibited, and this applies equally to classificatory kin. The children of two sisters will thus never marry, nor even have sex with one another.

Msuwani (plural asuwani, Yao msiwani) FZS, FZD, MBS, MBD. The children of a brother and sister call each other *msuwani*, without gender differentiation. Cross-cousin marriage is widely enjoined as the preferred form of marriage, and with respect to all matrilineal communities in Malawi, but especially the Chewa and Yao, there is a strong tradition of it. This implies, in essence, a moiety system, a tradition of 'dual clan organization', as Marwick (1965: 123) calls it. In the historical traditions of the Maravi, which forms an underlying pattern found throughout Malawi in the rural areas, the two archetypal matriclans (*mafuko*), Phiri and Banda, are linked by a relationship of 'cross-cousinship' (*chisuwani*). While Marwick suggests that, among the Chewa, there is a greater emphasis on a man marrying his mother's brother's daughter (1965: 124), while Mitchell writes that the Yao in practice give preference to the marriage of a man to his father's sister's daughter (1956: 197), in essence this is the same kin category. Although marriages may not in fact be with real cross cousins, informants do give the impression that cross-cousin marriage is the norm, and in many rural areas villages are linked by a continuing pattern of affinal relationships forming a moiety pattern of intermarrying villages. In the Zomba district this was expressed in many initiation songs, reference being made to the village (that is, the matrilineal core) with whom an ongoing relationship of *chisuwani* was established. Lawson writes of cross-cousin-marriage 'between pairs of nearby villages' (1949: 18), and in the Dedza district Mair noted how the preference for cross-cousin marriage led to the great majority of marriages being either in the same village or with neighbouring villages (1951: 105). Although there is a good deal of mobility among people at the present time, in rural areas a pattern of 'continual integration' between two local matrilineages (villages) still obtains to some extent. In the past, however, cross-cousin marriage formed a fairly high percentage of the total number of marriages, the couples being resident either in the same village or in neighbouring villages linked by affinal ties (Bruwer 1955: 120).

Between cross cousins there exists a relationship of familiarity and teasing, what is known in the anthropological literature as a 'joking relationship'. Particularly cross-sexually, this relationship varies, as Mitchell puts it, from 'ribald joking to sexual advances' (1956: 197). For a man to be addressed, in the Malawian context, by a woman he does not know well as *msuwani* rather than *bambo* or *achimwene* registers a personal and intimate interest. As cross-cousinship is a potential marriage relationship, sexual connotations always have salience, and a cross cousin may be addressed as *mkazi wanga* 'my wife', or *mwamuna wanga* 'my husband', even when they are not married.

The relationship between cross cousins, who are always potential sexual or marriage partners, is an egalitarian one, of easy familiarity and teasing. They may be rude or insolent towards one another, and often mock and swear at one another. They address one another with the term *iwe*, 'thou', normally used to address children and considered a somewhat disrespectful form of address.

Children

Mwana (Plural ana, Yao mwanache) S, D, BS, BD. All children are called *ana*, and the term has very general usage, not being restricted to the kin categories denoted above. Gender is indicated with the suffixes *mwanawamkazi* (female child) or *mwanawamuna* (male child). The first-born child is referred to as *mwana wa chisamba*, a reference to the first pregnancy ceremony that a young woman undergoes (*chisamba; ku-samba*, to wash the body). But significantly, in the matrilineal context, the children of a sister or of the women of the matrikin are termino-logically distinguished and may be referred to as *mdzukulu* (their mother's brother being *ambuye*). A man's sister's son is known as *chipwa* or *mphwanga* (younger brother, the suffix depending on the person speaking and the context), his sister's daughter as *mfumakazi* (female chief).

Affinal Relations

Husband/Wife. A woman calls her husband *mwamuna wanga*, my male/man, but when speaking in his presence refers to him as *bambo* (father), either 'our father', *bambo wa kwathu*, or as 'father of a child', *bambo wake* (his/her child). In a similar manner a man calls his wife *mkazi wanga*, my female/woman, but he addresses her either as the mother, *amai wache*, of the youngest child or by her clan name, *nabanda, naphiri*. In a public context relations between spouses tend to be formal. The Yao have a term for spouse (*asono*).

Mkamwini. In a kinship context where cross-cousin marriage is widely practised and uxorilocal residence is the norm, the son-in-law, the in-marrying affine, is a key figure. From the perspective of the young man's matrikin, he is their ZS (*chipwa*); from the point of view of his affines, he is the daughter's husband or the son of his wife's mother's brother. The kin term derives from *ka*, small, plus *mwini*, guardian. But the essence of the role of the *mkamwini* is that he is an outsider, a visitor (*mlendo*), in his wife's village, and that his function should be simply to beget children. He has limited rights over his spouse, and no rights over the children, for they 'belong' to his wife's matrikin. His role is simply 'to plant seeds only' (*kubyala mbeu chabe*) (Marwick 1965: 181). His power within his wife's matrilineage, with which he resides, is strictly curtailed, and his sexual function is highlighted, especially during initiation rites. He is referred to as the cock (*tambala*), hyena (*fisi*) or billy-goat (*tonde*).

Mkamwana SW. This term is used for a woman's daughter-in-law.

Mlamu (plural alamu). WB, WZ, BW, ZH, FBSW, FBDH, MBS. All these categories refer essentially to affines of one's own generation, and

Matrilineal Kinship

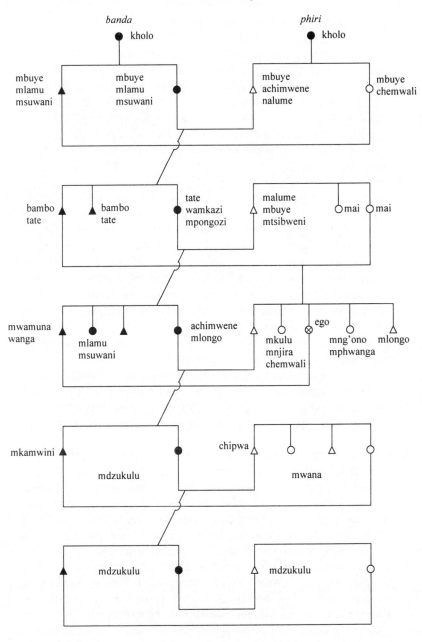

Figure 1. The Kinship System as an Ideal Structure

as there is a close correspondence between these and one's cross cousins (*asuwani*), given the marriage rule, relations with *alamu* are also of a familiar and joking pattern. Cousins may therefore be referred to as 'siblings-in-law' (*alamu*) or jokingly described as a spouse, *mkazi* or *mwamuna wanga*. The term *mlamu* is always reciprocal, and usually used with reference to one's own age group, but it may be extended to the grandparental generation – with whom an easy, egalitarian relationships is usually expressed – and a person's father's mother (FM) and mother's father (MF), neither whom are member's of one's matriclan, may be addressed as *alamu*.

Mpongozi (plural apongozi; Yao, akwego) WM, WF, HM, HF, MBW, ZHM. This kin term essentially focuses on a person's mother-in-law (WM, HM), who, given the moiety system, will also be a person's father's sister (*tate wamkazi*, Yao *atati wakongwe*). Conversely the father of a person's spouse will tend to be equivalent to a mother's brother, and thus be kin. The relationship between a person and his or her mother-in-law (*mpongozi*) is hedged with restrictive prohibitions. Their relationship with her must be reserved, they neither speak in her presence nor eat with her, and must attempt always to keep their distance. There must be no familiarity with her, and they must not approach her sleeping mat. Similar though less stringent restrictions apply to one's own father.

Sanderson regarded the Yao kinship nomenclature as evidence of past 'group marriages' (1920: 375). There is in fact little evidence for such marriages, but their kinship terminology is clearly consistent with a matrilineal system with an implicit moiety system and cross-cousin marriage as the norm.

In speaking to a person of the opposite sex, people will usually address them as the mother (*amai*) or father (*bambo*) of a child (often the first born) using the personal name, e.g. *amai d'dereki* 'mother of Derek', *abambo a emmi* 'father of Emmi'. In addressing a person younger than themselves people will often use personal names, but not if they are senior, when they will use kin terms such as *mai, bambo, achimweni or chemwali*.

Although cross-cousin marriage was preferred in the past, the essence of Malawian kinship is that a person must marry outside the matriclan (*pfuko*), or at least outside the local matrilineage (*mbumba*, or *chirongo*). With its emphasis on matrilineal descent, succession in the male line passes down through kinship (*abale*) from the mother's brother – who may be the guardian of the *mbumba* – to his younger brother or sister's son. Such a kinship pattern may allow marriage across the generations. These are mentioned by early ethnographers, and may still be encountered, though they are infrequent. The first is the marriage of a man to his grandaughter, his daughter's daughter, who, consistent with the moiety system, would not be a member of his own matrikin. The other involves the marriage of a man to his mother's brother wife, on the mother's brother's death. The sister's son in a sense inherits the widow (*chikolo*) of his *malume*. This too is consistent with the kinship pattern. One of my close friends in Malawi was born from such a second marriage of his mother. One may note too that on the death of his wife, a man may be offered a marriage with one his wife's matrikin, often a sister of the first wife, with whom, as a cross-cousin, he is often familiar.

What, however, is important in the Malawian context is that ties of blood (kinship) and affinity are interdependent, as Lawson noted long ago (1949: 181). This means that marriage is an important institution, regulating relationships between intermarrying lineages (villages), as well as providing a supportive framework for the relationship between the two spouses. Indeed, the parents of the respective partners – who themselves unite in marriage the two matrilineages – call each other *asewera*, from the verb *ku-sewera*, to dance or play. There is a good deal of warmth and co-operation between them, which is focussed around the institution of *unkhoswe*. Rangeley (1948: 27–8), Mair (1951) and Bruwer (1955) have all written at length on this institution, and we need only give a summary here.

The *unkhoswe* institution is premised on the notion that the matrilineage is a corporate unit, though not in any sense holding property in land. This corporate unit, expressed as the *mbumba*, is usually under the guardianship of a senior brother, who is responsible for the health and social well-being of his sisters and his sister's children. The oldest living male member of the matrilineage is, in theory, the guardian (*mwini*) or advocate (*mkhoswe*) of the entire matrilineage, but in practise these roles fall on younger, but still senior, men in the matrilineage. In fact, who becomes the guardian or the marriage advocate is very much in the hands of the senior women of the matrilineage, who constitute the core of the *mbumba*. In practice, too, the *mwini* (guardian) *mbumba* will often delegate a younger member, his elder sister's son, to act as *mkhoswe* (advocate) in the marriage negotiations of members of the matrilineage. It is important to emphasize that such negotiations between two matrilineages take place in a context where, through cross-cousin marriage, there may often be long-standing affinal ties between the two groups. Marriage, then, is to an important extent a 'factor of mutual interest' between two matrilineal groups (Bruwer 1955: 120).

Preliminary negotiations between two intermarrying groups are initially carried out by the maternal grandparents, especially the grandmother's (MM's) brother, *mkokowogona* (the sleeping log), or by a close relative of the potential bridegroom. The latter is known as *mkupamame* (the killer of the dew), who, after making the preliminary gestures, takes no further part in the negotiations. These are conducted by the *ankhoswe* of the bride and groom, who are, as noted, invariably their elder brothers and are ritually appointed at a communal beer-drinking ceremony involving the two matrilineages. This beer is known as *mowa waunkhoswe*, 'the beer of advocacy', and the ceremony is described as 'binding the marriage negotiations' (*kumanga unkhoswe*). The key to a formal marriage is the payment of a chicken (*nkuku ya kwati*, chicken of the marriage) by the boy's *mkhoswe* to the relatives of the bride. The payment may be made in cash, and the marriage is often sealed by a church ceremony. The *ankhoswe* or 'marriage sponsors', as Mair (1951) describes them, are responsible for the well-being of the marriage, for giving support and advice, and they act as 'go-betweens' with respect to the two matri-lineages. Their most important duty, however, is to deal with and somehow resolve any difficulties the marriage may encounter. The marriage is in practice finally cemented when the man completes the construction of a house in his wife's village, for uxorilocal residence (*chikamwini*) is the norm. But, as noted earlier, the village headman or *mwini mbumba* may bring his wife or wives to live with him in his own village, and this kind of marriage is known as *chitengwa* (*ku-tenga*, to bring, take). Although with paid employment and cash-cropping this form of marriage is becom-ing increasingly important, nevertheless in rural areas matrilineal kinship and *chikamwini* marriages still obtain. Studies during the colonial period certainly confirmed that the majority of marriages were uxorilocal, the majority of women residing together as matrikin (Bruwer 1949: 196; Mair 1951: 105). Villages I knew well in the Zomba, Thyolo and Mulanje districts all conformed to this pattern, the village consisting of a core of matrilineally related women, men being inmarrying affines, even though the contemporary social situation is complex and diverse, men often alternating between living with their matrikin and with their spouses.

Marriage and the role of the father, both in procreation and in the upbringing of children, is strongly affirmed and emphasized in Malawi. Sexual fidelity is also culturally affirmed, and should a man have extra-marital sex during his wife's pregnancy, this is seen has having dire consequences for both the mother and child, who become susceptible to mystical misfortune. Nevertheless marriage in Malawi is a fragile insti-tution, and divorce is common. Many women in rural areas have a series of transient but stable partnerships, and all the women I know well in Malawi, both professional and rural women, have had children by several husbands or partners. Many writers have attested to the high divorce rate among the matrilineal peoples of Malawi and to the 'looseness' of the marriage tie. To divorce is referred to as *ku-sudzula*, a widely used term meaning to finish an enterprise.

Over thirty years ago, Mitchell wrote that 'The divorce rate is high among the Yao and a typical family of five uterine siblings may have three fathers' (1956: 186). This statement has been certainly confirmed by my own more recent observations (cf. Marwick 1965: 176–9).

Although the *chikamwini* relationship has often been interpreted as a kind of brideservice, the productive work of the inmarrying affine is centred on the *banja* household. It is within this unit, focussed on a dyadic, reciprocal relationship between husband and wife, that the gender division of labour is enacted. Women are expected to perform certain domestic duties for the husband: they must prepare food and cook for the husband and serve him with food; and they must draw water and collect firewood for the household. Preparing warm water for the man's late afternoon bath is a 'duty', or perhaps custom (*nkhuwo*) would be a better word, that carries with it a warm, and deep resonance for both partners in a stable relationship. The nurturing and care of young children is largely in the hands of the mother, although her own mother and sisters take responsibility for the children for long periods. In return, the husband is expected to protect and care for his spouse, support her economically and provide shelter in the form of a house, built by himself with the help of his kin, in his wife's village. But crucial to the role of the husband, as *mkamwini*, is to beget children for his wife. And as many writers have suggested, a crucial emphasis is placed on the bearing of children, which is a 'matter of intense personal and social significance', as Mitchell describes it (1962: 38). The importance of children is expressed in conversation and rituals, and a man or woman who is unable to have children is held in low esteem. The conjugal bond is personal and individual, and, as already noted with regard to agricultural tasks, there is no pronounced division of labour.

Although bridewealth is practiced by both Ngoni and Sena, it is generally looked upon with extreme disdain by the matrilineal peoples of Malawi. The payment of *lobola* (*ku-lowola* or 'to go away', in the case of a woman marrying into husband's village) is often described as like the 'selling' of a relative (*amati kulowola ndi kugulitsa m'mbale wako*).

Social Change and Matriliny

Although, as we have discussed above, matrilineal kinship is still an important social institution in many rural areas of Malawi, over the past 150 years it has been subjected to the influences of profound social change. In an important essay on the 'matrilineal family' among the Chewa, Kings Phiri (1983) has discussed these fundamental historical changes under four headings: the development of the slave trade with the East African Coast; the intrusion of various 'patrilineal groups' into Malawi at the end of the nineteenth century; the influence of Christian missionaries and the socio-economic changes that accompanied colonialism; and the development of capitalism. It is unfortunate, however, that he uses a term like 'matrilineal family', for the family is a grouping based on affinal ties, not on kinship. We may discuss each of these influences in turn.

Outlining the Chewa family and lineage system as an 'ideal construct', Phiri suggests that matriliny among the Chewa is a complex of several variables: the nature of marriage, residence patterns, the exercise of domestic authority, and the control and custody of children. And the picture he portrays is very much what we have described above, though he has little discussion of the clan system (*pfuko*) or the family-household (*banja*). Thus Phiri emphasizes the supreme importance of matrilineal ties, the Chewa tracing their descent from a common ancestress, the widespread pattern of uxorilocality, and the avunculate – the importance of the authority of the elder brother as the guardian of the *mbumba* and as the *nkhoswe*. Seeing matriliny as an 'ideal' and as something of a past historical phenomenon, he thus concludes that all these features taken together suggest 'that the Chewa family was seen as an integral part of the wife's rather than the husband's lineage. In other words, the locus of control of the productive as well as reproductive capabilities of the Chewa nuclear family lay within the woman's group' (1983: 259). He views this structure as emerging out of specific economic circumstances which he never specifies, though he notes the importance of controlling labour in a situation where land was generally plentiful, and the importance of slaves, goats and iron goods as factors of production.

The important point, of course, is that historically matrilineal kinship in Malawi was typical of a situation where hoe agriculture under the control of woman was combined with the importance of trade and hunting focussed around men and where there was an incipient development of state systems in the form of chiefdoms.

But Phiri notes the importance of virilocality (*chitengwa*) even in the 'traditional' setting, and the conflict experienced by Chewa men between conjugal loyalties and loyalties to their own matrikin. Phiri suggests two ways in which this conflict was 'ameliorated'. The first, also suggested by Rita-Ferreira (1968) and Schoffeleers (1976), was the importance of the Nyau societies, for these 'may have given a sense of solidarity and even considerable influence to married men in (the) matrilineal context' (1983: 261). The second was the importance of cross-cousin marriage in the past and the more widespread practice of marrying within one's own neighbourhood. Even today, he writes, the majority of Chewa men 'marry within a five-kilometre radius of their own matrikin' (ibid.: 262).

The importance of slavery and long distance trade probably goes back several centuries with respect to Malawi, and Kandawire indeed suggests that domestic slavery came in with the Marave (Phiri) invaders around the sixteenth century. The evidence he presents for this is the existence of slavery among the Bakongo, from whose territory the early invaders are reputed to have come (1980: 140). But the emergence of a powerful Kalonga Chiefdom based at Mankhamba at the southern end of Lake Malawi in the sixteenth century probably had less to do with an invading conquering clan than with the control of long-distance trade between Central Africa and the east coast ports. However, during the early part of the nineteenth century, there was an important development of the slave trade throughout the upper Zambezi region. This slave trade, as Phiri writes, 'enabled matrilineages to accumulate slaves or pawns (*akapolo*) where productive and reproductive services were then appropriated by the lineage in question' (ibid.: 263). Drawing on the important essay by Douglas (1964), the suggestion is that the head of a matrilineage who had acquired domestic slaves or pawns could keep his male kinsmen in his own village by marrying them to female *akapola*. Phiri notes that during the nineteenth century in south-east Africa, a premium was put on women as slaves, ranking with ivory, cows and guns as important items of trade. During that period women were more highly valued than men as slaves: a slave dealer paid 12 iron hoes or 24 yards of calico for a woman slave, as against 10 iron hoes or 20 yards of calico for a male. The village headman or *mwini mbumba* could sell any younger members of his matrikin who were considered deviant or recalcitrant, while expanding his own matrilineage by the incorporation of female slaves. Only important chiefs and trading entrepreneurs who controlled 'administrative' (as Kandawire calls them) rather than 'kinship' villages (1979: 100–1) seem to have acquired slaves, and this involved an extension of virilocal residence to other male matrikin. Evidence from European missionaries like MacDonald (1882) suggests that the villages of the more powerful chiefs consisted of both their own and 'slave' (*akapola*) lineages. But importantly, the incorporation of slaves was analogous to *chitengwa* marriage, for the children belonged to the father, and thus to the lineage of the village chief, the *mwini mbumba*. The relationship between the head of the lineage and the children of female slaves was that of *mbuye/ mdzukulu*, which is why early writers spoke of *mbuye* as meaning not only mother's brother (also *malume*) or grandfather, but also master or lord (Scott 1929: 284). Phiri suggests that towards the end of the nineteenth century, the practice of marrying female slaves to male members of the matrilineage was widespread, so that village headman, the lineage heads, were able to avoid the dispersal of their male matrikin, while their sisters remained with them through uxorilocal marriage. Importantly, too, there was no discrimination against the children of slave women, for they were incorporated into the matrilineage.

In his study of the Yao village, Clyde Mitchell suggests that with the advent of colonial rule and the pursuance of an active policy against both domestic slavery and the possession of guns, the power of the territorial chiefs was broken. 'When the slave caravans stopped', he writes, 'the chief's source of wealth disappeared, and with it much of his power' (1956: 38). Thus the large administrative villages, under powerful territorial chiefs, tended to break up, even though such chiefs were recognized by the colonial authorities as principal headman. In contrast Kandawire argues that the system of values associated with 'domestic slavery', which he sees as a mode of production alongside that of 'domestic husbandry', was not abolished 'at one stroke' with the coming of colonial rule but, he implies, was continued by colonial rule itself (1980: 142).

The important point, of course, is that the 'domestic slavery' that was associated with the nineteenth-century slave trade did not lead to the demise of matriliny – if anything, it strengthened matrilineal kinship. It was, as MacGaffey writes (1983: 185), a form of 'acquired descent'.

At the end of the nineteenth century, another important influence on Chewa matriliny and that of other matrilineal peoples in Malawi was their interaction with groups of people who came largely as invaders and whose kinship patterns were essentially patrilineal. These include the Chikunda, Swahili traders, the Ngoni and the Kololo.

The Chikunda were not a 'tribe' or ethnic community but rather warrior slaves who lived on the Zambesi *prazos* or crown estates, to which they were attached. They entered Malawi in the last decades of the nineteenth century mostly as elephant hunters. Isaacman (1972) indeed writes of the Chikunda as not only being the militia of the *prazeros*, but as having played an important role as long-distance traders and as the principal elephant hunters in south-central Africa (1972). The Chikunda were drawn from a wide range of ethnic groups, such as the Chewa, Nsenga, Mang'anja, Sena, Tonga and Chipeta. Not all of these were patrilineal in social organization, but all these bands of roving traders and hunters were, as Kings Phiri records (1983: 266) absorbed with the passage of time into Malawian cultural life.

The Swahili traders were even fewer in number. They settled along the lake-shore, and many of the leading merchants established themselves as political leaders who were able to assert hegemony over the local people, whether Chewa or Nyanja. One of the best known of these traders was Salim Bin Abdallah, otherwise known as the Jumbe of Kota Kota, who between 1840 and 1870 controlled trade in ivory and slaves across Lake Malawi (Shepperson 1966). Jumbe and his Swahili retainers governed through a system of indirect rule, were important in introducing Islam to the area, and intermarried with local women. Virilocal residence was practised. But again, as with the Chikunda, the influence of the Swahili on the kinship patterns of the local people seems to have been minimal.

The Ngoni were very different. These pastoral and patrilineal people, whose history has been briefly but lucidly discussed by Desmond Phiri (1982), were an offshoot of the Nguni people who fled from the impis of Shaka in the 1820s. A group under Zwangendaba is said to have crossed the Zambezi in 1835, another group, the Maseko Ngoni, some years later. Various groups eventually settled in Malawi, especially near Mzimba, Dowa, Dedza and Mchinji, and established political hegemony over the local people. But in spite of their political and military dominance, the Chewa kinship structure, Kings Phiri maintains (1983), continued to thrive within these Ngoni states, to the extent that uxorilocal residence and matrilineal descent were adopted by the Ngoni themselves, along with the Chewa language. Where Ngoni influence was pronounced, virilocal marriage and bridewealth (*lobola*) payments were practised, as in the Dowa district, but nonetheless the conclusion one must draw is that the Ngoni cultural impact on the Malawian matrilineal system has been minimal.

The Kololo influence on Malawian culture was even slighter. The Kololo were in no sense an ethnic group but simply the Sotho porters, numbering some 25 individuals, who were left behind in the Lower Shire by Livingstone in the 1850s. Equipped with guns, they were able to assert their authority over the local Mang'anja villagers.

In an important sense, therefore, none of the invaders with patilineal kinship had a major impact on Malawian matriliny, and the other two important groups of immigrants to Malawi, the Lomwe and Yao, were both matrilineal.

The third important influence on the Malawian kinship system has been that of the Christian Missionaries, who first arrived in Malawi in the 1870s. By the 1920s, most of Malawi had been settled by Christian missionaries, the country being essentially divided up between the spheres of influence of the Catholics, the Scottish Presbyterians, the Anglicans and the Dutch Reformed Church as the main missionaries. In one way or another, the missionaries exerted tremendous pressure on the basic values and institutions of Malawian society, as Stuart (1974) has explored in relation to the Chewa. The institution of matriliny in particular came under attack with all its associated social correlates: polygyny, initiation rites and Nyau ceremonies, the emphasis on matrilineal ties and the subsequent looseness and fragility of the conjugal bond, the fact that marriage was essentially a bond between two groups mediated by *ankhoswe* rather than an individual affair with the husband/father having an authoritative role. All these were seen as 'inimical', as Stuart (1974: 28) puts it, and contrary to what the missionaries saw as basic Christian principles. They put a focal emphasis not on kinship but on marriage, not on the unity of a sibling group focussed around women but on the family under the control and authority of the husband. The missionary teaching on marriage stressed the sacred context and indissolvable bond between husband and wife, and laid emphasis on parental control of and responsibility for children (Phiri 1983: 268–9).

Although Christian influence and propaganda has undoubtedly had an impact on the cultural and social life of Malawi, especially through the educational system, this has by no means led to the demise of key social institutions such as matrilineal kinship, initiation rites, ceremonies associated with the spirits of the dead and the widespread use of medicine (*mankhwala*).

However, the impact of socioeconomic changes associated with the development of a capitalist economy within Malawi has been profound. Of special significance has been the introduction of a cash economy in the form of agricultural estates and cash crops, the imposition of hut or poll tax, which necessitated engagement with the market economy, urbanization, and labour immigration, both within (to estates) and outside Malawi. Throughout the colonial period, migrant labour, especially to Rhodesia and South Africa, was an important aspect of the colonial economy, at times actively encouraged in spite of opposition from the missionaries and local European planters. But importantly, although the deterimental effects of labour migration on family life were emphasized by missionaries, colonial officials and anthropologists like Margaret Read (who worked among the patrilineal Ngoni; cf. 1942), in fact the absence and mobility of husbands – now labouring abroad rather than hunting and trading – was a crucial aspect of the matrilineal system.

The impact on matriliny of the other aspects of developing capitalism – urbanization (though limited in Malawi), the production of cash crops (almost entirely in the hands of men) and wage labour on agricultural estates – has however been profound. And there is no doubt that where these developments have taken place matriliny has declined, virilocal marriage has become the norm, and the conjugal family has taken the place of the matrilineage, with the husband exerting control over both his wife and children.

Kings Phiri has suggested, in an interpretation of Kandawire's study of Chingale in the upper Shire Valley, that the intrusion of patrilineal peoples, Christian Missionary activity, colonialism and the modern capitalist economy has completely transformed the matrilineal system, such that it 'no longer exists as a functional unit'. It has been replaced, he suggests, by the nuclear family, comprising husband, wife and children. Phiri doubts whether such a 'radical transformation' has occurred among the Chewa of Central Malawi. But when one examines Kandawire's study, one finds that he does not argue such a thesis. His main concern is the colonial economy, particularly the *thangata* system, which was a form of forced labour on European agricultural estates. Distancing himself from Mitchell's account of the Yao, who he alleges had an 'insatiable thirst for primitivity' (1979: 147), Kandawire relegates kinship to an 'insignificant place' in his study, and offers no substantial analysis of either the family – as the 'smaller producing unit' – or the 'sorority group' both of which are only mentioned in passing (1979: 96–7). Although Kandawire's study has a historical dimension, he makes no mention at all of long-distance trade nor of 'domestic slavery,' which is given such prominence as a 'mode of production' in his paper on class formation in southern Malawi (1980). His central focus is on land tenure, the *thangata* system, and local politics among the various chiefdoms. Kandawire thus offers no evidence at all that matriliny had 'ceased to exist' as a social institution in the Upper Shire Valley.

But it is not simply a question of matriliny declining under the pressures of urbanization and the growing of cash crops: subtle efforts have been made to suppress matriliny. This was highlighted by Rogers (1980) in her discussion of the Lilongwe Land Development Program, seen as a model scheme for agricultural development in Africa. Sponsored by the World Bank, it focussed specifically on tobacco-growing and involved the privatization of land, as well as a strong bias towards men in the distribution of development inputs and in who was designated the 'household head'. In 1970–71, around 70 percent of the growers were men, even though many were living uxorilocally, and Rogers concluded that the land allocation programme was a deliberate plan to entrench individual ownership of land and to suppress matriliny, which the surveys suggested was still a thriving social institution. The programme was 'tantamount to an all-out attack on a people's way of life' (ibid.: 134).

Gender and Agriculture

Early in the century a missionary wrote of the Yao: 'While the men spend their time hunting, the women occupy themselves in the fields and in household cares' (Mills 1911: 229).

Evidence from the colonial and pre-colonial periods suggest that social life in Malawi was structured around an explicit gender division, with women being mainly engaged in agricultural work, in the processing and cooking of food and in basic childcare, while the men were away for long periods, especially in the dry season, actively employed in fishing, in long-distance trade or in what was a crucial activity for men of all ethnic communities, the hunting of the larger mammals. The gender division was thus an important organizing principle, as it still is, though at the present time hunting is a peripheral activity, even in rural areas.

In recent decades, the concept of gender has become an important topic of intellectual debate within anthropology, and 'gender studies' is a growing discipline within the social sciences. Although a relatively new analytic category, gender has long been implicitly recognized in anthropology and among sex-role theorists in sociology, particularly in discussions around the 'sexual division' of labour. Although issues of sex and sexuality were not entirely neglected, even the ethnographic writings of, for example, Malinowski, Kenyatta and Schapera did little, as Pat Caplan suggests, to theorize either sexuality or gender (1987: 13).

Social scientists have long recognized a distinction between biological *sex* – accepting the fact that humans are, like other animals, a sexually dimorphic species – and *gender* as a cultural definition of behaviour defined as appropriate to the sexes in a given society or historical period. Thus gender is seen as a 'cultural' or 'socially constructed' category focussed around the concepts of 'man' and 'woman' – as Simone de Beauvoir put it in the famous phrase, 'one is not born a woman, but, rather, becomes one' (1973: 301) – as distinct from 'female' and 'male' as biological categories. Although men, as sexual beings, are not capable of bearing children, this does not determine that women should be the primary child-carers (Lerner 1986: 238).

Because biology does not determine gender in any direct or simple fashion, many anthropologists and sociologists, in reacting against the biological determinism that is ubiquitous in Western culture, have either denied that there is *any* connection at all between human biology and gender (or kinship) -thus advocating a rigid dualism that divorces humans from their bodies – or have suggested that biological 'sex' itself is a cultural category, meaning that the sex-gender distinction is redundant or 'fundamentally misleading' (Moore 1994a: 813). Becoming aware of what has been common knowledge for a long time, namely that theories of sex and reproduction are culturally variable and diverse, and that sexuality itself is a social construct and to some extent influenced by human agency, such post-modernist anthropologists simply invert the premises of the 'sexual tradition', as Weeks describes it (1986: 17), and propound a rather monolithic cultural determinism. This post-modernist perspective seems to suggest that because 'sex' (as biological difference) can only be articulated through cultural theories or categories, it therefore follows that either 'sex' does not 'exist' or is itself simply a cultural 'construct'. It thus presents not some 'new vision' (as Moore prophetically proclaims) but old-fashioned cultural idealism of the neo-Kantian variety, which completely oblates biology. Just because we cannot think of a thing – whether it be sex, a human being or an elephant – without having some conception of it, and because cultural beliefs and categories, arising from social praxis, influence our perceptions and understandings of the world, including 'sex', this does not imply that all that exists are only ideas, concepts and discourses, and that sex, humans and elephants are therefore not natural. In his critique of Nelson Goodman's idealism, Putnam expressed this rather well :

Why should one suppose that reality can be described independent of our descriptions? And why should the fact that reality cannot be described independent of our descriptions lead us to suppose that there are only the descriptions? (Putnam 1992: 122)

For many post-modernist anthropologists and sociologists, any suggestion that gender *is* connected with biological facts or that gender may have a 'foundation' or 'basis' in biology is misleadingly interpreted as 'essentialism', that is, as a form of biological reductionism or theoretical manoeuvre that equates sex with gender (Connell 1987, Yanagisako and Collier 1987). Although many cultures – Western cultures in particular –

have an inherent tendency to 'naturalize' social inequalities, it is not a response to this to lapse into cultural idealism. Needless to say, the 'new vision' of post-modern anthropologists (Strathern 1988, Yanagisako and Collier 1987, Moore 1994) is replete with conceptual contradictions, as they continue to take sex differences for granted as natural facts recognized by all cultures (Stolcke 1993).

Henrietta Moore, in a recent critical survey of anthropological knowledge on sex and gender (1994), suggests that contemporary research in biology has suggested that 'biology is a dynamic component of our existence', which presumably implies our existence as social beings. She offers a quotation from Anne Fausto-Sterling's study, *Myths of Gender*: 'an individual's capacities emerge from a web of interactions between the biological being and the social environment . . .. Biology may in some manner condition behaviour, but behaviour in turn can alter one's physiology'(Fausto-Sterling 1985: 8).

Apart from those, like the sociobiologists, who tend to advocate a form of biological determinism, and those symbolic and cultural anthropologists who suggest a radical dualism between culture and biology and thus veritably deny the fact that humans are biological beings, almost all *social* scientists over the past half century would have agreed with this supposedly 'new vision'. Even anthropologically informed sociobiologists like van den Berghe (1979) and Freeman (1984) would advocate such an 'interactionist' approach, even though such approaches tend to underplay both social praxis and human agency (cf. Morris 1991: 138–42).

One regretably has to acknowledge, then, that the world is not entirely of human making and that sex differences are real among human beings, as they are among elephants and chickens. One cannot but agree with Howell and Melhuus in their criticisms of the post-modernists and their 'open-endedness' with regard to biological sex. They write, 'Although theories of procreation certainly vary dramatically, this does not mean that physiological differences between men and women are not universally acknowledged' (1993: 46).

In her important study of African metallurgy, Herbert emphasizes the importance of gender, with men almost universally being associated with iron-smelting, smithing and hunting, and women with pottery. But while she stresses the fluidity of gender identities (paternal aunts, for example, have the status of males, and women may become female husbands; see Amadiume 1987), she is clearly puzzled by an apparent 'paradox' in that African people both recognize the essential biological differences between female and male – thus she describes tham as partaking of 'essentialism' – and view gender as socially constructed and relational (1993: 224). If recognizing the existence of biological differences between the sexes makes one an essentialist, then, most people in the world, apart from certain self-proclaimed post-modernists, are essentialists. Of course the concept of essentialism has a more specific meaning, relating to the theory that there is an isomorphic or reductive relationship between sex and gender.

In Malawi people recognize that both gender and humanity – they are distinct notions – are grounded in nature, in the sense that they are attributes with which one is born (*ku-bala* to bear children, fruit, *badwa* to be born, *balitsa* gender (Zambesi Mission 1980: 62). Yet one is not simply born a human being, and a child is referred to as a thing (*chinthu*) in the early days of its life. Not until it has undergone the *kutenga mwana* (to bring the child) ceremony and has been incorporated into the kin group is it considered a human being. If the child dies before the ceremony it is not given a funeral but is quietly disposed of in the bush or on an ash heap as a 'thing'. Yet in being born, humans are still considered to be natural beings, for they do not articulate an either/or dualism, and the characteristics of a person are described as being part of their nature, in the sense of their having been born that way, (*chibadwa*, the Latin term for nature, *natura*, has similiar roots, for it primarily meant 'to be born'). A person's sexual identity is viewed in similar fashion, and people speak of being born as either a male (*-amuna*) or a female (*-akazi*). Sexual differentiation is not, of course, limited to humans but is seen as an essential aspect of the world, especially in relation to mammals and birds; and the more important of the larger mammals, like the baboon, elephant, kudu, as well as domestic animals (*chiweto*), are commonly distinguished by sex. Metaphorically, sexual diamorphism is applied to certain trees – even to trees that belong to different species but are closely allied – to divining instruments, the iron smelter (*nganjo*), fire-sticks etc. The sexual categories are also used, with a personal prefix, to describe a man (*mwamuna*) and woman (*mkazi*), such that there is a close identity between sex and gender, and spouses carry the possessive pronoun 'my' or *anga*, thus 'husband' is *mwamuna wanga*, 'wife' *mkazi wanga*. The human person or *munthu* is not gendered, and this term is rarely used to refer specifically to men, nor are the sexual terms *-kazi* 'female' or *-muna* 'male' used as noun-based adjectives, as they are with children, birds and mammals. One does not normally speak of a male or female person but of a man (*mwamuna*) or woman (*mkazi*). As we shall see, many of the kinship categories are not gendered, and both sexes may take the role of the opposite gender: mother's brother *malume* is a 'male mother', father's sister *tate wamkazi* a 'female father'. It is important to note here that the initiation rites are not specifically geared to making a person into a 'man' or a 'woman' but into a sexual adult, the boy as an affinal male and a potential father (*bambo*), the girl as a mother (*mai*). The common and polite form of address in Malawi towards one's own or the senior generation are the gender forms *bambo* for a man and *mai* for a woman. Figure 2 summarizes these gender categories.

Both gender (the cultural marking of biological sex) and sexuality, though they cannot be completely divorced from biology, are socially constructed. As they essentially form separate but overlapping domains, I shall treat them separately. I shall conclude this chapter by examining gender roles and briefly explore their relationship to subsistence agriculture. I examine cultural beliefs associated with sexuality in the companion volume already mentioned.

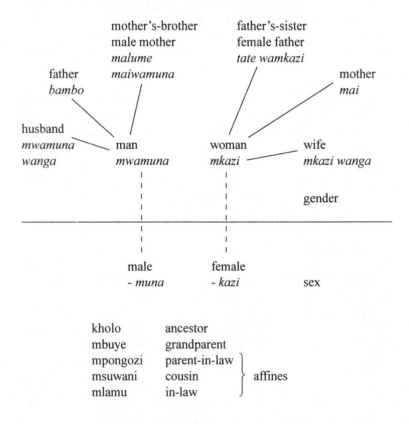

Figure 2. Gender and Neutral Kin Categories

In the pre-colonial period, Malawian people, like other people of east-central Africa, were essentially subsistence hoe-cultivators. Although farming patterns were complex and varied according to different regions and localities, two systems were widely practiced: the *dimba* system of wetland agriculture, found near streams, low-lying areas (*madambo*) and at the edges of the major lakes, and dryland cultivation (*munda*), which depended on annual rainfall. Slash-and-burn (shifting) agriculture (*visoso*) was extensively practised, this was still the case in some areas until comparatively recently, with the clearing of the Brachystegia (*miombo*) woodland being mainly the task of men who used iron axes (*nkhwangwa*) and bush knives (*chikwanje*). Women were the main cultivators, although not exclusively so, for the tasks of hoeing (*-lima*), heaping the soil into mounds or ridges (*-pandilira*) and weeding (*-palira*) were also undertaken by men as husbands attached to the matrifocal household. But women were the primary cultivators, and even today men are described by women as helping them (*thandiza*) in the fields (*munda*). Women also assumed the primary responsibiltiy for the planting, harvesting, processing and storing of the crops. Boserup's contention (1970) that African shifting agriculture was largely a woman's farming system is largely borne out by Malawian historiography, although it must be stressed that the pre-colonial agricultural system was both complex and diverse, and that men were actively engaged in the main cultivating tasks. The suggestion commonly made by economists and feminist anthropologists recently, that subsistence or smallholder agriculture is being 'feminized' and that there is a 'growing incidence of female-headed households' – as if these were comparatively recent phenomena – is highly misleading in the Malawian context. Historically, agricultural production was always the primary concern of women, and matrifocal or female-headed households were perhaps the norm. Contemporary scholars, when describing female-headed households at the present time, always define them in terms of women who are unmarried, divorced or with absent husbands, and seem unable to conceive of a household where a woman is the head, and yet has a husband attached and in residence. This was undoubtedly the norm in the past, the household being a constituent part of the *mbumba*, the sororate or matrilineal group.In rural areas such households are still found, and women conceive of the household or *banja* as ideally having an attached male (husband). Women describe a marital break-up as *banja yatha*, 'the family-household is "finished"'. In the past it seems evident that not only were women the principal farmers and largely associated with agriculture both practically and symbolically, but also that agricultural production was focussed around a matrifocal household (*banja*), which was to an important degree under the control of the woman, to which were attached in-marrying male affines who cleared the woodland and contributed agricultural labour to supplement that of the woman (see Spring 1990: 114, Safilios-Rothschild 1994, on the suggested 'feminization' of agricultural production). The main crops cultivated during the pre-colonial period were the staple cereals finger millet, *mawere* (Eleusine curacana), guinea corn, *mapira* (Sorghum bicolor) and pearl millet (Pennisetum americanum), such cultivated legumes as pigeon pea, *nandolo* (Cajanus cajan), haricot bean, *mbwanda* (Phaseolus vugaris) and the pea *sawawa* (not bitter) (Pisum sativum), as well as sweet potato, pumpkins, sesame (*chitowe*) and various gourds. Rice, tomatoes, groundnuts, sugarcane and coco-yams were grown in *dimba* gardens. During the nineteenth century, two other crops became increasingly important as staples – maize or *chimanga* (Zea mays) and cassava or *chinangwa* (Manihot esculenta). Maize eventually became the main staple, the porridge (*nsima*) made from its flour being universally liked, while cassava became an important security crop because it is drought resistant, can be cultivated on poor soils, yields a high calorific value per acre and, being stored in the ground, can be harvested at any time. Nowadays, people may also grow cassava as a cash crop to sell it in order to buy maize (Williamson 1975, Vaughan 1982).

But craft industry was well-developed during the pre-colonial period, and there were extensive trade networks, both local and long-distance. The production of iron and cotton goods and the hunting of the larger mammals were largely focussed around men, while salt production and pottery-making were undertaken by women. Both men and women were thus involved independently in trading and industrial activities.

The end of the nineteenth century, as already discussed, was a period of social and ecological disclocation in Malawi, with the expansion of ivory and slave trade, the intrusion of Yao, Swahili and Ngoni immigrants into the country and the formation of powerful, though small, chiefdoms. This led to a disruption of the population and the concentration of people in secluded or fortified villages, with the subsequent spread of woodland and tsetse fly, and finally the alienation of land to European settlers (Vaughan 1982, Smith 1983, Vail 1983)

Together with an expanding human population, such changes had a profound effect on local agriculture, resulting in growing land shortage, which put an end to shifting cultivation in many areas, a decline in soil fertility, increasing social differentiation and problems of food security for rural people. It also lead to a diversified economy, which, as many scholars have explained, consisted essentially of three sectors: a large-scale plantation or estate sector, focussed particularly around tea and tobacco and utilizing low-wage labour; a peasant sector focussed around progressive farmers (*achikumbi*), who produced groundnuts, cotton, maize or tobacco for sale as crops as well as food for their own use; and a subsistence sector. While during the colonial period the estate sector used the *thangata* system as a form of labour rent to maintain and control a supply of labour mainly consisting of Lomwe people, the peasant sector expanding with the development of tobacco and cotton as cash crops in the central region and the Lower Shire Valley especially, the subsistence sector was associated with migrant labour. Indeed, throughout the colonial period Nyasaland was a recruiting ground for wage labour, i.e. young adult men leaving the country to work in the South African mining industry. It must be stressed, however, that the subsistence sector in Malawi has never been conceived as separate from the market economy, for rural people have always been actively involved in market relationships through the sale of meat from hunting (by men), the brewing and selling of beer (*kachaso* strong, *mowa* mild, *ntobwa* sweet) by women and through petty trade and the marketing of garden produce, particularly that of the *dimba* gardens like groundnuts, tomatoes and chillies. With income obtained from such market transactions, people bought, and still buy, necessary commodities such as soap, cooking oil, clothing, sugar, milk powder and sometimes even maize.

An excellent portrait of the economic life and social conditions of rural Malawi during the colonial period is given in the Report of the Nyasaland Nutrition Survey of 1938–39. The following observations are noteworthy:

1. Although shifting cultivation was still in evidence in the Dowa hills, it was being replaced by a restricted 'bush-fallow' system.
2. The average land-holding (crop area) of an individual household (*banja*) was 2.7 acres.
3. There was a clear division of labour, with men largely engaged in fishing (on the lakeshore), hunting and basket-making and in the initial bush-clearing. But men were actively engaged in agricultural work and during the rainy season (December to March) did as much work as women in the gardens, if not more: 2–3 hours per day. This was still the norm some forty years later (cf. Clark 1975: 82). However, women's agricultural work was more continuous throughout the year and they did most of the planting, weeding and harvesting of the crops. In addition, women collected firewood for the household – a journey was made to the woodland every two or three days to fetch a headload

of firewood of around 25 kg – as well as bringing water daily, often assisted by young girls. They also spent considerable time pounding maize and processing other foods, as well as brewing beer, cooking and caring for young children. Women were also actively engaged in the production of crops for sale.

This pattern of economic activities still largely obtains in rural areas at the present time. Suggestions of 'involving' women in the 'development process' – that is to grow more cash crops – can only increase the already heavy burden that most rural women carry.

4. In more than half the households there were no men, as a large proportion of the male population were employed elsewhere, mostly on the Rand, as migrant labourers, whereas in the past men had often been away hunting, particularly during the dry season. During the colonial period, a large proportion of men were away for long periods as labour migrants. It is estimated that, according to district, between 10 and 40 percent of the adult male population were migrants or 'lost ones' *mchona* (Tew (Douglas) 1950: 42–3).

5. Crop cultivation was organized on a 'quasi-communal basis' and there were close inter-village links. Hoeing parties were organized, payments being made in the form of beer (*mowa*), and there was a strong emphasis on food-sharing, in terms of kinship (*chibale*), friendship (*chibwenzi*) or neighbourliness (*chinansi*). The report notes that one of the most striking features about agricultural work in the Dowa and Nkhotakota districts, where the research was conducted, was the system of 'collective labour' which was engendered by a 'community spirit' bolstered by social sanctions and cemented by beer (Berry and Petty 1992: 62–87).

There has been, as Vail (1983) suggests, a 'structural continuity' in the Malawian economy between the colonial and post-colonial period. Although both the *thangata* system and the migrant labour system came to an end at independence – in 1974 the government prohibited labour recruitment by the South African mines – subsistence agriculture has continued to be an important though neglected sector. Indeed, the main characteristic of the post-colonial years has been the massive expansion of the estate (plantation) sector at the expense of subsistence agriculture. This expansion, focussed mainly on tobacco, has since independence (1964) been phenomenal, being based mainly on the 'tobacco boom' of the 1970s. At independence private estates occupied one percent of the cultivated land and employed around 43,000; by 1979 the estates occupied 13 percent of the land and employed 143,000 workers. This land was obtained by the granting of leases on customary land and led to the creation of a new landed elite, for the new estates were largely under the control of the then President Banda and his 'entourage'. Despite this massive increase in employment on tobacco estates, wages were kept exceedingly low, and their real value has probably declined. There was also an expansion of peasant agriculture centred on the Lilongwe Land Development programme, which focussed on the commercial production of tobacco, groundnuts and especially maize. This was an attempt on the part of the state, backed by the World Bank, to foster a group of wealthier farmers or *achikumbi*, 'great cultivators' along the lines of the 'Master Farmer' scheme of the colonial period, which attempted to create a 'yeoman' class of farmers (Kalinga 1993; on the economic transformations of the post-colonial period, see Vail 1983, Kydd 1984, Mkandawire 1983, Cromwell 1992.)

The effect of these changes on the subsistence sector were significant. It involved the alienation of customary land for tobacco farming, the withdrawal of labour from the subsistence sector, and an undermining of matrilineal kinship and the power and autonomy of women within the household. While on independence Malawi was broadly self-sufficient in food, by 1980, when the harvest failed in the southern half of the country, large quantities of food had to be imported. Since then, with cycles of poor rains, food security has been problematic for many people in rural areas. *Njala* (hunger) is on the lips of many people who depend entirely on subsistence agriculture, particularly women.

Although it is clearly problematic to generalize about Africa as a whole given its diversity of cultures, feminist anthropologists who do generalize about African social life seem to suggest completely contradictory portraits when it comes to the issue of gender. Writers like Amadiume (1995), following the perspectives of Cheikh Anta Diop and his theory of African 'matriarchy' (see my critique of the notion of matriarchy in relation both to Diop and eco-feminists, Morris 1998) suggests that Africa is the 'cradle' of an 'archaic' system which is 'pro-female' and matricentric. Thus the 'core production' unit is seen as the 'matricentric unit'. Women share power with men and have a high degree of autonomy, such that they are able to participate fully at all levels of formal politics and have independent women's organizations which control and organize market trade and their own cultural and ritual associations. There is also a 'collective neuter gender' which allows flexibility and mediates the male and female roles. Following Diop and in Afrocentric fashion, Amadiume suggests that African 'matriarchy' is characterized by 'love, harmony, peace and co-operation' (1995: 47). While Diop is an apologist for state power, suggesting that the pre-colonial African states did not exploit their subjects, Amadiume emphasizes the resistance to 'centralism' of uncentralized peoples. She even suggests that African people did not value firearms or domesticate wild animals because of this matricentric ethos. State power, state violence and gender hierarchy are thus seen as 'imports' to Africa.

On the other hand, and in contrast, some feminist scholars have emphasized the ubiquity of 'African patriarchal authority' and have accused nationalist scholars, like Jomo Kenyatta, of concealing oppressive gender relations and legitimizing the perpetuation of these relations. African cultural tradition is thus seen as essentially patriarchal and as involving oppressive gender relations, which facilitated the exploitation of southern Africa by capital (Meena 1992).

Given the cultural diversity of Africa and its complex history it is difficult to generalize about the continent, as Meena acknowledges. Both portraits probably reflect aspects of the truth, the co-existence of gender equality and reciprocal relations between men and women *and* the subordination of women through gender hierarchy. In the same way – as we shall discuss in relation to hunting – reciprocal, complementary relationships between kin and affines in the subsistence sphere co-exist within a political hierarchy focussed around the power of territorial chiefs.

From the historical record one finds a similar ambiguity with respect to gender relations in Malawi. Observing the rituals of submission and obeisance expressed by a woman towards her husband (at a public gathering), or by a woman to a visiting male (of which I have often been the recipient) in which the woman greets the man in a kneeling position while shaking hands, writers like Duff MacDonald see such gestures as indicating the 'inferior' position of women in the local culture. The contribution which women made to agriculture was all too apparent to early missionaries in Malawi – though 'invisible' to contemporary development planners and economists (Salilios-Rothschild 1994) – and this led MacDonald to suggest also that Malawian women were treated no better than 'beasts of burden'. Women do all the work, he wrote, and hold a 'inferior position' to that of men (1882: 35).

Other writers suggested that Malawian women in the earlier period were not oppressed or subordinate to men, and that the ritual expression of humility and respect for the husband did not imply servility. Hans Coudenhove, an administrator at Chikala, remarked that the relationship between men and women was not based on the idea of inferiority of one sex to the other but on a division of labour, of which the crucial aspect, more emphasized by the Yao and Lomwe than by the Maravi people

(Chewa, Nyanja and Mang'anja), was the association of men with trade and hunting and women with the local subsistence community and agriculture. Men were not divorced from agriculture, but, as already noted, were actively involved in clearing land and hoeing the soil. However, male identity was very much linked with the woodland, with the hunting of the larger mammals and – as affines – with being outsiders. Coudenhove noted that sometimes on a trivial excuse a woman would, in public, humble herself before her husband – but this indicated, he suggests, her recognition of him as her spouse rather than her subservience to him. He noted that Yao and Nyanja women enjoyed great 'freedom' (1925: 76–7). In similar fashion, Joseph Thomson wrote that Makua (Lomwe) women 'seem to occupy a very independent position, and advocates of women's rights might take a few hints from them' (W.Y.Campbell n.d.: 92)

Evidence thus seems to suggest that among the matrilineal people of Malawi, women historically had a great deal of power and autonomy within the domain of subsistence agriculture and the village/ household or *banja*. Although women carried heavy responsibilities in terms of child-rearing, domestic work and agricultural production, they had a degree of control over their own lives, living among their matrikin with access to their own land and in control over their own labour produce and grain-bin. The *mbumba* sororate group often constituted a residential group in rural areas, a hamlet within a village community consisting essentially of a group of women who were sisters under the guardianship of their brother. Through her *nkhoswe* a woman had a high degree of control over her marriage, on the break-up of which she remained in her natal village, retaining the house and her children. In political terms, women also had a good deal of power: some chiefs were women, and it was common for a village head (*mfumu*) to be a women. Women could, in their own right, attend and participate in court cases (*milandu*). Women also organized their own rituals, particularly the girl's initiation ceremony (*chinamwali*). This is a crucial ritual among all Malawian ethnic communities, and it was entirely under the control of women through the local chief, and the senior woman or *namkungwi*, often a sister of the chief, was important as an informal advisor in community affairs. The family-household (*banja*) was essentially a matrifocal unit, though it was seen as complete only when a husband shared the house.

Although all this is written in the past tense and seems to echo Amadiume's theory, in rural areas of Malawi much of it still holds: residence is still commonly matrilocal, hamlets are still focussed around an *mbumba* matrilineal group and women still attempt to retain some power and autonomy. But many of the social changes discussed above, coupled with the emphasis that church leaders, development planners and politicians give to the ideal of a conjugal family under the authority of a male, have seriously undermined the autonomy and power of women in recent decades.

Although agriculture provides some 90 percent of Malawi's export earnings, mainly from sugar, tea and tobacco grown on the large estates, the majority of the population still derives its livelihood from small scale agriculture. Around 50 percent of rural households, however, cultivate less than one hectare of land, and over 30 percent of these households are described as 'female headed', in the sense of having no attached male. Recent surveys suggest that women contribute the majority of labour in small-scale subsistence agriculture and make the agricultural decisions in many rural households. Because of increasing male mobility, Spring concludes that the basic smallholder farm unit in Malawi is still the matricentric family consisting of a woman and her children. Many of these households are unable to meet their food requirements, and with little access to cash, many rural women and their families in Malawi are experiencing increasing poverty at the present time (Spring 1990; United Nations Report on Poverty in Malawi 1993).

Both economic and social activities in Malawi are organized around the seasons (*nyengo*), of which four are widely recognized. The rainy season (*dzinja*, a term that also refers to a deserted village or uninhabited woodland) extends from December to March. This is the main planting season. The ground has already been hoed prior to the rains, and both men and women are actively engaged in hoeing, planting the seeds, weeding and applying fertilizers if they can afford to buy them. As with other communities throughout east-central Africa, 3–4 maize seeds are placed in a single hole, 'one for the bush pig (*nguluwe*), one for the guinea fowl (*nkhanga*) and one for ourselves' (Marwick 1965: 40). The main planting of cassava and beans is from January onwards, but maize is always planted early in the season. The early part of the rainy season is typically a time of food shortage – the *njala* (hunger) season – as many households use up existing stocks of food. It is at this time that mushrooms (*bowa*), which are gathered by women collectively from the Brachystegia woodlands, become important as a relish (*ndiwo*) (see Morris 1987).It is during the rains too that flying termites (*ngumbi*), universally used as a side relish, are captured from the termite mounds (*chulu*) by men or young boys. The trappings of small mammals by men and boys and the gathering of wild vegetables by women takes place thoughout the year. But it is towards the end of the rainy season that women collect the leaves of wild plants for drying – of which *mfutso, Vernonia adoensis*, is the prototype – for future relish, and such plants as *kakombwe (Pistia stratoites)* and *chetsa (Cyperus alternifolius)*, water plants which are dried and burnt to make potash (*chidulo*) for cooking purposes.

Towards the end of the rains, around March and April, the time of the harvest season (*masika*), people in Malawi are actively engaged in protecting their crops not only from birds, but also from the depredations of wild mammals.In some areas, people build small huts (*msasa*)on the boundaries of their fields, especially if adjacent to Brachystegia woodland, and many virtually abandon the village to spend long hours watching their crops. It is thus important to understand that as subsistence cultivators, Malawian attitudes towards mammals incorporates opposition and hostility rather than an attitude of control and domination, one of keeping animals out of the village domain, which includes the gardens. Such depredations are such an important part of Malawian cultural life that I have discussed them more fully elsewhere (see Morris 1995). At the end of the harvest, people often sell their produce in the local market (*nsika*), especially such crops as pigeon pea, cowpea, *khobwe (Vigna unguiculata)* and groundnuts. As harvesting the crop and its marketing are closely associated by Malawians, sharing the same root, *sika*, it must be recognized that there is no clear division among rural people between subsistence and the market economy. Early one morning at daybreak, I came across a group of women collecting firewood from the forest at the top of Machemba Hill near Phalombe. They were collecting this wood not for the household, but to sell in the local market, in order to buy their basic subsistence requirements for the day. Malawians have thus long been incorporated into the market economy.

Between May and July is the period often referred to as *nyengo ya chisanu, chisanu* meaning cold or coldness. This is the time when both men and women begin cutting (*-mweta*) the grass, which is then laid out to dry in the village ready for thatching (*-folera*) the houses and grain stores (*nkhokwe*) prior to the rains. Bamboos, poles and firewood are also gathered from the woodland to be used in the making of baskets and bricks. From May onwards men begin to repair or build huts or brick houses (*nyumba*), the final plastering (*-mata*) always being done by women.

The dry season (*chilimwe, malimwe*) begins from around August when the leaves begin to fall (*mphakasa*) and extends until the break of the rains. This is the time of festivities, when initiations (*chinamwali*), weddings (*ukwati*) and commemorative rites of the dead (*sadaka, bona*) are held. It is also a time when the woodland is fired. In the past this was done in a ritual ceremonial conducted by local chiefs. Nowadays the bush is usually burnt by local hunters, for *chilimwe* is the main season for hunting the larger mammals. Although not as important as in the past, and now seriously engaged in as a 'profession' only by a minority of men, hunting is still important in rural areas. I discuss the sociology of hunting fully in the next chapter.

As the dry season draws to a close, people become increasingly involved in cultivating *dimba* gardens, thatching and repairing their houses, visiting friends, marketing their agricultural produce and hoeing and preparing the ground ready for the next planting season. The preparation is stimulated particularly by the coming of the first thunder showers some time towards the end of November, which are described as *kokalupsya*, 'the pushing (washing) away of the ashes'. The verb -*psya* has a wide meaning in Chewa, being used with reference to burning, cooking and roasting, as well as to be ripe, mature or ready.

It is of interest that when discussing with Malawians the subsistence tasks associated with men and women, people tend not to use the gender categories 'man' (*mwamuna*) and 'woman' (*mkazi*), but the kin terms 'father' (*bambo*) and 'mother' (*mai*).

–2–

Hunting Traditions

Introduction

In this chapter I outline the cultural traditions relating to hunting in Malawi, focussing specifically on subsistence hunting. The chapter consists of six sections.

In the first section I discuss hunting from a historical perspective. I focus particularly on the hunting traditions of three African communities, the Bemba, Lele and Ndembu, and note certain themes that have specific relevance to my own studies: the communal nature of hunting, the importance of meat sharing, the use of medicines to ensure hunting success, the salience of ritual prohibitions and finally, the close association between hunting and male gender identity. I explore the gender aspect more fully in the following section, which focusses on hunting and masculinity. After a brief discussion of the literature on masculinity, I explore two conceptions of masculinity in Malawi, one associated with the matrilineal kin group, the other with men as male affines. In the latter, men are closely associated with hunting and symbolically identified with the woodland and with the larger mammals, the emphasis being on their fierceness, virility and courage.

In Section Three I provide some background material on hunting in Malawi, on hunting during the iron-age period, the importance of hunting in Malawi culture and the digging out and trapping of mammals.

In Section Four I discuss the two main forms of hunting in Malawi, hunting by solitary individuals and communal hunting (*uzimba*). I stress the importance of hunting dogs, the empirical skills of Malawian hunters and the organized nature of communal hunts, which involves the sharing of meat. I conclude the section with a brief discussion of poaching in Malawi.

Section Five explores the important ritual aspects of hunting in Malawi, for hunting is never a purely empirical activity. I suggest that although there is a symbolic opposition between hunting and sex in Malawi, this does not imply a negative attitude towards hunting, for as I go on to explore, hunting is a rite of transformation akin to iron-smelting, pot-making, beer-brewing, initiation and human procreation. I note the spiritual aspects of the hunt and the importance of the disease *chirope* (blood), which is caused by the blood of a wild animal which has not been killed with appropriate ritual respect. I specifically highlight the affinities between iron-smelting and hunting as rites of creative transformation.

In the final section I look at the political aspects of hunting in Malawi, particularly from a historical perspective, for hunting at the present time is largely centered on subsistence. I thus discuss the various professional hunting and trading groups which were centrally involved in the ivory trade in the nineteenth century, such as the Chikunda, Bisa and Zimba.

Historical Perspectives

Hunting plays an important role in the subsistence economies of horticultural societies throughout the world, although, as Susan Kent remarks, its significance relates as much to its symbolic value as to its economic importance. However, in emphasizing its symbolic role, this should not lead us to deny completely the economic value of wild animals to human communities (Kent 1989; 12). With reference to tropical America, some writers have suggested that the advent of horticulture creates habitats that support higher densities of small mammals than are found in the surrounding undisturbed areas, giving rise to what Linares (1976) has described as 'garden hunting'. Thus, in economic terms, hunting may be no less important among subsistence agriculturalists as a source of protein than among hunter-gatherers. Evidence suggests that this is indeed the case, and a 'passion' for meat has been noted in many horticultural societies (Siskind 1973, Kensinger 1989, Kent 1989: 6–7; for a discussion of the literature on hunter-gatherers and a critique of eco-feminist perspectives on hunting see Morris 1996c).

Hunting among African peoples has undoubtedly declined in importance since the end of the nineteenth century. Prior to this, however, its significance had less to do with its role in the provision of basic subsistence, or indeed its symbolic role, than with the crucial part hunting played in the procuring of trade goods such as leopard skins, rhinoceros horn and of course ivory. The hunting of African elephants for ivory goes back into antiquity, but the ivory trade began to develop crucially between the twelfth and sixteenth centuries, with the growth of trade between the East African Coast, centred on such ports as Sofala and Kilwa, and the African interior. This led to the subsequent development of tributary states between the Limpopo and Zambezi Rivers, based largely on this trade. From the end of the eighteenth century the ivory trade expanded even further, most of the ivory being taken by African hunters. Fierce competition often developed between such peoples as the Bisa and Yao (Alpers 1975, Hall 1987: 78–9).

From the turn of the present century, the decline in larger game animals because of increases in the human population, the creation of game sanctuaries and the imposition of game laws by the colonial authorities specifically forbidding the hunting of large mammals except under licence severely curtailed the hunting of mammals for trading purposes (Morris 1996b). The ivory trade, and the hunting associated with it, is now illegal and undertaken secretly. Hunting for subsistence, however, continues to flourish throughout Africa, even though, strictly speaking, it is illegal in many countries.

John MacKenzie (1988: 55–81) has discussed the role of hunting in African societies during the colonial period, drawing mainly on early traveller's accounts. He notes that all African peoples hunted in one form or another, whether to protect crops, for basic subsistence or for trading purposes. Interestingly, he also discusses, even though briefly, the opportunity hunting gave indigenous elites to control the labour of others and to create centralized polities from the profits of trade, as well as symbolizing 'dominance over the environment'. He also reflects on how the destruction of game by European hunters, the creation of game reserves, and the demise of hunting rights for Africans – even though then, as now, the game laws were never fully enforced – must have had a significant effect on the local economy, particularly on African nutrition. I do not want to replicate his wider discussion here. I shall focus instead on the hunting traditions of the matrilineal peoples of Central Africa, making reference to some classic ethnographies.

As the tsetse fly was historically widespread over much of the wooded savannah region of south-central Africa, few domestic animals were kept apart from goats, sheep and chickens. Thus meat from wild animals, both large and small, formed an important part of the diet of many communities. Although meat was of minimal significance in terms of calorie intake, from a social and cultural standpoint it had a primary value. Richards wrote that the Bemba had a longing for meat that amounted to a craving and that their reaction to it was quite out of proportion to its nutritional value (1939: 56–7). This reflects the fact that meat was not only valued as a relish but also had a social significance that went beyond mere subsistence. Hunting therefore had a prominent role in Bemba culture: Richards writing that 'every Bemba is a hunter by desire and enthusiasm' (ibid.: 342), though her remarks refer essentially to men, and it is probable that not every man hunted.

But what is clear from such accounts is that the communities of Central Africa had essentially a dualistic economy consisting of subsistence agriculture focussed around a group of matrilineally related women and hunting (or fishing) centred around men. The latter 'sector' was implicated in trading networks and politics, as well as being geared to local subsistence. The gender division was, therefore, a basic axis around which social life revolved, and hunting was intrinsically associated with the male gender. As Douglas notes with reference to the Lele of Kasai: 'The separation and interdependence of the sexes is a basic theme of their social organization and ritual, and one which is reiterated in almost every possible context' (1954: 2). She also writes of the Lele 'craving for meat', but emphasizes that hunting is fundamentally a ritual activity. It also focusses on the communal hunt in the forest, and Douglas notes that the village community is ultimately a political and a ritual unit because it is a single hunting unit. For this reason, she writes, hunting is considered their most important activity, and the Lele think of themselves as first and foremost a 'hunting culture' (ibid.: 16).

The Ndembu of Zambia display a similar social pattern. Victor Turner, who wrote a number of path-breaking studies on these people, described them simply as 'shifting hoe cultivations and hunters' and described the Ndembu social system as 'pivoted on the importance of hunting' (1957: 25). Turner emphasized the contradiction between the two major principles of Ndembu social life – matrilineal descent and virilocal marriage – and notes how these are related to the 'structural opposition' between women and men in this society. While the cultivation of cassava tends to be the women's sphere and little ritualized, hunting is a purely masculine pursuit that is highly ritualized and valued socially above its objective contribution to Ndembu diet. He writes: 'In the idiom of Ndembu ritual, hunting and masculinity or virility are symbolically equivalent, and the symbols and gear of huntsmanship are reckoned to be mystically dangerous to female fertility and reproductive procreation' (1957: 27). Turner quotes the Ndembu as saying: 'For the man, huntsmanship; for the woman, procreation'. Hunting for the Ndembu, therefore, is not simply an economic or even a sporting activity, but intrinsically connected with ritual activities and with 'cults of affliction'. Turner notes that these rituals emphasize the father-son bond, thus providing a patrifocal element in a basically matrilineal society (1967: 5).

Hunting for the Ndembu is therefore a 'male monopoly' intrinsically related with masculinity. Given its past links with trade and the origins of states, hunting is also associated with high social status. Kent has noted more generally that hunting confers male identity and status among sedentary horticulturists, and there is a pervasive dichotomy in many such communities between male/hunting and female/farming (1989: 7). It must, however, be borne in mind that this is a ritual categorization. Among the Ndembu men are engaged in subsistence agriculture, particularly in clearing the woodland, and while ritual hunting tends to be communal and cult-like, subsistence hunting is more individual. Moreover, 'masculinity' relates primarily to the role of a man as an affine, the emphasis being on virility and outsider status. Turner gives an interesting discussion of the contrasting ideal personalities of the village headman (brother/kin) and the professional hunter (affine). The good headman should be generous, hospitable, helpful and democratic: the hunter is a 'wanderer', boastful, a loner, fierce, with sexual potency (1957: 202–3).

Given the importance of trade and professional hunting during the nineteenth century – such hunting being closely identified with the power of certain chiefs – it is not surprising that hunting guilds or cult fraternities developed in many central African societies. These professional hunters wielded great power, and with their focus on trade goods were often independent of the subsistence sector. Richards noted that the Bemba formerly had organized hunting guilds, with specialist elephant hunters. But as the ivory trade was no longer an economic activity in Zambia in the 1930s, such guilds no longer existed, although ritual hunts were still performed (1939: 342). Alpers (1975: 11) notes that during the nineteenth century, the Makua in southern Tanzania had specialist hunting societies devoted respectively to the hunting of the elephant and buffalo. He surmised that hunting the latter indicated Makua dependence on hunting for food rather than simply being geared for the ivory trade. Yet in the last decades of the century, 'Makua' had become essentially a generic term for itinerant professional elephant hunters. In the 1950s, however, although hunting cults among the Ndembu also contributed to basic subsistence in the provision of meat, they were focussed specifically on ritual activities. Turner describes two such cults: the Chibinda (bows and traps) and the Chiyang'a (guns). The latter consisted of professional hunters – Turner described it as a vocation – who hunted by means of muzzle-loaders. They hunted larger mammals such as buffalo, eland, hartebeest, roan and sable antelope, as well as smaller game, either in partnerships or leading small parties, perhaps spending several weeks on a hunting expedition.

Where the hunting of large mammals still plays an important role in the subsistence economy, as among the Bisa of the Luangwa Valley, professional guilds of hunters may be found. Marks (1976: 61–9) describes four such fraternities among the Bisa focussed on the hunting of the elephant, hippopotamus, lion and antbear respectively. He notes that with the advent of the muzzle-loader in the middle of the nineteenth century, hunting became more of an individual pursuit, and the professional guilds declined in importance. Much of his material on these specialist hunting organizations therefore relates to the past.

What is also evident from the literature on the Central Bantu is that the hunting and trapping of mammals took diverse forms. Besides a whole range of snaring and trapping techniques, many of them geared to the protection of crops as well as to the procuring of meat, hunting also involved many different techniques. Hunting could be individual or collective, involve nets, spears, harpoons, muzzle-loading guns or bows and arrows, and be undertaken with or without the aid of a hunting dog. Prey ranged from locusts, small birds and mice to larger mammals such as the elephant and buffalo (Richards 1939: 344–7; Scudder 1962: 197–200; Marks 1976).

Of particular interest is the hunting of the elephant in the past, without the aid of firearms. Three basic methods were employed. In the first, a group of men under a leader (Chibinda) and assisted by dogs hunted elephants with special spears (*kalongwe*) which were poisoned. With a blade about a foot in length, the spears were roughly eight feet long. After the leader had hurled the first spear at a selected elephant, the other hunters and the dogs then moved in and harried it until it succumbed. The second method was a variation of this. One of the hunters, equipped with a iron spear embedded in a heavy piece of wood, would lie in wait in a tree whose branches extended over a water hole or a path frequented by elephants. When a unsuspecting elephant passed underneath – the hunters' associates sometimes driving a herd in the direction of the tree – the hunter would thrust the heavy spear between the shoulder blades of the elephant, striking the spinal cord. If poison was used, death followed in a matter of hours; otherwise hunters aided by dogs closed in on the animal; hurling more spears until it collapsed.

The final method of hunting elephant required much skill and courage. The hunters concealed themselves in the long grass near to an elephant trail. When a chosen elephant was driven past, selected hunters took it by surprise, and using special axes, which were sometimes poisoned, cut the tendons of the elephant's hind leg. This method of hunting, which involved hamstringing the animal, seems to have been practiced in Africa for many centuries (Verney 1979: 87).

It is of interest that the elaboration of trapping techniques seems to be far more complex among horticulturists than among hunter-gatherers. In an earlier study, I noted that among hunter-gatherers such as the Andamanese and the Hill Pandaram few traps or snares are used (1982: 79), and Lee likewise reports the limited use of snares among the !Kung as compared with the Bisa (1979: 209). Hitchcock, in his studies of the Basarwa of the Kalahari, reports similarly that sedentary communities tend to exploit a wider variety of mammals than nomadic hunter-gatherers, depend more on smaller mammals and use a wider variety of traps and snares (cited in Kent 1989: 3).

Ritual hunts (*libanda*) are held involving a large-scale game-drive using nets among both the Bemba and Ndembu. Organized by the village headman, these hunts are held annually and involve burning the bush during the dry season. Both men and young boys are engaged in the hunt, which ritually confers prosperity on the village, and the meat is shared and ritually eaten at the end of the hunt (Richards 1939: 344–5, Turner 1957: 29–30).

Group hunting with dogs specifically to obtain meat for subsistence seems to have been widely practised throughout Central Africa. Dembeck described the 'pact' with the dog, fashioned during the palaeolithic period, as 'one of the greatest events in human history' (1965: 29), and Ingold has described hunting with dogs as perhaps the most widespread of all human hunting practices (1980: 66). Hunting dogs are certainly common in the region.

Richards, though she spoke of hunting as 'the romance and delight of Bemba life' (1939: 350), recognized that it was not simply a food-producing activity but intrinsically linked to other aspects of Bemba social and religious life. Some of these aspects are worth highlighting.

First, a fundamental emphasis was placed on the sharing of the meat. Although the hunter, as a prototypical affine, was seen as a 'wanderer' and as beyond the bonds of matrilineal kinship, nevertheless no hunter could selfishly consume the meat himself. Often there were strict rules as to its division. In the case of larger mammals, the chief was entitled to a hind leg. The same applied to the Ndembu, the consumption of game meat always being collective, the meat being subdivided among the married men of the lineage. A hunter who was deemed to be 'greedy', retaining his own kill, could be expelled from the village (Turner 1957: 32). Marks, with respect to the Bisa, records the distribution of meat from one impala antelope: the hunter gave a hind leg to the village headman, his maternal uncle, and the rest went to his mother, his maternal nieces and the wives of his nephews (1976: 25). He retained the chest, intestines, head and hind leg for himself, that is, for his own immediate family. In other words, the distribution is not simply an exchange of 'meat for sex' but involves a wide range of kin and affinal relatives. As Marks put it, 'a hunter's obligations are primarily to his matrilineal relatives, and through his wife, to her relatives if he happens to be resident in her village' (ibid.: 124).

Secondly, the hunting of mammals always involved the utilization of medicines to ensure hunting success, protect the hunter against sorcery and counter the harmful effects that might stem from animals' 'spirit', which was always co-present in the hunting of the larger and initially more powerful mammals. Thus, as Richards writes of the Bemba, every form of hunting has its 'magic rites', various medicines and charms to ensure the success of the trap or snare, or of the hunt. Animals themselves are thought by the Bemba to have medicinal properties. Parts of their skin or bones are therefore used as activating medicine (*chishimba*) in many charms or medicinal concoctions (1939: 343). Hunting medicines are also discussed by Turner (1967: 288–90) and Marks (1976: 107–11) for the Ndembu and Bisa respectively. The latter describes three kinds of medicine: *chilembe* (Euphorbia Decidua), to prevent the game from escaping; *ulwito lia nama*, to call or lure the game (the roots of various trees are used); and *mfenzi*, to hide the hunter from dangerous game.

Thirdly, certain mammals are believed by many Central African people to possess ritual power. They must therefore be approached with respect, and powerful medicines are necessary to protect the hunter from any possible misfortunes that may arise from killing one of these game animals. Before the hunt, offerings should be made to the spirits of the dead (*mzimu*) and the hunter must enter the savannah woodland in 'good heart'. There must be peace and tranquility within the kin group – quarreling is seen as putting the hunter in a 'hot' condition – and the hunter must abstain from sexual activity prior to the hunt. Again sexual intercourse is seen as making the hunter 'hot', and this has serious consequences for the hunt: either no game will be taken or the animal, in becoming a spirit (*chibanda*), will make the hunter sick or even mad. Richards writes that some animals 'are described as being Ifibanda (sing. Ichibanda) or haunting spirits, or else are thought to turn into Ifibanda when killed, and they are feared on that account' (1939: 343). She notes that the bushpig, bushbuck, rhinoceros, eland and antbear are all associated with the spirits. Among the Gwembe Tonga, Scudder notes that the elephant, hippopotamus, eland, kudu and pangolin are the only animals to whom these people regularly attribute shades (spirits *mizimu*). Thus unless due medicinal protection is used, the power of these animals may cause disaster to either the hunter or his family (1962: 195).

In his discussion of the animals ritually important to the Bisa, Marks mentions the elephant, lion, hippopotamus, antbear, eland and rhinoceros. He writes of the 'power' of these mammals, the rituals associated with them being in the nature of 'appeasement ceremonies' (1976: 120). Of interest is that Bisa do not normally hunt these animals, though they may be important as medicine. In terms of subsistence, and the game animals most frequently taken with muzzle-loaders on hunts, the most popular meat among the Bisa are the buffalo, warthog and impala. Bushbuck, waterbuck and zebra are also taken occasionally, but though they are common, the meat of these three species is not well-liked by the Bisa (1976: 205–10).

Finally, it is worth noting the ritual contrast that exists between sexuality and hunting. If a pregnant or menstruating woman comes into contact with a gun, this may cause the gun to malfunction and inhibit hunting success. As already mentioned, under no circumstances must a man have sexual relations prior to the hunt. If a hunting expedition is unsuccessful, hunters may suspect that one of their party did not abstain from sex prior to the hunt, or alternatively, that their spouses may have committed adultery in their absence (Richards 1939: 349, Alpers 1975: 12). It is important, therefore, for the hunter to remain in a 'cool' condition when hunting, coolness being associated with the spirits and the woodland (Marks 1976: 115).

Hunting and Masculinity

The distinction between biological sex and gender has, according to Herbert, come as something of a 'revelation' to western scholars (1993:19), although the distinction has been implicitly recognized by people in all cultures and was clearly evident in the work of Margaret Mead. The suggestion that there is only a 'contingent' link between sexual anatomy and 'maleness', recently heralded as a new insight by anthropologists (e.g. Cornwall 1994), is a truism that ordinary mortals have long acknowledged, which is why, many years ago, I had to undertake certain rituals in order to become a 'man'. But Herbert notes that the ethnographic literature on initiations in Africa has long indicated that Africans themselves recognize that gender is socially, not biologically, created. Thus Herbert concludes that Africans partake both of 'essentialism', in recognizing the essential biological differences between male and female, and of the view that gender is relational and socially constructed (ibid.: 224). If essentialism is defined as the recognition of sexual difference, then – apart from a few post-modernist anthropologists like Moore (1994:819), who seem to deny the existence of sex – most people throughout history have been 'essentialists'. Usually, however, essentialism has a more specific meaning implying an equation between sex and gender via some form of biological reductionism (Cornell 1987: 67–71).

In recent years there has been a surge of interest in 'masculinity' and in 'men's studies', much of it in response to feminism. Some of this literature has been a guarded reaffirmation of male authority, an example being Robert Bly's popular book on masculinity, 'Iron John' (1990). In an earlier anthology of poetry, Bly (1980) prefaced the work with a quotation: 'One day the master imagined a new blossoming'. This, in essence, encapsulates his plea for a new conception of masculinity, neither 'soft' and 'effeminate' nor stridently 'macho', but 'wild'. Focussing his discussion around the Grimm fairy tale about 'Iron John', Bly advocates the recovery of some form of male initiation, a bonding of men, a return to the forest and hunting and the reaffirmation of the 'wild man', fierce, robust, energetic, independent (especially from the mother), but not aggressive, brutal or expressing dominance over women. 'To be fierce', Bly wrote, 'does not imply domination' (1990: 27). Bly's ideal man is associated with the wilderness, with hunting, and is a disciplined 'warrior', wielding 'male authority" for the sake of the community. Small wonder that some feminist anthropologists have seen this as a new version of 'macho masculinity' and as a realignment of the general association of masculinity with power (Cornwall and Lindisfarne 1994: 16). Although the hunting of large mammals is largely gender-specific and still carries a mystique even in urban contexts, particularly in its guise as a blood sport, it is of interest that hunting is rarely mentioned in studies of masculinity, even when these have a comparative ethnographic focus (e.g. Cornwall and Lindisfarne 1994). Gilmore's lucid and readable study of cultural conceptions of masculinity, 'Manhood in the Making' (1990), is, however, noteworthy in that it includes a discussion of hunting.

All societies, Gilmore suggests, distinguish between male and female, as well as providing 'institutionalized sex-appropriate roles' for adult men and women. Manhood he therefore defines simply 'as the approved way of being an adult male in any given society' (ibid.: 1). Drawing on earlier feminist anthropology, Gilmore makes a distinction between bio-logical sex and gender as a cultural category, affirming that these are distinct concepts which 'may have a relationship but not an isomorphic identity' (ibid.: 22). Conceptions of masculinity are, then, seen as cultural constructs, 'collective representations that are institutionalized as guiding images in most societies' (ibid.: 29), and are not simply 'products of anatomy'(ibid.: 23). Although Gilmore has a unitary conception of manhood with respect to any given society, for him the notion that 'men' exist as a 'natural, unmediated category' (Cornwall and Lindisfarne 1994: 27) is somewhat misleading. 'Men' and 'masculinity' are not natural, they are ''social facts', ideological forms that reflect the material conditions of life. Thus the Tahitians and Semai are not overly concerned with 'manhood' (ibid.: 217). Masculinity, then, for Gilmore is a 'cultural ideal' to which men must conform, and in a comparative analysis of a diverse range of societies, he suggests that there is a constantly recurring notion that 'real manhood is different from simple anatomical maleness, that it is not a natural condition that comes about spontaneously through biological maturation but rather is a precarious or artificial state that boys must win against powerful odds' (ibid.: 11).

To become a man, boys have to pass a 'critical threshold', involving physical hardihood, courage and stamina, for real men are not born but made. Gilmore is critical of both biopsychological reductionism and the notion that masculine ideologies are simply mystifications that validate male dominance and the oppression of women. Like Bly, Gilmore wishes to decouple masculinity from ideologies of male power. In his discussion of hunting, he therefore emphasizes that while hunting is frequently a metaphor for masculinity, the connection between hunting and manhood expressed by many hunter-gatherers is not simply a justification for violent or aggressive tendencies, nor simply an expression of male dominance. Nonetheless he stresses the sexual metaphors that are associated with hunting, the provision of meat as a source of protein, the importance of stamina and risk-taking in hunting as evidence of manliness and the fact that in many hunter-gathering communities, the hunting of large mammals provides a threshold – initiation – into manhood. (1990: 113–17).

Gilmore's study of masculinity has been the subject of a good deal of criticism, particularly from anthropologists who specialize in the Mediterranean region (e.g. Hart 1994, Loizos 1994). It is suggested that he views masculinity as a unitary phenomenon 'grounded' in biological dispositions, that he assumes the 'hegemonic form' of masculinity to be the only form of masculinity in a specific society and that he therefore does not explore the multiple or diverse forms of masculinity that may be present in any ethnographic context.

Masculinity in Malawi is often talked about as if it were a unitary conception, as if there was an identity between sex and gender. People will speak of *ubwamuna* in terms not only of semen but of 'manliness', with connotations of virility, courage and fierceness. But essentially, masculinity in Malawi takes two forms, for as Connell writes, masculinity is not so much an essence as a way 'of living certain relationships' (1987:179).

The first kind of masculinity links the male person (*mwamuna*) with his kin relations, specifically in terms of his kin group (*ulongo, mbumba*), as a brother or mother's brother. In terms of these relationships a man is not associated with hunting but with the village community. *Ulongo* is a relationship between a brother and sister, and is essentially reciprocal and egalitarian. Ideally, therefore, a man's relationship with his sisters, as well as with his male kin (*abale*), must be one of caring and regard (*-samala*) and of support and protection (*-sungira*). In a formalized sense, when the relationship takes on a political dimension, this form of masculinity is conceptualized in terms of the concept of possession or ownership (*mwini*). The term implies stewardship or guardianship rather than dominance, being widely used to describe oneself or selfhood: *mwiniwache*, 'he himself', is a familiar phrase. Masculinity in this sense is especially associated with the role of the mother's brother or village headman whose disposition must be that of a guardian – amiable, un-assertive, non-aggressive, always seeking peace and harmony – and whose authority is that of a male mother (*mai wamwamuna*). It is of interest that among the Yao, according to Sanderson (1954: 272), masculinity is associated with the term *ulume*, which is derived from the kin term *akwelume*, the maternal uncle.

The contrasting form of masculinity in Malawi is closely identified with affinity and with hunting. It is important to note, however, that hunting does not form a critical threshold in the assumption of an adult role for men. Children are incorporated into the kin group at a very early age, essentially via the *kutenga mwana* ritual, which also imparts person-hood. In the early years of life gender is not emphasized, and there are no terms for 'boy' or 'girl' other than by reference to sex (i.e. *mwana wamwamuna*, a male child). But boys begin associating together at an early age, forming hunting parties among themselves or participating in communal hunts: many thus develop hunting skills and become aware of the ritual aspects of hunting long before they reach puberty. Many boys also undergo initiation rites before they reach puberty, and the essence of such rites, as I describe in a companion volume, is to separate the boy symbolically from his own kin group and to affirm his identity as a male affine. Important in this process is the emphasis on fierceness, virility, bravery and the induction of the boy into a male fraternity that puts a focal stress on their opposition to women. The boy thus comes to be symbolically associated with the woodland and identifies with the mammals that are found in this environment, the emphasis being on their 'wildness' (*chirombo*, wild animal). The rituals enact the identification of men with mammals; the young boy symbolically becomes the substance of the larger mammals, particularly antelopes such as the impala, roan and kudu, and in the girls initiation rites and in public ceremonials, they assert, as animal structures, their sexuality, fierceness, wildness and opposition to the women as a kin collectivity. Such rituals emphasize that men are outsiders, from the woodland (*thengo*). Thus in their role as affinal males, men emphasize a form of masculinity that is akin to that described by both Bly and Gilmore. This form of masculinity associates men with the woodland – as opposed to the village community – with wild mammals, with hunting and thus with the provision of meat.

Although, in reality, few men in rural areas are ardent hunters, hunting is seen as prototypically a masculine activity and is closely associated with affinal status. In Malawi the male affine, the in-marrying spouse, is conceived symbolically as an animal – the *kamwini* may be referred to as a goat or hyena – and as an outsider (*mlendo*). The hunter too is viewed as an outsider, and significantly the term widely used in Malawi for a hunting expedition or safari is *ulendo*, a journey, derived from the term *mlendo*, stranger or visitor. Throughout Malawian history, therefore, the founding of chiefdoms and dynasties, has been described in terms of an outsider who was able, through his hunting abilities, to establish political authority (Ntara 1973: 67, 119). It is also noteworthy that in the past, when colonial district officers toured their districts on *ulendo*, they were expected by local people to shoot game and thus provide meat for local communities.

The close association postulated between men as affines, and the woodland environment, and the 'identification' that is made between men and the larger mammals, means that the killing of such animals is seen as akin to homicide. The hunting of animals must thus be protected with medicines and sanctioned by the ancestral spirits. Yet in other contexts, it is women who are associated with game animals, and the act of hunting is analogously linked with sexual intercourse. Some episodes in the initiation rites have men as hunters shooting with bow and arrows mammals conceived as human females, and an equation is often made between 'searching' after women and after game. *Mpalu* is a term that describes a skilled man or a hunter (though it may also be used metaphorically to refer to a thief – the hyena again is a crucial association) and the correlative verb *ku-pala* is used to describe a person seeking a lover or friend. We may note that there are often semantic links made between the male penis and hunting implements.

Hunting in Malawi contributes little to basic subsistence, although meat is eagerly sought after and enjoyed by both women and men. But as elsewhere in Central Africa, hunting is important as a social and ritual activity, and in terms of the male affine, hunting and masculinity are closely associated. By means of the boy's initiation rite, and through hunting, especially the communal hunt, *uzimba*, men as affines come to be associated with the woodland and with wild mammals, and an ideal of masculinity is culturally expressed. This contrasts with the domain of woman – agriculture, village, matrilineal kinship – and with the masculinity that is implied by kin relations. It is an ideal that is specifically emphasized in relation to the middle years of a man's life and focusses on such attributes as male virility, independence, bravery (*umuna*), fierceness (*ukali*), firmness and strength (*-khwima*). In the Malawian context hunting (and masculinity) does not imply a Promethean attitude towards nature, nor control over the biotic domain, nor does it of itself imply male dominance. But both hunting and affinity have the inherent potential for the development of social hierarchy, male aggression and what Poewe refers to as 'productive individualism' (1981: 15). As affinity is a group rather than an individual concern, so hunting is not conceived as a purely 'individualistic' form of productivity: hunting in Malawi is essentially a collective enterprise undertaken by a group of men and boys. Nor is hunting seen as an act of aggression: though considered to be dangerous (*-opsya*), it is not perceived as any more 'aggressive' than cutting firewood or cultivating the earth. The Eurocentric equation made between predation and aggression does not apply to the Malawian context, any more than it does to the mammalian world itself. The cultural domains of hunting and agriculture, men and women, the affinal males as a 'cult' or hunting fraternity and the kin group focussed around a core of matrilineally related women are conceived essentially as reciprocal and interdependent, involving what Poewe describes as a pattern of 'sexual parallelism'.

Hunting and its associated masculinity do not therefore imply dominance, whether over nature or over women. When Cartmill defines hunting as the 'deliberate, direct, (and) violent killing' of wild mammals, and the hunt as 'an armed confrontation between humanness and wildness, culture and nature' and as representing 'a war waged by humanity against the wilderness' (1993: 30), his views reflect a Eurocentric bias, not how hunting is perceived in Malawi.

Hunting in Malawi: Background and Techniques

Hunting in Malawi goes back into prehistory. For both the pre-Bantu hunter-gatherers, the Akafula or late stone age people, and the early iron-age communities in Malawi, hunting played a significant role in their economic life. Savannah woodland is a fairly rich environment with regard to the larger mammals, and by all accounts the transition to farming was a long and gradual process, as iron-age cultivators gradually replaced the earlier foraging peoples. Evidence suggests that the earliest cultivators reached Malawi in the second century AD, but for many centuries after this these early iron-age farmers co-existed with the hunter-gatherers. But importantly, hunting remained a very significant part of the economic pattern of the early Iron Age cultivators. As elsewhere, there may have been a definite shift in the transition to farming, with the increasing exploitation of smaller mammals and the wider use of traps and snares than in earlier foraging period (Clark 1972: 23–5, Mgomezulu 1983: 54–5).

There have been two important studies on the zooarchaeology of the early iron-age period in Malawi, both focussed on the Dedza highlands. Mgomezulu's excavations were made in the area of Chongoni Mountain, to the east of the Linthipe river, while Crader's study focussed on Chencherere rock shelter, 13 km north of Dedza. Although entitled *Hunters in Iron Age Malawi* – and although the excavations unearthed pottery and even maize from a later period – the latter study was felt to deal with material culture relating to people whose subsistence base included only hunting and gathering (1984: 174). However, the radio carbon dates obtained for the Chencherere rock shelter range from 500 BC to AD 800. The two studies are based on bone fragments collected from rock shelters. Mgomezulu's material relates to six shelters in the vicinity of Chongoni Mountain (dating from 130 BC), while Crader's deals with the Chencherere material. From their analysis it is evident that ungulates constituted the main animals hunted during the early iron age period. I list below (Table 1) the number of individual mammals that their excavations indicated, as these relate to the more important species.

From their analysis, it can be seen that hunting focussed essentially on six mammals – grey duiker, klipspringer, bushpig, zebra, hare and hyrax – which constituted some 41 per cent of the bones found in the rock shelters. Other important mammals included ungulates (sable, hippopotamus, red duiker, impala, waterbuck, sharpe's greysbok), as well as antbear, lion, jackal, serval, wild dog and hyena. From the evidence, it is clear that Burchell's zebra was once plentiful in the Dedza Highlands. Other animals noted in these studies which are no longer to be found in the area include the suni (1), wildebeest (2) and cheetah (2), and three species were recorded from this early iron-age period for which there are no contemporary records from Malawi: Thomson's gazelle, steinbok and springbok. Among the small mammals noted were gerbil (11) mole

Table 1. Mammals Hunted at Iron-age Sites

Species	Minimum number of Individuals			
	Chongoni Mountain	Chencherere	Total	%
grey duiker	26	17	43	5.9
klipspringer	14	12	26	3.9
bushbuck	12	3	15	2.0
reedbuck	4	9	13	1.8
hartebeest	2	6	8	1.0
eland	4	4	8	1.0
oribi	2	11	13	1.8
bushpig	44	9	53	7.3
warthog	–	10	10	1.4
zebra	48	17	65	8.9
rhinocerus	4	–	4	0.5
buffalo	–	7	7	1.0
hyrax	52	14	66	9.0
hare	42	8	50	6.8
bushbaby	30	2	32	4.4
slender mongoose	2	3	5	0.7
porcupine	8	2	10	1.4
total	294	134	428	59.0
other species	192	106	298	41.0
TOTAL	486	240	726	100.0

After Mgomezulu 1983: 44–5, Crader 1984: 46–7).

rat, (9) and cane rat (12). The bones of tortoise (19) and monitor lizard (2) were also found in the Dedza rock shelters.

The evidence from the early iron-age period presented above shows a very similar pattern to that of the present time, as will be detailed below: although as larger mammal species are now confined to game sanctuaries or hill forest, they are less frequently hunted than perhaps they were in the past.

The term for hunting in Malawi is *ku-saka*, and the general term for game animal is *nyama*, which also means meat. But *nyama* means any edible animal, and 'to hunt' in the Malawian context does not specifically relate to the larger mammals. It will thus be used to describe the hunting of small mammals, such as rodents, even though the 'hunting' simply entails digging field mice out of burrows. But prototypically, hunting consists of a collective drive by a group of men and boys with dogs. To 'drive' animals into a net is *ku-sakira*. Hunting however is distinguished both from fishing *(ku-wedza)* and trapping *(ku-chera)*. The capturing of animals, large and small, is also described as *ku-sodza* (to catch fish or small game), *ku-gwira* (to hold or capture) or to kill (*ku-pha*). A clear distinction is made in Malawi between being killed and dying a natural death, and usually a distinction is also made between the deaths of animals (*ku-fa*) and of humans (*ku-mwalira*, to die or be lost).

Hunting is essentially the prerogative of men, but women will hunt smaller game, and any small animal discovered during agricultural activities is invariably killed by the women themselves using sticks or their hoes. If they come across the burrows of gerbil (*phanya*) or the multimammate mouse (*kapuku*), they will invariably dig them out. Women will usually affirm that they do go hunting, but always with respect to rats and mice (*mbewa*), locusts (*dzombe*) and freshwater crabs (*nkhanu*). Women will often form a small hunting party to collect the crabs from streams. The hunting of locusts, however, is usually the dry-season occupation of male youths hunting in small groups with bows and arrows, the arrows being long staffs of *bango* (*Phragmites*) reed or bamboo, armed with 3–4 prongs made from the spokes of a bicycle. During the dry season, young boys are also actively engaged in the trapping of small birds using 'bird-lime' (*ulimbo*) (see Morris and Patel 1994).

The importance of animals and hunting in Malawian culture can be gleaned from the fact that they play a prominent role in *Mtunda I*, the Chewa reader for standard one pupils. Not only are gender roles specifically outlined in the reader, but such animals as mice (*mbewa*), locust (*dzombe*), crocodile (*ng'ona*), duiker (*gwape*), shrew (*swiswili*), rat (*khoswe*), hare (*kalulu*), leopard (*nyalugwe*) and baboon (*nkwere*) are mentioned, and there are specific lessons on both elephants destroying maize crops (*iononga chimanga*) and on a young boy, Bibo, hunting and trapping (*atcha msampha*) a hare. It suggests that while the boy captures animals, the girl does not know how to trap (*Susi sadziwa kutcha msampha*) but knows how to collect relish (*kuthyola ndiwo*). It may be noted that whereas animals are described as being killed (*ku-pha*), plants are referred to as being broken or destroyed (*ku-thyola*).

Likewise, the early vernacular texts on the history of the Mang'anja, Lomwe and Yao, all give prominence to hunting activities (see, for example Chafulumira 1948:22, Soka 1953: 69–72, Abdallah 1973: 11).

The simplest form of hunting, which is specifically undertaken by boys, young men and older men, is the digging of small mammals out of their burrows. This is particularly focussed on the category *Mbewa* (rats, mice and elephant shrews), and in rural areas many Malawians, particularly some older men, have extensive knowledge of the biology and ecology of *mbewa*.

Given the importance of rats and mice in their diet – and this is particularly pronounced in Mulanje, Thyolo, Dedza and Dowa districts (at least this has been my experience) – it is hardly surprising that this interest is deeply reflected in both the language and culture of the people of these regions. In the northern region of Malawi, among Tumbuka-speakers, there seems, for some reason, to be little focus on rats and mice. Many Tumbuka, even people extremely knowledgeable about wildlife, seem to recognize only three categories: *fukuzani*, the mole rat; *sezi*, the cane rat; and *mbewa*, which seems to cover all the other species of rats and mice, including the black rat. But there are Tumbuka terms for many of the *mbewa*, and these are denoted in the text.

Among Chewa-speakers there is a rich vocabulary specifically focussed on the category *mbewa*. Not only are there widely recognized names for all the common species, but words are used that specifically relate to mice which have no direct English equivalent. The loose earth or clay with which a mouse shuts up its hole is called *chifule*; to leave a thin layer of earth to hide an escape hole, making the escape easier, is *kunenekeza*; the escape hole itself is called *mbuli* (from the verb *kubulika*, to break out); rat and mice tracks or marks are *mizimbe, mleka* or *mpita*, while mouse droppings are *nchimbiri*.

People who regularly trap or dig up mice have an extensive knowledge of their ecology and habits. There are basically two ways of capturing small mammals, digging (*ku-kumba*) and trapping (*ku-chera*). The digging up of mice is a skilled affair, and the techniques employed depend on the species involved. Some mice are easily obtained; others, like the giant rat (*bwampini*) and mole rat (*namfuko*), demand forethought and skill, otherwise much time and energy may be wasted or even no animals captured at all. I have spent several hours with local people at Zoa digging out giant rats and was always amazed at the amount of time and energy people are willing to devote to digging in order to obtain a small amount of meat. The mole rat is a particularly difficult mammal to obtain by digging. It is a prodigious burrower which can excavate soil at an alarming rate. Loveridge records how, with two assistants, he attempted to dig out a mole rat on the Nyika, and after digging for some sixty feet and for several hours failed to obtain a specimen. The right procedure for capturing a mole rat was divulged while sitting around the fire in the evening later: rat was then divulged.

Gently brush aside the soil so as to expose the opening, then insert a stick through the roof of the burrow a foot or so from the entrance to prevent the rodent retreating. Blow with as much force as you can muster into the hole until the blesmol, allegedly sensitive to breezes, returns to block the entrance when a second stick should be suddenly thrust downward immediately behind it and the disconcerted animal quickly seized (1954: 120).

Digging out mice is largely the concern of men and young boys, as is the trapping of mice, but nevertheless women are often knowledgeable about *mbewa*. The main season for digging mice is during the dry season (*chilimwe*), and scrub vegetation and woodlands may be deliberately fired prior to digging. In the case of *mbewa* like the multimammate mouse (*kapuku*) or gerbil (*phanya*), which are communal (several individuals often being found in a burrow), the burrows themselves may be smoked out prior to digging, and the same may be said of the pouched rats. By observation and smelling the soil (for its urine) or even by raking for parasites in the soil, skilled diggers are able to determine the presence of particular species of mice. Mice vary a good deal in their mode of burrowing, with regard to depth, whether or not they place loose earth on the surface (as with *phanya* and *namfuko*), whether or not they have 'sealed' entrances (*chitseko*), and whether or not they have escape 'hatches' or bolt holes. The burrow of a mouse is usually described as a *una* (hole or burrow) or *dzenje* (pit) – even occasionally *mgodi* (mine) – while the nesting chamber is referred to as *pfunkha* or *chipinda* (room) and the nest as a *chisa* (or *masa*).

At Zoa and Mulanje, I have spent many hours with Malawians digging up mice and have always marvelled at their intuitive knowledge of the habits of particular species.

The main species obtained by digging are *bwampini* and the two other species of pouched mice (*jugu, yungurukuve*), the mole rat and the two commonest species of field mice (both of which are found in scrub Brachystegia woodland and abandoned cultivations), *phanya* and *kapuku,* the gerbil and the multimammate mouse.

Like subsistence agriculturalists elsewhere, trapping is an important social activity among rural Malawians. Although primarily focussed on the acquisition of both large and small mammals for meat, trapping is also undertaken to protect village gardens from the ravages of herbivores, and livestock from predators such as hyenas and leopards (on wildlife depredation in Malawi see Morris 1995). During times of acute food shortage, the trapping of small mammals and birds may proliferate, and woodland areas near the village may be strewn with traps and snares. A wide variety of traps are used to obtain mammals, the setting of which demonstrates great skill and ingenuity. I shall outline below the main kinds of traps used, the construction and setting of which is mainly the prerogative of men and boys.

Khwekwe (khokwe, gango; Yao likwekwe, chitawa, litambula). This is a simple noose made of string or wire set across an animal path, in gaps along a fence deliberately constructed of branches and grass in the woodland or along the edge of cultivations. A fence will often be made along streams, with the noose set between uprights at specific stream crossings or watering places. The noose may be fastened to a stake, bent sapling or log, depending on the mammal species for which it is intended. To snare or trap a mammal or bird is described as *ku-tchera*, a verb which also covers the plucking of leaves or fruits from plants. Such loose snares are widely used, and although often common in scrub woodlands near villages, they may also be encountered far from human habitations. I have come across wire snares at the headwaters of the Katete stream in the Dzalanyama range, as well as in the middle of such game sanctuaries as Kasungu, Mwabvi, Nkhotakota and Lengwe, sometimes several miles from the nearest village. The trapping of mammals is thus an organized occupation for many men, who may sell the meat they have captured. A wide variety of mammals are caught by wire snares: hyrax, hare, grey duiker, bushbuck, bushpig, porcupine, baboon and monkey are the main species taken, but larger antelopes such as sable and reedbuck may also be caught, as well as carnivores such as hyena or leopard. Few animals are killed by the wire nooses, and many may experience a slow and painful death, particularly if they drag around the stake or log. But usually the trapper doing his rounds dispatches the animal with a spear or knobkerry. As recalled to me by many hunters, such occasions are eventful, even dangerous, particularly if the trapped animal is a hyena, bushpig or porcupine. I have heard men pass critical comment on those who neglect their snares and do not visit them regularly.

Msampha (Yao *lukonji*). This is the common spring tap, which, though based on the same principle, may vary in size from small traps set in pathways to catch the veld rat (*thiri*) to large spring traps that are set in fenced areas to capture large mammals like the bushbuck or klipspringer. Their size thus varies according to the species. Those designed to capture small mice are made from a spring sapling about 70 cm long, usually of a locally obtained wood, perhaps a sapling of *mtombozi* (Diplorhynchus) or *mpoloni* (Heteromorpha). The sapling is staked in the ground and bent over the pathway of the mammal, where an intricate contraption is delicately constructed. It consists of a trooped sapling about 10 cm high, a trip bar, a toggle and noose, the mice being captured as it springs the trap. Visitors to Mulanje and Zomba plateaus will see lines of these traps set in the montane grasslands, usually spaced about 3–4 metres apart and placed along the pathways of the fieldmice. The four striped mouse (*mphera*), along with brush-furred rat (*chitwa*) and veld rat (*thiri*), are the main species caught this way, often by forest workers who augment their relish (*ndiwo*) by trapping mice. I have found traps on hills even at the highest altitudes, well over 2000 metres. But similar, larger traps are used to capture cane rats and elephant shrews. Stannus (1922: 355–6) records such traps being utilized to obtain the creek rat (*mende*) and elephant shrew (*litawala*).

Similar spring traps, of varying sizes and with a noose, trip line and toggle (called *kachala* or *kasangandewu* (*msanga*, quickly, *ndewu*, stripe) are also used to trap both birds, especially the francolin (*nkhwali*), guinea fowl (*nkhanga*) and dove (*njiwa*) and larger species of mammals. Among the latter the klipspringer, hyrax, civet, grey duiker and Sharpe's grysbok may be mentioned. Again, it is worth noting that much time and effort may be invested in the making of spring traps. Not only does one find trapping lines far from human habitations, in remote forests or on the tops of high mountains, but in specific areas numerous traps may be set. In October, in an area of scrub vegetation at the base of Litikala peak, Mulanje Mountain, at an altitude of 1950 metres, I came across twenty carefully set spring traps. Set within an intricate pattern of fencing, and with spring saplings about 150 cm long, it was difficult to see where a klipspringer or bushbuck could move without encountering a snare. On Zomba and Mulanje Mountains I have regularly counted around fifty spring traps for field mice set in as many metres on firebreaks in the montane grassland.

Although such spring traps for vlei rats are important in augmenting the protein intake of local people, they seem to offend many Europeans, who may themselves be avid meat-eaters. I have known Europeans who destroy, perhaps wilfully, every trap they come across.

Diwa (Yao, *liliwa*).   This is a stone fall trap with an intricate device made of small sticks which is baited (for small mammals, usually with ground nut or roasted maize). To attract rats and mice fried bran is often placed in the vicinity. The main support stick is referred to as *jirikiro* or *mphanda*, the trip toggle as *kaphirimwana* ('child of the small mountain:) and the bait *nyambo*. The main species caught by this kind of trap tend to be small mammals: the fat mouse (*kapeta*), giant rat (*bwampini*), pouched rat (*jugu*), the multimammate rat (*kapuku*), gerbil (*phanya*), red velt rat (*mpakadzi*) and elephant shrew (*sakhwi, deng'a*). Larger versions may be used to trap the rock hyrax (*zumba, mbira*), sun squirrel (*ngorogoro*), porcupine (*ngungu*) and monkeys (*pusi, nchima*). As already noted, fried bran is often used to attract mice or rats to the trap. Stone fall traps are often set during the rainy season (*dzinja*).

Chigwenembe.   This is a trap made from the hollowed root of the *mpefu* or *chigwenembe* tree (Albizia antunesiana), into which is inserted a strong bent sapling made from a variety of trees. At the mouth of the trap is a noose (*khwekhwe*) and a taut string which prevents the mouse from reaching the bran (*madea, chigaga*), or roasted maize placed at the end of the hollow root (tube). To reach the bait, the animal gnaws through the string, which is often made of the bark of the *kachere* (*Ficus natalensis*) or *mombo* (*Brachystegia longifolia*) tree, and is then caught tight (*ku-sindikiza*) by the noose. The small mammals mainly taken by this form of trap include the multimamate mouse (*kapuku*), bushveld gerbil (*phanya*), creek rat (*mende*) and single striped mouse (*mphera*). Neither the fat mouse (*kapeta*) nor long-tailed forest mouse (*sonthe*) are said to be caught in this way. A smaller type of trap using the same method is called *chipoto*.

Ngombera [goba, ndeka, lilesa (Y) mujere (L) lukombelo (Y)].   This is a trap for small mice made from thin strips of bamboo, loosely woven into a narrow cone-like basket about 32 cm long. It is not baited but is placed in the runs of the mice, who freely enter the trap, being prevented from retreating by the sharp, inward pointing bamboo spikes that are fixed on the rim of the trap. The rim is the same circumference as the body of the mouse and the mouse can enter it but not go back. If it struggles, as it often does, it becomes even more firmly held in the narrow end of the trap. The main species caught by this method are the single-striped mouse (*mphera*), veld rat (*thiri*) and creek rat (*mende*).

Nkhoka (Yao lukoka).   Using the same principle as the *diwa*, this large spring trap is baited with a variety of items, depending on the mammal for which it is intended. The name of the trap is derived from the verb *ku-koka*, to pull. The trap is built with two rows of stakes between 30 and 60 cm apart, depending on the mammal, and with a heavy log supported at one end. The log is held by an upright at the other end, which collapses when the crossbar holding the bait (*nyambo*) is moved, crushing the mammal. This kind of trap is used to capture giant rats (*bwampini*) mongooses (*nyenga*), civel cats (*chombwe*) and cane rats (*nchenzi*), as well as such large carnivores as leopards (*nyalugwe*) and hyenas (*fisi*) when the trap is baited with meat.

Mbuna. This term is usually employed to denote the game pits used for capturing large mammals such as bushbuck (*mbawala*). But it is also used to describe the small traps that consist of a sunken pot filled with water and baited, which is used to trap multimammate mice in cultivations or in and around human habitations. The game pit is used to capture larger mammals and is commonly seen in evergreen forests, such as Mt. Chipata or Mt. Mchesi, where they are designed to capture such antelopes as the bushbuck and forest duiker (*kadumba*). The sides of the pit may slope inwards, making it difficult for the animal to move, or the bottom may be staked. From oral traditions and historical records, it is evident that in the past elephants and other large mammals were often caught in staked pits. These pits were a metre or so across and up to two metres deep, being concealed by long grass or herbage. The stakes were not usually poisoned, but the elephants were often eventually killed with spears and arrows. Duff speaks of pits used for elephants as being up to four metres deep, and writes of there being 'great drives' organized to drive game animals – buffalo, elephant, zebra and antelopes – into these pits (1903: 300–1, Maugham 1910: 350).

Mchera (Yao nyemba). This is the falling spear trap. The verb *ku-chera*, as already noted, has a wide range of meanings, signifying the plucking of fruit or leaves, as well as to set a trap. But *mchera* (plural *zera* or *michera*) specifically signifies a large trap, widely used in the past to kill elephant, hyena, hippopotamus and leopard. It consisted of a beam of wood up to two metres long, armed with an iron spike or spear, which was usually poisoned. The beam was suspended in an overhanging position over the animal track, especially near paths leading to watering places. The beam was held by a strong cord over a forked pole, the cord being attached to a trip mechanism at ground level. When released by the passing mammal, the weighted spear forcefully penetrated the animal's spine. Both Livingstone and Kirk mention that the banks of the Shire River in the middle of the nineteenth century were 'dotted' with this kind of trap, especially during the dry season. Elephant and hippopotamus were the main mammals trapped, animals which not only had high value as meat and for their skins and ivory, but tended to create havoc in the *dimba* gardens of the local people (Livingstone 1865: 94).

The *mchera* harpoon was commonly set on the path which hippopotamus took on their way to the feeding grounds. The trap was sprung by the animal catching its feet on the string, which acted as a trigger. The harpoon then fell, wounding the animal, which died within a few hours as the poison took effect. The poison only affected the wounded part, which was removed before the hippo was eaten. The hippo invariably took to the water, where it died, floating to the surface after a short time. The trap was set mainly during the dry season. Lowell Procter, who journeyed up the Shire in 1861, noted parties of hippo hunters and remarked that they would go immense distances in order to reach the stricken hippos. Both crocodiles and hippo were then plentiful in the Shire, especially in the 'Elephant Marsh' (Foskett 1965: vol.1/142, Bennett and Ylvisaker 1971: 59).

Ukonde (*khombe*).   Game nets (*ukonde*) are frequently used, as we shall note, to capture mammals during communal hunts. But large hand nets, two to three metres in diameter and held by long pieces of bamboo, are also often employed to net bats (*msanasana*; probably *Rousettus aegyptiacus*). The bats are caught at dusk as they emerge from rock crevices or caves (*phanga*) on the hills around Dedza, or on Ngala hill near Nathenje. Several hundred bats may be caught this way. As the caves are high on the mountains, often on precipitous rock faces, the netting of bats can be a highly dangerous enterprise. The bats are roasted and sold in the local markets at Dedza, Nathenje or Lizulu for about 10 tambala each.

Individual and Communal Hunting

The hunting of larger mammals in Malawi is essentially the prerogative of men and consists of two basic types. The first type is the kind of hunting undertaken by a solitary man, sometimes accompanied by a younger male,

HUNTING IN THE OLD DAYS

and usually by a dog. The second is a communal hunt, which in the past was often organized by a local chief or headman and involved the ritual burning of the bush. Although not as elaborate as in the past, communal hunting with either nets or dogs is still commonly practiced in rural areas. Hunting takes place throughout the year but is mainly a dry-season activity (June to October), especially regarding communal hunts.

All men are potential hunters, but within any community there are normally one or two men who are recognized as more specialist hunters (*mlenje*), because they go out regularly, either on their own account or in a semi-professional capacity, selling meat locally. The latter usually possess guns (*mfuti*), mainly shotguns or locally made muzzle-loaders (*mfuti za gogodela*). The latter contraptions may be made from the tubing of bicycle frames and can be lethal weapons to use. Many professional hunters bear the scars of injuries caused by the misfiring or disintegration of muzzle-loading guns. Gunpowder is made from dried hyrax urine (used as a substitute for saltpetre) together with charcoal and sulphur, and shot is made by cutting up iron rods. Hunters possessing firearms tend to be secretive about the fact, since throughout the colonial and post-colonial periods there have been severe legal restrictions on their possession, particularly rifles. During the nineteenth century, guns seem to have been plentiful and widely used by both Europeans and local hunters. Those used by the latter seem to have been of a variety of shapes, and Scottish missionaries at Mulanje noted that many guns possessed by local people had done duty at the Battle of Waterloo or bore the legend 'Tower' or '42nd Regiment'. Some of these guns are still around. The missionaries noted that it was not an uncommon sight at the Sunday service to see as many as twenty guns ranged along the wall of the church, together with ammunition pouches and powder horns (Life and Work in BCA, July 1902, MNA). Hunting in game sanctuaries – poaching to the authorities – is still widely practised, for both meat and ivory. But many men hunt armed only with bow and arrow or a spear, although invariably accompanied by a dog.

All serious hunters own a hunting dog (*garu*), which is, typically, an ordinary village dog, a creature which spends most of its days hanging round the family compound sleeping and most of its nights acting as a very efficient guard dog. Any disturbances or human movements at night is invariably highlighted by the ever-watchful dog. But they are not particularly aggressive animals – but they are loyal, tenacious and have great endurance. I had a pet village dog at Zoa, and he regularly followed me on my motor-cycle, running anything up to thirty miles within a few hours. The village dogs are of the Basenji type. They are medium-sized dogs, with a short, thick, silky coat, which is usually a rich chestnut brown in colour, sometimes darker. The breast and paws are white, and so is the tip of the tail, which curl's back. At the withers they stand about 42 cm. The muzzle is also white, and their forehead characteristically wrinkled. The breed is reckoned to be the only dog in the world that does not bark (cf. Maugham 1910: 323) – and though normally silent while hunting, those in Malawi do bark when threatened or disturbed, especially at night, particularly those of mixed breed.

In a survey carried out in the Mulanje and Zomba districts only about twenty percent of families possessed a dog, and this was usually because the man in the household was a keen hunter. Cats are far commoner, around fifty percent of families possessing them. (Coudenhove described Nyasaland as a 'land of cats' (1925: 176). Although superficially dogs appear to fend for themselves and are little cared for, they are in fact considered part of the household, and fed by their owners – who may be of either sex – and are usually well-treated. Most dogs are associated with men who hunt and accompany him on hunting expeditions. Dogs are considered the friends of a person (*bwenzi la munthu*) and their company is enjoyed. Hunters state that they like their dogs to accompany them on their trips, and one remarked to me that some people trust (*amakhulupirila*) only their dogs! Dogs often have small kennels built for them in the compound or else are given a mat or hessian bag to sleep on, and they are provided with food in the way of scraps: porridge, beans, maize, bones and fish. When asked, hunters suggest several reasons for keeping (*ku-sunga*) a dog: as a guard dog for protection against thieves and wild animals, for beautifying the household, as a flower (*amakongolesa pakhomo ngati maluwa*), and, most importantly, to help a man in his hunting pursuits. When it comes to using dogs as hunting aids, the prey invariably mentioned are the hare, bushbuck, duiker, vervet monkey and mice.

The names given to the hunting dog all tend to be of a personal nature, derived from personal association or habits or from specific incidents relating to the dogs'owner. Examples are *mfiti za limba* ('the strong witch'), *zilipano* ('it is here', so called because a relative was thought to be bewitching (*matsenga*) his children), *alekazao* ('leave theirs'), and *miseche* ('slander').

Although dogs are eaten elsewhere in Africa (cf. Ojoade 1990), Malawians do not eat them, as its meat is considered not to have a good smell (*ilibe pfungo la bwino*) and because they were not eaten by their ancestors (*makolo*). I was informed of one old Lomwe man who was said to eat dogs, but this was unusual. The association of dogs with rabies is well known, and the term *chiwewe* is used to refer either to the disease or to a mad dog (*garu cha chiwewe*).

Men frequently go hunting, accompanied only by a dog or with perhaps a younger partner, armed with only a spear. Hunting may often be combined with trapping, especially in the setting of wire snares, and is normally undertaken at daybreak or early morning. Some men hunt alone at night, often without the aid of a lamp or torch but always with one or even with two or three dogs. Some night hunting, however, takes place with the aid of a lamp. Men who hunt frequently are skilled in woodcraft and have a detailed knowledge of the ecology, habits and movements of wild mammals. As with women in respect to the gathering of mushrooms and wild herbs, skilled hunters have extremely good eyesight and are able to detect the signs and presence of mammals at some distance. Their sense of smell and hearing is also acute, and most hunters with whom I was acquainted could both recognize and mimic the calls of birds and mammals. As with hunters throughout Africa, Malawian hunters are skilled trackers, and their ability to discover the whereabouts of mammals is based both on skills in woodcraft and on a wealth of empirical knowledge, much of which is memorate, although it is also gained through the tuition of an older male with whom the hunter may have been acquainted in his early years.

Anthropologists are just discovering what naturalists and ethno-biologists have long known and emphasized, namely that African peoples have a wealth of empirical knowledge relating to practical affairs and subsistence, especially to the hunting of mammals. Field biologists and European hunters have long relied upon the tracking skills of local hunters and game guards, and their knowledge of wildlife and 'bushcraft' has long been acknowledged even while being appropriated (Walker 1981).

In tracking animals or in simply wandering through the Brachystegia woodland in search of game, hunters never simply track but are con-tinually on the look-out for the marks or signs (*chizindikiro*) of wild animals. These signs maybe visual, trampled vegetation, broken branches, tracks and droppings, or they may be aural, the alarm cry of a baboon or monkey, the bark of a bushhuck, the cicadas ceasing to sing. Experienced hunters are able to recognize the tracks of mammals and, from my own experience, many are skilled at this and can make an accurate assessment not only of the species, but also of the type of animal and the age of the track. Hunters are also adept at recognizing the identity of animal drop-pings, for scatological signs and habits vary according to different species and give a good indication of the animals likely whereabouts. Many hunters will smell the droppings, to obtain a sense of their age. The study of animal droppings, as G.D. Hayes once remarked, is not an 'unpleasant pastime', but to the Malawian hunter it is of inestimable value and essential to a successful hunt. Hunting has been described as a 'battle of wits' between the hunter and the animal, but essentially the very nature of hunting implies that the hunter identifies with the animal and attempts to ascertain its mode of thought and action. In contrary fashion, in describing animal behaviour hunters will often humanize them, giving them human language. Hunters also recognize the crucial importance of animal scent and of moving into the wind. Hunters invariably ascertain wind direction by picking up a portion of dry dust and letting it fall from the fingers, noting the direction in which it drifts.

Although a boy may learn his hunting skills by accompanying an older relative on a lone hunting expedition, often his mother's brother or father, such skills are learnt less through apprenticeship than by shared experiential knowledge. As most young boys in Malawi are initiated, hunting is not a rite of passage, and as already noted, most boys begin hunting while still quite young. Boys will form hunting parties of three to six individuals and go foraging and hunting together in the woodlands and in abandoned gardens around the villages. They will 'hunt' for crickets with bow and arrow, for field mice by digging, and for small mammals – hare, duiker, hyraxes, elephant shrews – by hunting with dogs. But most of their hunting skills and empirical knowledge on the ecology and identification of the larger mammals will be learned when they accompany a group of older men on communal hunting expeditions. Such skills and knowledge are thus gained informally, experientially, while engaging in shared, social practices, in much the same way as young girls gain knowledge (*nzeru*) of fungi and wild food plants by accompanying elder women on collecting expeditions. It is thus from personal experience that boys learn the importance of walking silently through the woodland, of listening and looking for animal signs, and it is through shared experience too that they gain knowledge of the habits, distribution and ecology of the various mammal species and of the practices and rituals of the hunt.

Uzimba is a general Chewa term for the collective hunt, although it may also be referred to as *ulenje, liwamba, kauni* or *buwa*. During the colonial period, the communal hunt was an important and widespread method of capturing mammals. Hayes was to describe it as an 'abominably cruel method of hunting" (1978:50), echoing sentiments that had long been expressed by colonial administrators, many of whom made serious efforts to have this form of hunting proscribed. The general practice was to leave a large area of grassy woodland unburnt until around October;

while the immediate vicinity of the woodland had all been fired. Some-times during the day, but mostly at night, local people, including women and children, would set alight the three sides of woodland area, while the men and boys waited on the open side armed with spears, bows and arrows and knobkerries. Assisted by dogs, they would kill the animals as they emerged from the flames. Often the animals were seriously burnt in the process. All species of mammals – large and small, ranging from field mice and elephant shrews to large antelopes – were captured in this fashion. On one occasion, an early administrator recorded that a herd of elephants happened to be in the area set aside for burning. As the elephants would neither cross the flames nor face the human barrier, they milled around, attacking the flames. They were so badly burned that they had to be destroyed later by the administration.

Although many Europeans in the colonial government seemed to have no objection to local people hunting with dogs and spears – 'We must allow them some form of sport', one noted – hunting by fire was the subject of much critical debate. When, in October 1930, the then Governor of the Protectorate went on tour to the Bua River, a favourite hunting ground of Europeans – Bua, it may be noted, means 'hunt' – he and his entourage were greatly dismayed to observe a large-scale hunt by local Africans taking place. One member of the party, the game warden Rodney Wood, noting that this type of hunting was found throughout the Pro-tectorate, appealed to the Chief Secretary to put a stop to this 'barbarous method of hunting'. It could not be condoned, he argued, merely because it was a time-honoured local custom. This led to a directive from the Governor to all district commissioners to take all possible steps to put an end to this mode of hunting, which was seen as being in direct contra-vention of Rule Four of the 1927 Game Ordinance (MNA/NC1/10/1).

Such hunting by means of fire is still widely practised, but on a much smaller scale, usually at night by a group of men and boys assisted by dogs and armed with spears, bows and arrows and knobkerries. Local men and boys often congregate on the sugar estates of Dwangwa and Nchalo around the month of May, when the sugar fields are fired prior to cutting, equipped with the above hunting weapons as well as with sticks and stones. As the animals flee from the burning vegetation they are speared or hit by the waiting hunters. Besides birds and the monitor lizard (*ng'anzi*), the main mammals taken in this way are the vlei rat (*thiri*), creek rat (*bvumbe*), porcupine (*nungu*), civet (*chombwe*), genet (*mwili*), mongoose (*nyenga*) and occasionally duiker (*gwape*) and bushpig (*ngu-luwe*). But the main animal captured is the cane rat (*nchenzi*), which makes its home in the sugarcane fields.

There are wide variations in the nature of communal hunts, according to whether they are organized through the local chief (*mfumu*), whether they use fire or nets, and with regard to the number of participants. From my own experience a hunting party consists usually of between five and sixteen men and boys, accompanied by around three or four dogs. The hunters carry bows and arrows, spears and knobkerries. The bows (*uta*, plural *mauta*) are around 1.5 metres long and are made from such trees as *mtalala* (*Zanha africana*), *mwanambewe* (*Markhamia obstusifolla*), *mlunguchulu* (*Fagara macrophylla*), *tenza* (*Grewia micrantha*) and *mposa* (*Annona senegalensis*), all durable wood species. The bow string (*nsinga*) was traditionally made of twisted animal skin or tendons, but nowadays people tend to use plastic cord. The tendons of such antelopes as the kudu, eland and hartebeest were those most favoured in the making of the bow string (Stigand 1909: 40). Arrows (*mbvi*, plural *mibvi*) are some 90–120 cm long, usually made of bango reed or bamboo, and with a metal arrow head made of locally forged iron. Some 20 cm long, this is inserted into the bamboo shaft (*bano*) and bound with cord; it may or may not have barbs. The arrow is usually flighted with guinea fowl feathers. Arrows without barbs are called *mpaliro, ndumba, psimo* or *chisonga*, those with barbs *ncheto* or *nkhaka*. In the past arrow poison was made from the *liane Strophanthus kombe* (*ulembe, kombe*).

Some hunters still use arrow poison, but this form of hunting is now rare, and at the present time communal hunts do not involve its use. Livingstone, when travelling up the RIver Shire in 1863, found hunting with poisoned arrows to be common and remarked that the local men who hunted were 'deeply imbued with the hunting spirit, and follow the game with steady perseverance and cunning, quite extraordinary'. When the poisoned arrow was shot into an animal, the shaft usually fell to the ground or was brushed off by the animal, leaving the iron barb, which was covered with *kombe* poison, in its flesh. After the wounded animal had succumbed to the poison, the portion of meat round the wound was cut away, but all the rest was eaten (1865: 466).

The arrow poison was usually described as *chaola*, a term also used to describe a plague or sudden death. As with other hunting utensils, for its 'heat' and power to be preserved it must not come into contact with a menstruating woman. The arrow poison was made from the crushed seeds of the Strophanthus vine, which at the end of the nineteenth century were a major export from Malawi. Other sources of arrow poison in the past were the bark of *mlunguchulu* (*Fagara macrophylla*), the root of *katupe* (*Boophone disticha*), the fleshy stem of *nyakalambe* (*Adenium obesum*) and the woody climber *mkuta* (*Adenia gummifera*). The latter plant is still widely used as a hunting medicine.

The Strophanthus plant carries the Chewa name *mbolo*, which proto-typically means penis, derived from the verb *ku-boola*, to pierce, sting, make a hole. The knobkerry, which is also important in hunting, is called *mbolomondo*, although the more common term is chibonga (plural *zibonga*). On tea estates workers all carry their baskets by means of a knobkerry, a stick with a clubbed head, which quickly comes into action should a mammal – civet, hare, elephant shrew, mongoose – be disturbed while working in the tea fields. Several hundred workers may then spon-taneously abandon their plucking, weeding or pruning activities to chase the unfortunate animal, which is rarely able to make good its escape. The final piece of hunting equipment taken on a communal hunt – for guns are essentially used by solitary hunters or small groups – is the spear (*mkondo* or *nthungo*). These are usually made of thick bamboo (*nsungwe*) but vary in structure, weight and size. On a hunt there are always several men carrying large-bladed knives or billhooks (*chikwanje*), which are used to cut paths through the woodland undergrowth.

A communal hunt is initiated either by a local chief or village headman (*mfumu*), or by a local hunter who takes it upon himself to organize a hunt. He is then known as *mwini wauzimba*, the owner of the hunt. As in the organization of initiation rites, a group of men with whistles (*pintu*) or reedpipes (*khweru*) will go around the village attempting to drum up support, indicating the time and place of the hunt. Often the men of neighbouring villages will be invited along. The area where the hunt is to take place will be associated with a particular kin group, and one of the senior males will be nominated the *mwini watchire*, the owner of the woodland. This person is often also the leader of the hunt.

At the appointed time the men gather at the gardens, and on a large communal hunt as many as two hundred men and boys may join in, armed with spears, bows and arrows and knobkerries, and accompanied by several dogs. The hunts I have experienced, however, were on a much smaller scale, although I have been informed of large-scale communal hunts in several areas, near Phirilongwe Mountain especially. Only men and boys participate in the hunt, it being suggested that women lack the strength (*alibe mphamvu*) to climb the wooded hillsides (although they regularly do so to collect mushrooms and firewood) or to throw the spears and knobkerries (*satha kuponya zibonga*).

It is of interest that the verb *ku-ponya*, to throw, covers not only the hurling of spears and knobkerries at the animal but also the shooting of arrows. In contrast, to fire a gun is *ku-omba mufti*, a verb which also covers the beating of a drum, the crowing of a cock (*tambala*), the clapping of hands, the moulding of a clay pot, the sound of a waterfall, and in causative form (*ku-ombeza*), to divine.

On entering the woodland, the hunting group will divide into several parties, forming a line of beaters (*liphondo*) on each side of the woodland. They will be referred to as *mbali ya ku m'mawa* (side of the early morning) and *mbali ya ku madzulo* (side of the evening), the east and west flanks respectively. If fire is used, all the surrounding woodland will already have been fired, leaving a large 'island' of untouched woodland where the large mammals will tend to congregate, as the grass undergrowth will afford protective cover for them.

The burning of the woodland (*kuocha tchire*) by the hunters is seen in positive terms. While ecologists and foresters, and Europeans generally, see it as a destructive activity, hunters accord it a quasi-religious significance, and do not regard it simply as a pragmatic activity. It is described as warming the place (*kufunda malo*) and is seen as essential to the regeneration of the woodland with the coming of the rains in late November and December. Thus the optimal time for the communal hunt is at the end of the dry season, in September or October. In symbolic terms the firing of the bush is analogous to sexual intercourse, both of which generate heat and are creative acts. Similarly, ritual intercourse at the end of a mourning period, the completion of initiation rites and the ceremony to conclude the childhood period (*ku-tenga mwana*, to bring forth the child), is also described as 'warming the place' (*kufunda malo*).

Driven by the fire and the beaters – young boys playing a prominent part in the hunt, normally armed with sticks and knobkerries – the mammals are driven out of an area of woodland. They are then set upon by the dogs, who often hold them at bay while they are speared or beaten by the hunters. All types of mammals may be taken this way, but the principal ones sought in the communal hunt, depending on the location, are the duiker (*gwape*), hare (*kalulu*), bushbuck (*mbawala*), sable (*mphalapala*), porcupine (*nungu*), Sharpe's grysbok (*kasenye*), vervet monkey (*pusi*) and bushpig (*nguluwe*). Although the communal hunt generates much excitement and seems to be enjoyed by all the participants – at least this was my impression from talking to them – such hunts are organized under the direction of the hunt leader.

Communal hunts may also utilize nets (*ukonde*), which are staked out in a line, the game animals being driven into it. Entering the nets (*kulowa m'ukonde*), they are killed (*kupha*) by spears and knobkerries. The line of nets may extend a hundred metres or more.

At the end of a communal hunt there is a formal sharing of the meat. The sharing is described In terms of a division (*ku-gawana*) of the game animals. Small mammals like the hare and elephant shrew are usually taken by the person(s) who captured it, but the larger mammals, like the sable, duiker and bushbuck, are formally cut up by the 'owner' of the hunt (*mwini wauzimba*). According to custom the village chief (*mfumu*) and the owner of the woodland (*mwini wa tchire*) are given a foreleg of the larger antelopes (*mwendo wa mwamba*), while the owner of the hunt himself gets a hindleg (*mwendo wa thako*). The person who first hits (*ku-mwenya*) a mammal is entitled to a leg, as is the man who deals the fatal blow (*msomoli*). All the rest of the game meat is shared out by the 'owner' of the hunt, and all participants receive a portion, varying in amount according to their involvement and status.

Although there is no formal rule forbidding the hunter from eating his 'own kill', there is a strong emphasis on meat obtained from hunting being shared. There is a general consensus among hunters I knew that the meat from large game animals, ranging from the duiker (*gwape*) to the buffalo (*njati*), should be allocated as follows (this specifically refers to meat obtained on solitary hunts): a foreleg of the mammal should go to the village chief as a mark of respect (*ku-lemekeza*), the back (*msana*) and neck (*khosi*) should be given to the mother's brother (*malume*); flesh without bones (*mnofu yopanda fupa*) should be given to the man's spouse (*mkazi*); and the rest of the meat, like the intestines (*matumbo*), should be given to the hunter's kin (*Abale*). In a communal hunt, it is the 'owner' of the hunt (*mwini wauzimba*) who directs the sharing of the meat; in a small hunting party, it is the man whose spear has killed the mammal or who is considered the senior hunter (*mkulu wa ulenji*).

An early historian of the Chewa, Samuel Ntara, spoke of an exchange of meat for sex (1973: 119), but generally speaking the sharing of meat does not simply reflect affinal ties between the man and his spouse, but political relations with the territorial chief, as well as kinship relationships. In the past the rights of mzinda, associated with the territorial chiefs, not only included rights over land and initiation ceremonies (*chinamwali*), but also rights over the larger game animals. Especially important were the skins of lions, leopards and serval – which only chiefs might wear – and rights over elephant tusks, the ground tusk being deemed to belong to the chief. As owner of the country, *mwini dziko*, the territorial chief was also entitled to a hind leg of all the larger animals taken on hunting expeditions, whether by solitary hunters or during village-wide communal hunts (Rangeley 1948: 24–5).

In the past, as now, if a large amount of meat was obtained from the communal hunt, it was cut into strips (*mizongo*), put on to drying platforms (*utao*), dried by means of a fire and then tied into bundles (*mtolo*).

Communal hunts are also organized to counter crop depredations, particularly by baboons. Such hunts are usually on a small scale but are considered much more effective than hunting baboons by muzzle-loaders or by trapping – baboons are intelligent and wary animals. The hunting of baboons is done at night, usually around October, when the woodlands have been fired and the baboons are sleeping together in wooded gullies or thickets. The animals are then easily surrounded with dogs and killed by means of spears and arrows, although not usually without a great deal of commotion and fight.

Hunting, whether communally organized or undertaken as a solitary pursuit, is a source of pleasure and excitement for the majority of Malawian men who live in rural areas. Meat is eagerly sought after, and I have often spontaneously come across scenes of great hullabaloo and excitement, only to discover a group of people, which may include women and children, surrounding some beleaguered mammal – a vervet monkey perhaps – who was being attacked from all sides. A lone buffalo which had wandered into cultivated land near Senga Bay was surrounded and eventually succumbed to a barrage of stones and spears hurled by a group of villagers. In a short story by J.W. Chadangalara, the hero Tasiya is described as a 'lover of hunting in the bush with his dogs' (see Young and Banda 1946: 110). It describes a communal hunt in which duiker, bushpig, reedbuck and eland were killed with the aid of dogs, and the great 'pandemonium' that occurred throughout the hunt, with shouts of '*psa-koka*! *psa-koka*!' (catch, hold, pull), as the dogs put up and chased the fleeing mammals. But importantly, as Mandala (1990: 39) points out, communal hunts were co-ordinated events, not general melees (in spite of the excitement they generated) and the hierarchical ordering of technical activities under the *mwini wa uzimba* was complemented by an unequal distribution of the game captured.

Large communal hunts seem to be a thing of the past, though, as already noted, small-scale co-operative hunts by men and boys and dogs are still quite common where wooded hlllsldes abound, especially the forested hills of such mountains as the Vipya, Phirilongwe and Michese. But even at the end of the colonial period *uzimba* hunts were witnessed by Europeans. In 1960 Bradshaw described one such *kauni*. It took place at night; the hunters, some thirty odd men and boys, held a lighted touch in one hand, a knobkerry in the other, which, he writes, can be thrown by most Africans with deadly accuracy at short range. Quoting from W. Robert Foran's book *A Breath of the Wilds* (1958), in order to suggest that Africans have 'no humane instincts' or 'ethics of true sportsmanship', Bradshaw concludes his short essay with the following words: 'And so "Kauni" still continues – constituting one of the age-old practices in which the African is still able to give full rein to his primitive and barbaric instincts in regard to wild life destruction'.

Yet significantly, in witnessing the share-out of the hunt, Bradshaw counted a half-grown duiker, three guinea fowl, four francolin, a 'mess' of finches, grasshoppers and mole crickets. Over twelve hours of 'dissipated wasted energy' had probably provided, he calculated, for each participant about two ounces of 'mess' i.e. meat (Bradshaw 1960: 6–7) – hardly an orgy of wildlife destruction, but no doubt important in the diet of subsistence agriculturists.

In the past, at the conclusion of a successful hunt, a dance called *chipalu* was generally held (Stigand 1907: 128).

It is worth noting, however, that hunters themselves are often aware that communal hunts can be destructive of mammal populations, for all animals within a given area may be taken. One hunter remarked to me that the depletion of large mammals on Phirilongwe Mountain in recent years had been largely due to *uzimba* – although it is probable that the depletion of zebra, elephant, eland, sable, kudu and lion has equally been due to the influx of hunters with rifles and the opening-up of the area to tobacco estates.

I conclude this section with a discussion of poaching.

Poaching is simply the unauthorized taking or collecting of wild mammals, whether by trapping or hunting. As hunting is forbidden in forest reserves, national parks and game reserves, which together make up some 20 percent of the land area (Bell 1987: 83), poaching is prevalent throughout the rural areas of Malawi. Thus a constant battle rages on the boundaries of all the major game sanctuaries, for local people do not recognize the legitimacy of government control over such woodland areas. With increased population pressure deforestation has become a serious problem, with the eradication of Brachystegia woodland throughout Malawi over the past four or five decades. Thus the only extensive areas of untouched woodland still to be found are the forest reserves and game sanctuaries. And it is in such sanctuaries that many of the larger species of mammals are to be found.

As local people are forbidden to enter the wildlife sanctuaries to hunt or trap mammals or to collect firewood and medicines, conflict eventually arises with the game guards. On the borders of the sanctuaries, village people are hostile towards the staff of the Department of National Parks and Wildlife, and many refuse to sell them food or be friendly towards them. People recognize that the government (*boma*) have reasons to protect the wild mammals of the woodland (*kuteteza nyama za m'tchire*) and that this brings in revenue (*ndalama*) from tourists (*anthu achilendo*). They will also suggest that it is not a good thing to enter the wildlife sanctuaries without permission, but almost no one I have spoken to who lives in areas adjacent to wildlife sanctuaries – at Mwabvi, Liwonde and Kasungu in particular – is happy with the situation. They feel that they should be free to enter the reserves and national parks to hunt animals and to gather firewood, medicines and wild foods. Many people said to me that the majority of people who live adjacent to the wildlife sanctuaries did not like (*samakonda*) the restrictions placed upon them, and felt that they should be allowed to enter these woodland areas for hunting purposes.

The wildlife authorities often sympathise with what they describe as the 'small time subsistence poacher', and there is no doubt that poaching by professional hunters who enter the parks and reserves in small groups armed with sophisticated high velocity rifles like the AK47 are a serious problem, particularly as their activities are focussed on the rhino and elephant. The Department of National Parks and Wildlife is doing all in its power to curb this kind of poaching: since elephant tusks and rhino horn are highly profitable commodities, the elephant and rhino are under serious threat throughout Africa. The Department is also mounting educational campaigns to reform poachers and is exploring ways and means of using wildlife resources profitably and sustainably so as to help local village communities, since currently profits from the sanctuaries in the form of tourist revenues invariably go to the national government. But it is a fact that most of the hunting and trapping in the wildlife sanctuaries – poaching – is undertaken for subsistence purposes (although the hunter may sell the meat) and such hunting and trapping is widely and extensively practised.

The situation in two game sanctuaries may be briefly discussed. A survey of Vwaza Marsh Game Reserve in 1982–85 estimated that mortality rates due to poaching amounted to about 72 percent of the total mortality, and included 66 elephant, 69 buffalo, 13 roan, 23 hartebeest, 10 kudu, 32 warthog and 12 hyrax, as well as numerous other species, including zebra, bushpig, porcupine, duiker, reedbuck and impala. Patrols of game guards within the reserve – three per month – reported seeing ten dead elephants, 36 groups of poachers, hearing 90 gunshots and finding 7 drying racks for meat and 112 snares or traps. Most illegal activities took place along the boundaries of the game reserve, and although the hunting of large mammals with firearms was common, almost all poaching activities constituted an integral part of the local subsistence economy. As poaching in the reserve was so widespread, and as local people were eager to make a number of boundary changes to the reserve, the wildlife biologist concluded that the Department of National Parks and Wildlife had not been very successful in influencing public opinion as to the reasons why the sanctuary exists and its value as a protected area (McShane 1985).

The same situation is found in relation to Liwonde National Park, where poaching within the sanctuary is widespread and seems to be on the increase. Elephants are constantly hunted by professional hunters for their tusks, using high-powered automatic guns. But hunters from surrounding villages are even more ubiquitous, their activities largely directed towards obtaining meat for local consumption. Antelopes such as kudu, sable, impala and waterbuck are hunted by muzzle-loaders or trapped by wire snares. In July 1989 intensified patrolling discovered some 150 wire snares, many close to Makanga camp. More recently, in the period September to November 1994, the game guards collected around 5,000 snares that had been set to capture mammals, as well as apprehending six men in possession of firearms (W.S.M. Newsletter, February 1995).

The hunting of mammals in wildlife sanctuaries and forest reserves is therefore an important aspect of the local subsistence economy, even though communal hunts are curtailed within such sanctuaries. Interestingly people refer to animals in such sanctuaries as *ng'ombe/nyama wa boma* (cattle/game of the government).

Hunting: Ritual Aspects

The woodland in Malawi is considered to be a cool (*ozizira*) environment, and it is therefore imperative for anyone entering the woodland to hunt to be and remain in a cool condition. Hunting is not viewed negatively or seen in oppositional terms to reproduction, but like all vital productive activities – child-bearing, the firing of pots, initiation, iron-smelting – it must be undertaken in a cool condition. Fire, sexual activity and contact with blood all make a person 'hot' (*otentha*); it is important, then, that a man whose wife is menstruating (*asambamo*, washing) should not go hunting. It is equally important that men should not have sexual inter-course with a woman prior to the hunt, nor must his wife have sexual relations with any other man while he is on a hunting expedition. Such illicit sex (*chigololo*) is viewed as extremely dangerous. Equally important, social relations within the village must be peaceful and tranquil

Table 2. Species of Mammal Trapped or Hunted in Malawi for Food

Species	Cultivations	Stream/River Edge; *dambo* Environs	Savanna Woodland	HABITAT Montane Evergreen Forest	Riparian Grass; Thickets	Montane Grassland	Rocky Hillsides
Carnivores							
3. Otter *katumbu*		x					
8. Civet *chomwe*			x		x		
9. Genet *mwili*			x				
10. Mongoose *nyenga*		x	x		x		
24. Serval *njuzi*			x				x
Unqulates							
26. Elephant *njobvu*			x	x			
27. Rhinocerus *chipembere*			x		x		
28. Burchell's Zebra *mbidzi*			x		x	x	
29. Warthog *njiri*		x	x				
30. Bushpig *nguluwe*		x	x		x		
31. Hippopotamus *mvuu*		x					
32. Blue Wildebeest *nyumbu*		x	x				
33. Hartebeest *ngondo*			x				
34. Red Forest duiker				x			
36. Blue Duiker *kadumba*				x	x		
Carnivores							
37. Klipspringer *chinkhoma*							x
38. Oribi *chowe*		x					
39. Sharpe's Grysbok *kasenye*			x	x	x		

Table 2. Species of Mammal Trapped or Hunted in Malawi for Food (*continued*)

Species		HABITAT					
	Cultivations	Stream/River Edge; *dambo* Environs	Savanna Woodland	Montane Evergreen Forest	Riparian Grass; Thickets	Montane Grassland	Rocky Hillsides
40. Suni *kadumba*					x		
41. Impala *nswala*			x				
42. Roan *chilembwe*			x			x	
43. Sable *mphalapala*			x				
44. Buffalo *njati*		x	x				
45. Kudu *ngoma*			x				
46. Nyala *boo*			x		x		
47. Bushbuck *mbawala*				x	x		
48. Eland *ntchefu*			x			x	
49. Reedbuck *mphoyo*		x			x	x	
50. Waterbuck *nakodzwe*		x	x				
51. Puku *nseula*		x					
Mbewa Cateqorv							
52/55. Elephant shrews *sakhwi*			x		x		
58/59. Cane Rat *nchenzi*		x		x	x		
60/61. Mole Rat *namfuko*		x	x			x	
62. Vlei Rat *thiri*		x					
63. Gerbil *phanya*	x	x	x				
65. Giant Rat *bwampini*		x		x	x		
66. Pouched Rat *jugu*	x		x				
67. Long-tailed pouched rat *yungurukuue*					x		

Table 2. Species of Mammal Trapped or Hunted in Malawi for Food (*continued*)

Species	Cultivations	Stream/River Edge; *dambo* Environs	Savanna Woodland	Montane Evergreen Forest	Riparian Grass; Thickets	Montane Grassland	Rocky Hillsides
				HABITAT			
69. Fat Mouse *kapeta*	x		x		x		
70. Spiny Mouse *kachenzi*			x				x
71. Creek Rat *bvumbe*		x					
72. Single-striped Mouse *mphera*		x	x				
73. Four-striped mouse *mphera*	x				x	x	
74. Water Rat *nthukwi*		x					
Mbewa Category							
75. Long-tailed Forest Mouse *sonthe*	x		x		x		
76/77. Pygmy Mouse *pinji*	x		x	x		x	
79. Brush-furred rat *chitwa*					x		
80. Mulanje rat *chitwa*				x			
81. Multimammate Mouse *kapuku*	x	x					
82. Redveld Rat *mphakadzi*			x				x
Other species							
87. Bat *msanasana*			x		x		x
89. Bushbaby *changa*					x		
90. Night Ape *kamundi*			x		x		
91. Baboon *nyani*	x		x		x		

Table 2. Species of Mammal Trapped or Hunted in Malawi for Food (*continued*)

Species	Cultivations	Stream/River Edge; *dambo* Environs	Savanna Woodland	Montane Evergreen Forest	Riparian Grass; Thickets	Montane Grassland	Rocky Hillsides
				HABITAT			
Other species							
92. Vervet Monkey *pusi*	x		x		x		
93. Blue Monkey *nchima*	x		x	x	x		
94/95. Hyrax *mbila*					x		x
96. Antbear *nkumbakumba*			x				
98. Sun Squirrel *gologolo*			x	x	x		x
100. Bush Squirrel *likongwe*			x		x		
103. Porcupine *nungu*			x				x
104. Scrub Hare *kalulu*			x				x
105. Red Rock Hare *kafumbwe*			x				x

(*ntendere*); there must be no conflict, and the hunter must thus have no anger (*kwiya*) in his heart. His disposition must be calm and gentle, and as the heart is the seat of the emotions, it is described as *kufatsa mtima*, to have a gentle heart. Blood, sex and anger are contrary to the disposition that is required of the hunter, who must be in a 'cool' (*ozizira*) state. As one hunter said to me, 'a person who is cool will kill animals well' (*akhala ozizira akuphabwino*).

Any contravention of these rules is seen has having dire consequences. The hunters may not find any game, or misfortunes may befall them. Accidents may occur, and a hunter may be seriously injured, even killed, by a wild animal. If game is not encountered during a hunt – and it is said that the larger mammals are able to smell semen – men may suspect that one of their party is 'hot', having had sexual relations prior to the hunt. Or – and this has often been suggested to me when accompanying hunters – a man's wife is having sexual relations with another man during his absence, and this is the reason that he has been unlucky and has not encountered or killed any game animal. This idea seems to be widespread throughout southern Africa (cf. Junod 1927: 61). Some men will not even carry metal coins when on a hunting expedition, for metal is associated with 'heat'.

There is then, in Malawi, a pronounced antithesis between sex and hunting, but it would be highly misleading to interpret this in gnostic fashion as implying a symbolic dualism between men and women, hunting and cultivation, such that hunting is seen as a 'life-taking' activity and sex and reproduction a 'life-giving' one (Rosaldo and Atkinson 1975). This kind of analysis tends to see both hunting and menstruation in negative terms and to conceptualize 'heat' likewise, as the negative side of a symbolic polarity that is associated with red, menstrual blood, fire, witches, sickness and sterility, as opposed to 'coolness', which is associated with white, semen, water, ancestral spirits, health and fertility (cf. Kuper 1982: 20 on the symbolism of the Southern African Bantu). Both accounts imply a radical gnostic schema of good and evil that is quite foreign to Malawian conceptions, which imply a complementary polarity between men and women, hunting and cultivation, and seek a symbolic balance between 'hot' and 'cool'. Hotness is a condition, not a disease (*nthenda*). It is associated with blood, fire and sex. But these are not viewed negatively, for they are essential aspects of both human life and ecological well-being. Thus hunting, like childbirth, menstruation, pot-making, iron-smelting and initiation, is not viewed negatively: being a creative activity that is associated with 'heat' (blood), it must be undertaken in a 'cool' condition. A hunter, a child, a menstruating woman, an initiate undergoing a transition ceremony, all have affinities with each other: they are in a vulnerable state and must not come into contact with anything that generates 'heat'. They must remain 'cool'.

In the past, among the Yao, a child was ideally born in the woodland where it was 'cool', and in the early years of life many young children came under the care of the grandmother, who is beyond child-bearing years and is seen as sexually inactive and thus 'cool'. A menstruating woman is also deemed to be 'cool' and can thus handle a child, while a sexually active person must not, especially if the sexual activity is considered illicit. A man who has sexual relations with a woman and then embraces his child is said to 'cut' (*kudula*) the child, and this has grave consequences for it. Although a menstruating woman may be described as *mkazi wa dothe* (woman of the earth) and the condition is referred to in terms of washing the body (*kusamba*), menstruation is not viewed by women as a negative state that is 'unclean' or 'polluting', nor as a disease (*nthenda*). A girl's first menstruation is a source of rejoicing and ritual affirmation, and although subsequent menstruations are seen as a loss (they may be described as *kugwa pansi*, to fall down), the menstrual flow is not viewed as the negation of life, nor is hunting. A menstruating woman is described as being in a 'cool' (*ozizira*) condition and thus vulnerable like a child, but also as potentially affecting others in an adverse way. She must not have sexual relations, either on her own account, or because she may adversely effect the man. He will contract a disease, usually referred to as *kanyera*, the 'blood' (*magazi*) of the women entering his body, which is associated with backache (*msana*), with a painful navel (*mchombo*) and a general weakness of the loins. The man has no strength and is unable to achieve an erection. He is deemed to lose weight, to become thin (*ku-onda*) and to have a very cold body, such that he is constantly desiring meat, salt and chillies and wanting to sit near the fire. A menstruating woman must also observe certain rituals associated with the fire: she must not put a pot on the fire, nor lean across the fire, nor put salt (*mchere*) in the relish (*ndiwo*) of her family, otherwise they will be 'cut' and contract the disease *mdulo* or *tsempho* (see Morris 1985).

Like a menstruating woman a hunter must also observe certain precautions. It is best that he places his hunting equipment – especially spears, guns, bows and arrows – where they can remain 'cool'. This is often on the verandah (*khonde*, a word that has linguistic affinities with both spear, *mkondo*, and war, *mkhondo*). Some hunters insist that hunting equipment must never be placed near the kitchen fire or even in the kitchen (*malokuphika*, the cooking place). Others feel that it must not be placed in the sleeping room (*malo wa gona*), where sexual relations take place, as there is a fear that this may 'cut' the spear or gun (*kuopa imatsem-phedwa*). Equally important, a woman must never step across a bow or spear, for it will then lose its vitality, its essential 'heat'.

When a man goes hunting, he must therefore enter the woodland in the correct ritual condition: he must be 'cool'. This is because hunting is thought to be a highly dangerous and risky enterprise, dependent on luck and open to spiritual influences, not only from the spirits of the dead (*mizimu*), but from the animals themselves. For a successful hunt, the hunter, or the owner of the communal hunt (*mwini wauzimba*), not only needs skill and good luck, but also protection against dangerous animals – even mammals like the male bushbuck or porcupine can be dangerous in certain circumstances – and against the negative influences that stem from killing certain of the larger mammals. This is associated with the possibility of contracting a highly dangerous condition termed *chirope*, derived from one of the terms for blood (*mlopa*), the other more common term being *mwazi, magazi*.

When going hunting, therefore, it is important initially to make offerings (*nsembe*) to the spirits of the dead, who are usually addressed as *ambuye* (grandparents). These spirits of the ancestors (*mizimu ya makolo*) are respectfully asked (*ku-pempha*) for help and support, so that a man may travel through the bush without difficulty and find game animals (*kupeza nyama*). Ideally, offerings are made by placing millet flour (*ufa*) at the foot of a tree, the *msolo* (*Pseudolachnostylis maprouneifolia*) and the *mpoza* (*Annona senegalensis*) being favourites, as these two trees are associated with spirits of the dead, but any tree will suffice. These trees are not held to be sacred, nor do they incarnate the spirits, who are said to reside in remote woodlands, but rather the *mizimu ya makolo* are said to like (*amakonda*) these trees, both of which are widely used for their fruit and for medicine. If offerings are not made then, this will adversely affect the hunt and it will be without luck (*mwayi*).

As I have discussed elsewhere, the use of medicines (*mankhwala*) permeates Malawian cultural life, and medicines – the roots, bark, fruit and leaves of plants – are widely and extensively used, not only for therapeutic purposes, but for all aspects of social life (Morris 1996a). It is hardly surprising, then, that medicines play an important and crucial role in hunting. Almost all hunters carry with them a small medicine bag (*chitumwa*), which is worn around the neck or carried in the pocket. This holds such ingredients as the dried leaves of *chisoni* (meaning 'compassion') (*Myrothamnus flabellifolius*), the dried roots of *palibe kanthu* ('it does not matter') (*Dicoma anomala*), hedgehog spines, leaves of *nyambata* (*Desmodium velutinum*) and some pieces of the stem of the small herb *muitana* ('you call') (*Galium bussei*). This medicine bag is believed to bring the person 'good luck' (*mwayi*), as well as to protect the hunter from accidents and dangers and the potential evil influences (*woipa*) of witchcraft (*ufiti*). But medicine is also put on the muzzle of a dog so that it smells well, on guns, spears and arrows so that they hit their mark, on traps and nets so that they capture animals, and on the hunter's body to protect it from the possible detrimental effects of killing the mammal (*chirope*).

These medicines come from a diverse number of plants, and knowledge of the more powerful medicines is restricted largely to *asing'anga* (herbalists) and to senior men. The owner of the hunt (*mwini wauzimba*) and men who specialize in hunting as an activity, are usually well known also for their knowledge of medicines. Indeed, the two go together, for knowledge of medicines complements skills in enabling a hunt to be successful. One plant which is especially associated with hunting medicines is *mpetu* (*Boscia angustifolia*), a small tree with orange roots that have a strong smell; its alternative name is *musaza* (*ku-sasa*, to be sour, have a bad smell).

The name generally given to hunting medicine is *chikoka*, which is a correlative of the term for the large dead fall trap *nkoka* (*ku-koka*, to draw, pull, drag). But parts of animals are also important in hunting medicines, both as good luck charms – like pangolin scales and hedgehog spines – and as strengthening medicines, *chizimba*, which I have discussed elsewhere. The *chizimba*, the animal substance – skins, bones, hair, dung – constitutes the activating agency of the plant medicines, whatever their purpose, for luck, protection against misfortune and sorcery, or to give the hunter insight and endurance.

Although men clearly enjoy hunting and although meat is highly esteemed as food by both men and women, hunting is nevertheless felt to be a highly precarious and dangerous enterprise. It is thus hedged with ritual. This is not simply because it is potentially dangerous and life threatening, nor is it because chance and luck play an important part in whether or not a hunt is successful, for even a skilled hunter may spend a whole day in the woodland without obtaining a single game animal. It is rather because the killing of animals – particularly large and more 'potent' mammals such as the kudu, bushbuck, eland, hippopotamus, elephant, impala, sable, roan, buffalo and, in the past, the blue wildebeest – may, without proper ritual precautions, have an adverse effect on the physical and mental condition of the hunter. For it is believed that the act of killing a game mammal is akin to that of homicide, and that the 'blood' (*chirope*) of the mammal may enact a kind of vengeance, entering the body of the hunter and bringing punishment (*kubwezera chilango*) in the form of a serious condition. One hunter told me that if a person who kills a close relative (*wapha mzake*) through conflict (*ndewu*) or a game animal (*nyama*), the eyes of this person will become very red (*wofiira*). If not treated the person will become blind (*khungu*) or mad (*misala*). The redness of the eyes and the hot condition of the man is due to the blood of the animal (*magazi wa nyama*). A man in this condition, described as *chirope* (*blood*), easily becomes angry (*sachedwa kupsya mtima*, 'soon burn the heart') and fierce (*amaopa*). He is therefore liable to engage in further killing, especially of his own kin. After killing the large 'potent' animals, medicines therefore have to be taken to counteract the 'heat' and power of the blood. These medicines are called 'medicines of the blood' (*mankhwala a chirope*), one important ingredient being the roots of the small tree *mlungamu* (*Brackenridgea zanguebarica* or *Ochna macrocalyx*). All hunters speak of *chirope* as a kind of disease (*nthenda*) that causes the red inflammation of the eyes and leads to a condition like madness (*ngati misala*), with a spinning head (*kuzungulira mutu*). However, it is explicitly seen as distinct from both true madness and from rabies (*chiwewe*). It is particularly associated with hunting large game animals, especially the larger antelopes, the hunting of which is surrounded with a good deal of 'mystique". To hunt such animals as the buffalo or kudu without first preparing protective medicine is seen as courting disaster, leading to madness or misfortune (*zobvutika*). Essentially the condition is expressed in terms of the blood entering the head or body of the hunter (*magazi imalowa mutu mwache*). Although some hunters may indeed speak of the spirit of the thing (*mzimu chachintu*) as entering or coming upon the body of the hunter (*chanyama chinatwera kuthupi lache*), normally hunters do not speak of the animal as having a spirit, nor do they say that it is the spirit of the animal that causes the hunter's madness. Rather it is the 'blood' of the animal entering the body of the hunter that makes him prone to violence and madness.

Thus a distinction is usually made between *chirope* as it effects hunters and homicides, and the spirits of people (especially hunters who have suffered accidental deaths), which may take the form of an animal. But such *chiwanda* or *mnyama* (personalized form of *nyama*) spirits invariably take the form of animal predators such as lion, leopard, hyena.

Because of these beliefs a young hunter's first kill and the cutting-up (kutumbula) of a large mammal is usually accompanied with a good deal of ritual, particularly in the form of a medicinal wash (*kusamba*) to ward off the 'blood' of the slain animal. The wanton killing of game animals or the killing of animals that have not reached maturity (*msinkhu*) is said to lead to *chirope*, or to the angering of the ancestral spirits. One hunter remarked to me that the killing of a dog was similar (*chimodzimodzi*) to homicide, and thus led to *chirope*. W.P. Young records in his memoirs of Nyika that one hunter said to him after killing an eland: 'You will not shoot an eland again; the spirit is angry if more than one of his oxen is killed' (1953: 47). This implies a spiritual restriction on the number of animals that may be killed during a hunt. I was also told that if a man kills many domestic goats his heart will become angry (*ku-psya mtima*), and if he does not take medicine he will be prone to violence.

But although the blood of the animals has the power to 'influence' the heart of the hunter, so that without 'cooling' medicines may lead to violence and madness, blood, like hunting itself, is not viewed negatively. For it is also seen as the epitome of life and vitality, and the partaking of blood is an important aspect of many spirit rituals, such as those of *nantongwe* and vimbuza (Boeder 1984: 47–9, Peltzer 1987: 180–90).

In her discussion of *chirope*, Werner (1906: 67–8) notes that this word is connected with *mlopa* meaning blood, and that it entails the idea that 'the spirit of the slain enters the body of the slayer'. This is even the case, she suggests, with animals, so it is the custom of the hunter to throw a small piece of meat on the fire and to eat it so that 'the spirit of the beast' does not enter the body of the hunter. But all hunters with whom I was acquainted spoke of the blood (*mlopa, magazi*) of the animal entering the body of the hunter, not some animal 'spirit', and all made a clear distinction between *chirope* as a condition and *chiwanda*. The latter are seen as malevolent spirits (*mzimu woipa*) who may take the form of animals, especially, as already noted, such carnivores as the hyena, leopard, jackal or lion. But such predators may nonetheless be described as *chirope* in the sense that their appearance (*maonekedwe*) may display fierceness and greed (*chirombo chalusa*).

In an article entitled 'Nyama, die Rachemacht' (Nyama, The Power of Revenge) Hermann Baumann (1950) offered a comparative survey of the concept of *nyama* in Sub-Saharan Africa. He noted that it was one of the most widely distributed of Bantu words, signifying not only game animals generally, especially the larger 'power' mammals, but also expressing notions that implied a sense of 'vital force' or 'power' inherent in the blood of the mammal or in a substance. *Nyama* was a conception that suggested the existence of a 'life-soul' or 'soul substance' present in animals, as well as in humans, trees and other substances. It was conceived of as 'half-spiritual, half-material', as localized in the blood and certain entrails (heart, liver, spleen), or as concentrated in the bodily extremities (horns, hair, skin, tail). He noted that *nyama* often took the form of a 'revenge-power', such that an equation was made between homicide and the hunting and killing of the larger mammals, especially the kudu, eland, elephant, duiker, hippotamus and rhinoceros (1950: 210–11; Baumann here drawing on the ethnographic writings of Junod on the Thonga). Because of this 'revenge power', he also detailed at length the various forms of ritual, found throughout Africa, whose raison d'être was to ward off or counteract the 'power' of the slain animal. Other scholars have noted that rituals that are enacted to protect the hunter against an animal's *nyama*, which is described as 'the force or energy inherent in all matter, animate and inanimate', and which is sometimes associated with intense heat. *Nyama* is also linked with the vital force found in the bloom of iron-smelting (Herbert 1993:177).

In Malawi, the term *nyama* prototypically refers both to meat and to game animals, but it is also used to describe the essence or substance of any object or thing, especially in reference to wood or iron. But when speaking of what Baumann refers to as 'revenge power', hunters in Malawi invariably use the term *chirope* (blood), not *nyama*.

The religious ritual that surrounds hunting was even more pronounced, it seems, in the past, when communal hunting of elephant was commonly practised (cf. Fraser 1923: 135–7).

We have suggested that hunting, like menstruation, must not be viewed negatively, as if it were the antithesis of life-giving human reproduction. But because it involves, prototypically, the firing of the woodland, the use of metal implements and the spilling of blood, as well as, in the past, the use of 'hot' arrow poison, hunting inevitably generates 'heat', which, in excess, is extremely dangerous and contrary to human well-being. Moreover, the larger mammals, such as kudu, roan and eland, are symbolically associated with the woodland and with the spirits of the dead (*mizimu ya makolo*), such that: the killing of these mammals is akin to homicide. It is thus imperative that a hunter, like a menstruating woman, remains in a 'cool' condition, that the spirits of the dead are harnessed for support (there must be peace in the village, and the killing must not be wanton or violent), and that medicines are used to protect the hunter not only against witchcraft and ill-luck, but also from the potential ill-effects of 'heat', expressed as *chirope*. 'Heat', whether generated by fire, blood, sex, salt, metal or meat, is absolutely essential to procreative processes and to human well-being; only in excess, uncontrolled, does it lead to sterility, sickness and misfortune.

Thus, rather than seeing sexuality/child-bearing (woman) and hunting (men) in gnostic fashion as antithetical activities, in the Malawian context human procreation and hunting are viewed analogously as similar positive social processes. Whereas the semen of the male affine activates the blood of the woman to produce a child – just as the rain activates the burnt woodland to produce new plant growth – so the hunter uses 'heat', in the form of poison, fire, spears and arrow heads, to produce meat (*nyama*). Hunting is therefore viewed not as the negation of life and procreation, but rather as a ritual of transformation, a social process analogous to cooking, beer-brewing, initiation, pot-making and iron-smelting, as well as to human procreation itself. This is highlighted by comparing hunting with that other social activity which is essentially restricted to men, iron-smelting.

When David Livingstone journeyed through Malawi in the 1860s he noted that the economy combined agriculture with hunting, but he was also clearly struck by the widespread occurrence of manufacturing industries, particularly iron-smelting and smithing. Iron-working was a prominent feature of economic life in Malawi, and he was greatly impressed at the quality of iron produced, for it was superior to that produced in Birmingham. Every village, he noted, 'has its smelting house, its charcoal burners, and blacksmiths'. They made good axes, spears, needles, hoes, arrow heads, bracelets and anklets. (Livingstone 1887: 82).

Iron-smelting may go back many centuries, and it is associated with the influx of 'iron-age' people into Central Africa between the second and fourth centuries AD. It came with agriculture and with what David Killick (1990: 40) has described as a 'package of technologies', including pottery and the domestication of animals. By the middle of the nineteenth century, iron-smelting and smithing formed a flourishing industry in many parts of Malawi, at a time when hunting and long-distance trade was also prominent. Around 1920, however, it suddenly declined, unable to compete with the importation of cheaper iron goods, especially metal hoes. The prominence of iron-smelting in the past life of Malawian people is reflected in the fact that the early chiefdom was called Maravi, which can be translated as 'the land of flames', and the ethnonym Mang'anja is derived from the stem ng'anja to smelt iron (Price 1963).

Iron-smelting is a skilled and difficult operation, and like both child-birth and hunting an extremely risky affair. It is necessary to maintain a high temperature, to have a reducing agent, charcoal, and an exact amount of air. Too much air may produce only slag. The lateritic iron ore is called *thale*, and the charcoal (*khala*) is made from such hardwoods as *mwanga* (*Pericopsis angolensis*), *mpala* (*Brachystegia spiciformis*) and *napini* (*Terminalia sericea*). The production of iron was accomplished in three stages. The large primary furnace (*ng'anjo*) was operated by means of an induced draft. These furnaces stood over two metres high, and good-examples can still be seen in Kasungu National Park, though long since abandoned. These furnaces produce not bloom, but slag with small pieces of iron, which is then re-smelted in a smaller secondary furnace (*chirambo*), driven by bellows, which produces the single bloom. The term for this bloom is *chuma*, which is a general term for wealth. The slag is described as *tubsi*, a word also used to describe dung or animal excretment (plural *matubsi, matubvi*). The final stage entails the reworking of the iron bloom into tools at a forge (*chipala* or *libvumbo*). The blacksmith is described as *munthu wa chipala*, or *chipalu*, a term that refers to any skilled person, including a hunter. It is of interest that *thale* (*Yao utale*), iron ore, also refers to the Termitomyces mushroom, both smelting and the mushrooms being associated with termite mounds. The forging of iron is *ku-sula*, and the manufactured iron is *chitsulo*. The smelter is described as *mfundi*, derived from the verb *ku-funda*, to warm, and this term may also be widely used to denote a skilled worker.

As with hunting and childbirth, iron-smelting is steeped in ritual prohibitions. Smelting always takes place in the woodland, often far from the village, and like hunting, the whole operation must be undertaken in a 'cool' condition. The smelter or *mfundi* too must remain 'cool' throughout the smelting process. Ideally, the initial firing of the smelting furnace must be done by means of fire-sticks – itself symbolically seen as a conjugal union – not with fire derived from the village. As with hunting, offerings must be made to the spirits of the dead (*mizimu ya makolo*) and special medicines used to protect both the *mfundi* and the smelting process, from witchcraft and evil influences, as well as for good luck. Offerings are placed at the foot of the *msolo* tree and a sacrifice is made of a chicken, often white in colour. Msamba and Killick (1992) interpret the whiteness of the chicken as a symbol of 'cleanliness and purity', but essentially it symbolizes the necessary 'coolness' of the woodland and the spirits (*mizimu*). Significantly the chicken was referred to as *tambala mtuwa* (*-tuwa* white as ashes).

The medicines involved in smelting are described as *msinkho* or *mtsiriko*, a general term for protective medicine (*ku-tsirika*, to protect with medicines). Van Der Merwe and Avery (1987) and Killick (1990:134) have discussed the medicines used in the smelting process. Important ones to note are the *chizimba* or activating medicines that are used in combination with the plant medicines, and are derived from animals – such as the porcupine (*nungu*), hippopotamus (*mvuu*), zebra (*boli*), honey badger (*chiuli*), hedgehog (*chisoni*) and antbear (*godi*). Also significant is the fact that many of the plants used are trees which are widely associated with male virility. These include *mwanga* (*Pericopsis angolensis*), *mvunguti* (*Kigelia pinnata*), *mwabvi* (*Erythrophleum sauveolens*), *msambamfumu* (*Afzelia quanzensis*) and *chipangala* (*Dichrostachys cinerea*).

Again, as with hunters, smelters must not have sexual relations the night prior to smelting, nor during the period of the smelting operation, which may last several weeks. To do so would generate 'heat' and destroy the product. Nor must a menstruating woman approach the *nganjo*. Killick has interpreted this in terms of the menstruating woman being 'unclean' and 'polluting', but such Judeo-Christian concepts are misplaced in the Malawian context, where the symbolism of hot and cold is pervasive. Because, as with hunting, smelting is a productive activity that involves heat, it must be kept 'cool'. Nor must these ritual prohibitions be interpreted simply in terms of the gender division. Sexually active men from the village must not approach the smelting operation, or be involved in hunting, and if the smelting is not a success its failure may be blamed on the sexual misdemeanours of one of the men involved in the smelting. On the other hand, young girls and elderly women past child-bearing can freely approach the *nganjo* because they are considered 'cool' and do so to provide the men with food.

Among the Tumbuka (Phoka) the smelting furnace is symbolically described as female – 'our wife' – and the smelting process is explicitly seen as analogous to human reproduction (van der Merwe and Avery 1987: 159). The development of the iron bloom within the furnace is thus seen as analogous to the development of the foetus (child) within a woman's womb. Killick could find no evidence in the Kasungu district that the furnace was seen as female, or that the growth of the bloom was seen as analogous to human gestation (1990: 123). Yet the verb used in Chewa to describe the forging of hot iron, *ku-sula*, is also widely used to describe the operation of medicines used in human reproduction. Also, the ritual prohibitions that surround childhood are akin to those that are associated with both iron-smelting and hunting, as well as with other transformative processes such as pottery-making, beer-brewing, the production of salt and the initiation of boys and girls. All these social processes must be undertaken in a 'cool' state.

Iron-smelting in Malawi was a very similar activity to hunting in being a specialist occupation, but undertaken largely on a part-time basis and during the dry season (July-December). It involved highly developed technical skills like hunting, and like hunting and childbirth was a rather risky affair. It was thus surrounded with ritual prohibitions.

In his classic study of alchemy, *The Forge and the Crucible* (1962), Eliade discussed the ritual significance of 'heat' as a 'magico-religious' transformative power and the symbolic equation made between iron-smelting and gestation. He noted the 'organic metaphors', the 'sexual symbolism', and the associations made between human reproduction and social activities involving fire, namely cooking and in particular metallurgy (1962: 38–42). He noted too that iron as a metal was often 'charged with sacred power' and was widely used for ritual purposes. But though emphasizing that metallurgy often takes on 'the character of obstetrics' (ibid.: 8), he does not discuss hunting. This omission has been rectified in a path-breaking study of African metallurgy by Eugenia Herbert (1993), who substantially develops Eliade's seminal insights.

Herbert suggests that underlying, or at least inherent in, the cosmologies of Sub-Saharan Africa is a 'basic paradigm' focussed around some of the most salient aspects of human existence – gender, age, life and death, fertility and power. This paradigm suggests that metallurgy, especially iron-smelting, is a 'transformative process' akin in its essential structure and symbolic aspects to other transformative processes such as hunting, the investiture of chiefly authority and pottery, and human procreation, all being expressions of a single 'procreative paradigm' or 'transformative model'. Drawing on a wide range of comparative material, Herbert describes in great deal the sexual imagery associated with smelting furnaces, which may either be gynaemorphic or embody both male and female elements; the analogies made between smelting and human procreation; the ritual prohibitions associated with smelting, which, as described above, entail the exclusion of menstrual women and interdictions relating to sexual relations during smelting; the hot/cold symbolism that is focussed around smelting; and the essentially ambivalent, even multivalent, nature of fire, iron, power, and menstrual blood. The 'procreational model' thus implies a propensity for anthropomorphism, a 'gendered universe' and the 'imposition of the human model of fertility on the world'. But though stressing the 'down-to-earthness' of African cosmologies and the symmetric nature of gender 'oppositions' – right/left, forest/village, hot/cold, earth/sky, spear/hoe – Herbert nevertheless emphasizes the 'exclusively male control' of fertility (ibid.: 127). This is expressed through what she describes as the 'tripartite representation of male power': metallurgy, the political authority of chiefs and hunting, all of which are 'quintessentially male-dominated activities' (ibid.: 165).

Herbert thus describes hunting as an exemplification of the 'procreative paradigm', a rite of transformation. The rituals and traditions of hunting, she writes, reveal a world where 'power is structured along the axes of gender and age', the 'realm of male fertility par excellence' (ibid.: 166). She emphasizes the affinities between smelting and hunting: the invocations to the spirits of ancestors; the widespread use of medicines and charms for protection and good luck; the ritual prohibitions relating to menstruation and sex; and the association of both activities with men and with the woodland. In an analysis of ethnographic material relating to hunting among the Lele, Ndembu and Kongo, she concludes that hunting is a transformational activity that can be 'equated' with human reproduction. She therefore questions the willingness of many anthropologists to stress the 'destructive' capacity of men as hunters and to set up a symbolic dualism between hunting and reproduction, such that we have the following pairing of oppositions:

MEN	WOMEN
HUNTING	AGRICULTURE
DEATH	LIFE
FOREST	VILLAGE

Rather, hunting, she argues, is analogous to human procreation, it is intrinsically linked to fecundity – as both Douglas and Turner imply – and it has a 'paradoxical symbolism' (ibid.: 170). Death is essential to life, and 'masculine powers', expressed in smelting and hunting, are essentially creative and indispensible to human life, though also potentially destructive. A symbolic 'equivalence' between hunting, smelting and human procreation is clearly evident in Malawi, thus confirming Herberts' analysis. But the relationship between gender and hunting is by no means transparent or monovalent, but indicates contrasting social identifications between men and animals.

Hunting: Political Aspects

The reflections expressed in the last section apply specifically to hunting as a subsistence and ritual activity. But historically hunting has also been important as a commercial enterprise, being implicated in long-distance mercantile trade and in the establishment of centralized polities and chiefdoms based on trade. The hunting of elephant, rhinoceros, buffalo and hippopotamus were important in this regard, and though the ivory trade was fundamental, the trading of animal medicines and skins were also important. As hunting with muzzle-loading guns developed throughout the eighteenth and nineteenth centuries, so a close relationship emerged between hunting, warfare and trade, focussed around the political hegemony of certain territorial chiefdoms. These chiefs combined the two forms of masculinity and established territorial villages (*mzinda*), which were essentially trading depots. Slaves were incorporated into the chiefly lineages, particularly women, whose children belonged to the chief's *mbumba* kin group. Thus during the nineteenth century (when Malawi was more, not less, centralized than in the past) a close identity obtained between hunting and warfare, and professional groupings also grew up which specialized in the hunting of the larger mammals and were particularly involved in the ivory economy. Five groups are of special interest in the history of the nineteenth century: the Bisa and Chikunda, who hunted in the central regions; the Phodzo hippo hunters of the Lower Shire; and the Zimba and Kololo, who were also associated with the Lower Shire Valley and came to dominate the ivory trade of that region.

As the weapons of war and armed conflict were also those of hunting – spear, bow and arrow and muzzle-loading gun – it is not surprising that historically there was a close connection between hunting and warfare. The term for armed conflict, *nkhondo* (Yao *ngondo*), is semantically close to the general term for spear, *mkondo*, and in the past similar rituals to those of hunting were enacted prior to taking up arms.

From the historical record there appears to have been no development of hunting cults in Malawi such as were found in other regions of central Africa: but there is plenty of evidence for the existence of certain groupings of professional or itinerant hunters which were attached to certain territorial chiefs or political authorities or, as with the Kololo, became politically dominant themselves. Early writers often speak of these hunting groups as if they were ethnic communities, but this is misleading. I will offer some brief notes on five of these so-called 'tribes'.

The Chikunda stemmed from communities living in the Luangwa valley of Zambia and were essentially attached, as warrior slaves, to the Portuguese Prazeros of the Zambezi region. During the nineteenth century they emerged as major elephant hunters in south central Africa and played an important role in long-distnce trade, particularly to the extent that this was focussed on the export of ivory. The ranks of these itinerant hunters included men from diverse ethnic backgrounds – Mang'anja, Chewa, Nsenga, Chipeta, Tonga – and they usually roamed in bands of about 15 to 20 men. Armed mercenaries as well as ivory hunters, they usually attached themselves to Chewa chiefs in the central region. The chief, as Langworthy writes, 'was usually happy to have the Chikunda around as he could benefit from their guns, either to protect his village or to serve to provide meat. In addition, he might expect that the ground tusk of all elephants shot in his area would be given to him as tribute' (1975: 23).The political dominance of Matekenya on the Lower Shire during the middle of the nineteenth century was based on the procurement of ivory and slaves by his Chikunda retainers (Mandala 1990: 68–72).

During the nineteenth century the Chikunda combined their hunting skills with commercial enterprise and armed force, becoming a major economic force in Malawi; their impact on the Zambezi slave and ivory trade was substantial (Isaacman 1972). Stigand described the Chikunda as 'great hunters' and noted that they hunted mainly buffalo and elephant with rifles (190: 37) With the establishment of colonial rule, the Chikunda became largely absorbed in the local Chewa and Mang'anja population.

The Bisa, the subject of Mark's important ethnography (1976), also originated in the Luangwa valley, but during the nineteenth century many Bisa entered Malawi as hunter/traders, particularly in search of ivory. Livingstone described them as 'great travellers and traders' (1865: 502) and noted that many Chewa and Mang'anja chiefs often had a retinue of Bisa hunters, with whom they entrusted their ivory to be sold at the coast. As the Bisa had guns and were skilled hunters, they were usually welcomed by local chiefs. One Bisa chief, Marenga, settled on the southern lake shore. Having a source of independent power, the Bisa may well have been a factor in the political instability of the region during the nineteenth century (Langworthy 1975: 12–13). Fraser attributed the hunting success of the Tumbuka to the fact that they obtained arrow poison from Bisa traders (1923: 135). E.D.Young, who led the Livingstone search expedition in the 1860s and who visited chief Marenga, suggested that by their enterprise, the Bisa controlled and transported a greater part of the ivory and slaves to the Mozambique coast (1868: 184)

Long before the arrival of Europeans in Malawi, the hunting of hippos for their meat and ivory had been a specialized activity undertaken by specific communities who lived on the banks of the Shire and Zambezi rivers. Livingstone had first met the Phodzo when journeying up the Zambezi in 1858, but when trade in the ivory of both elephant and hippopotamus began to flourish and expand in southern Malawi in the second half of the century, many groups of Phodzo moved into the Nsanje area, particularly around the Dinde marsh. This community, which constituted something of a caste (Mandala 1990: 88), specialized in the hunting of hippopotamus, the skilled hunter being known as *mkhombwe* or *likombe*. The hunting was largely done from a canoe using a harpoon made of iron some 45 cm long, with a razor-sharp one-sided barb at the end. The harpoon was called *chidamba* or *chibutha* (*chimuta*); its lower end was attached to a rope. The harpoon was tightly inserted into a long pole made of *tenza* (*grewia*) wood, which is very light. A rope encircled the pole, the rest of the twelve-metre rope being closely wound around the entire length of the pole and secured at the end. The whole harpoon plus shaft was called *mwaeyo*. The hunters also carried a spear or *nthungo*, with an iron blade 7 cm long, and a shaft of strong bamboo some 3–4 metres in length.

The hunting of hippo with harpoon was a highly risky affair. A team of two men would go out quietly in canoe, in daylight, and approach a sleeping animal. They would approach the hippo from the side, and the man at the bow would hurl the harpoon into its side, aiming to strike behind its foreleg, so that the barb could penetrate deep into its heart. Harpoon hunting needed great strength, coolness and accuracy. If the harpoon had struck deep, it would separate from its corded handle, the barb remaining in the hippo, which invariably dived, or else took to water if the hunting was being undertaken in reed beds. The effect essentially was that with harpoon detached, in the hippo, the rope came off the pole, which came to float on the surface of the water, indicating in which direction the hippo was swimming or diving. The pole would guide the hunters to the hippo until the animal was killed with spears, other men joining in the operation. The *mkhombwe* showing amazing skill and daring in harpooning the quarry – for not only are the hippos dangerous but there are many crocodiles in the Shire – as well as evading the hippo's attacks and in following it until it had been killed. The rope was never strong enough to drag the hippo, but it was strong enough to ensure that the pole remained attached to the harpoon. It thus acted as a float and marker to enable the hunters to keep in contact with the animal (Livingstone 1965: 38–9, Talbot 1956).

Like the Chikunda, the Zimba (or Mazimba) were not really an ethnic community, although today in the Nsanje district people still identify themselves as Zimba, as a group of mercenaries (warriors) and hunters who migrated into Malawi from the Lower Shire. During the sixteenth century, when there was acute rivalry between the Kalonga and Lundu chiefdoms for control of the ivory trade, the Zimba were described as the warrios of the Lundu chief. Around 1588 a 'band' of several thousand Zimba was described as attacking Kilwa (Alpers 1975: 46–52). But the term *mzimba* actually means 'hunter', being connected with *uzimba*, the communal hunt, and it was clearly used in the past to describe groups of itinerant warriors and hunters who were attached to the territorial chiefs, especially Lundu, in a professional capacity. Their activities were specifically focussed on the hunting of elephant for ivory.

The Kololo (or Makololo) were also in no sense an ethnic community. When Livingstone abandoned his Zambezi expedition in 1864, he left sixteen of his porters behind in the Shire Valley. These men, of mixed background, came from the Barotse kingdom of Sekeletu, although only two of the porters, Kasisi and Moloka, were in fact true Kololo. Left behind with guns and ammunition, the Kololo quickly established petty chiefdoms in the Lower Shire Valley based on the hunting of elephant and the ivory trade. Helped by their guns, they became rulers of the local Mang'anja people and for a short period at the end of the nineteenth century largely controlled the ivory trade, which, as MacMillan has written, was the basis of their wealth and power. Rivalry with the African Lakes Corporation and the collapse of the ivory economy at the turn of the century put an end to Kololo political hegemony (MacMillan 1975, Mandala 1990: 81–90).

It has to be noted, then, that in the Malawian context hunting has historically formed a part of two quite contrasting domains. On the one hand, as described above, it played an important role in the local subsistence economy. The pre-colonial economy in Malawi could in fact be described as a 'dual economy' combining subsistence agricuture, focussed around women and the local matrilineage, and hunting, focussed around a covert fraternity of men. Such men were conceptualized as affines, as outsiders (*alendo*) associated with the woodland (*thengo*). The relationship between the two economic spheres, as between the two intermarrying matrilineal groups, can essentially be conceived as one of balanced reciprocity. Hunting in this context was fundamentally a collective enterprise geared to subsistence and the provision of meat (and skins) for local consumption. The emphasis was on exchange.

On the other hand, hunting was a commercial enterprise focussed around the territorial chiefs, local rulers who combined political authority with their entrepreneurial activities. Although also highly ritualized, as Fraser's account (1923) of elephant hunting Ekwendeni shows, such hunting tended to imply a very different attitude towards the land and towards the game animals that were hunted. This may have been expressed in the term *mwini dziko*, but with the hunting of ivory, the relationship of the chiefs/ hunters to the country (*dziko*) and its fauna was less one of 'guardianship' than of control, ownership and dominance. This form of hunting was more specialized, more implicated in armed conflicts – some of Chizimba or Chikunda hunters were little more than armed mercenaries who specialized in hunting – and more individualistic. In a sense, commercial hunting by Malawians in the nineteenth century was akin to that of European hunting, but it lacked the emphasis on 'sport' and its religious and medicinal aspects were still pronounced. Indeed, early European explorers in the Shire Vally expressed amazement at the medicinal accoutrements of these local hunters. Henry Faulkner, who accompanied the Livingstone Search expedition of 1867, and who was an avid hunter himself, described one such hunter graphically as follows:

... an extraordinary figure in the shape of a native sportsman .... A high fez, so old and greasy that one could never have believed that its colour had once been red, adorned his head, and he carried a rusty gun about six feet long. Many belts, pouches, bags and knives of different sizes encicled his waist, and his powder horn hung from his neck.... Around his wrists he wore several rings of what appeared to be some root recently dug from the ground, and the stock of his gun was covered with the same article, that it was a mystery to me how he could shoot with it.

The hunter assured Faulkner that the medicine was necessary for 'straight shooting' and for protection against lions and elephants (1868: 173; see also E.D. Young 1868: 186–7 for similar reflections).

Hunting as a commercial activity, although it still carried mystical dangers with regard to the killing of the larger game animals, was, in essence, highly poiticized. It thus implied a hierarchical relationship in terms of both gender and the relationship between the village of the territorial chiefs (or hunter/chief, *mzinda*) and the local village communities. Moreover, the proceeds of the hunt were fundamentally under the control of the professional hunter, even though tribute was paid to the chief (the ground tusk of the elephant), while in contrast the meat obtained from the communal hunt within the subsistence sphere was widely shared. Since the advent of colonial rule and the demise of the ivory economy, hunting in Malawi has largely been geared to local subsistence needs, as I have described above.

It is important, however, to note that subsistence hunting differed fundamentally in its aims and ethos from that of European hunting during the colonial period.

Conclusion

Leaving aside the hunting of elephant, which in the past was a specialized form of hunting focussed on the ivory trade, hunting (*uzimba*) in Malawi is centred on subsistence. Although surrounded by ethical prohibitions and ritual, it is essentially focussed on the provision of meat for local consumption. It may be undertaken individually, but African hunting is a collective enterprise, and meat always has to be shared with kin and affines. In contrast, European hunting in Africa was very much an individualistic enterprise, and its reason d'etre is 'sport' and the acquisition of 'trophies'. R.C. Maugham, in his book *Wild Game in Zambezia* (1914), describes big game hunting as an 'extremely absorbing pursuit' (ibid.: 2). It also includes a photograph (ibid.: 316) of the 'results of a month's hunting', which shows four local Africans standing behind an array of trophies – hippo skulls and teeth, the horns of several buffalo, eland, sable, reedbuck and hartebeest, as well as smaller antelope, and the skins of lion and serval. While for Malawians the skins and horns of mammals are seen as having medicinal properties, and thus use, for the European 'white hunter' and 'sportsman', these trophies symbolize power and control over nature, as well as signifying the military prowess of the European. Both types of hunting are linked to masculinity, but with local subsistence hunting this masculinity has a reciprocal relationship with horticulture involving the exchange of meat, whereas masculinity among European big game hunters is associated with independence, control, transcendence, adventure, cultural dominance and what has been described as 'muscular Christianity'. In the minds of many 'white hunters', the hunting of large mammals and of local Africans was veritably equated, and in his autobiography *Lessons from the Varsity of Life* (1933), the founder of the Boy Scouts, Baden-Powell, lauds the excitement and emotional satisfaction of 'man-hunting' in the Matopo Hills while on the Ndebele campaign of 1896. Baden-Powell was an avid hunter, and although 'A scout is a friend to animals' is one of the Scout laws, there is a whole chapter in his autobiography devoted to describing how he stalked and killed everything from woodcock in Albanian woods to lions on the African plains, including a spirited defence of both pig-sticking and fox-hunting (cf. Morris 1983). In his memoirs of the Matabele campaign, Baden-Powell wrote: 'The longest march seems short when one is hunting game . . . lion or leopard, boar or buck, nigger or nothing' (cited in MacKenzie 1987: 52). MacKenzie notes similar sentiments expressed by hunters like Stigand. But though hunting among Europeans was associated symbolically with military prowess and cultural dominance, and the masculinity it embodied was completely divorced from the domestic domain, it was also, significantly seen as a scientific pursuit. Many of the well known European hunters in Malawi during the colonial period – Sharpe, Wood, MacPherson – saw themselves as hunter-naturalists. They thus combined the hunting of large game with natural history pursuits.

Hunting in Malawi must not be viewed in a monolithic fashion. It had diverse meanings, which can be understood only in terms of the varied contexts in which it was found.

–3–

Folk Classifications

Introduction

In the last two chapters, I have outlined two very contrasting attitudes towards wildlife that are expressed by Malawians. As subsistence agriculturists experiencing continual depredation of their crops by wild mammals, there is a pervasive sense that animals are in 'opposition' to human concerns and well-being. This opposition is expressed in many ritual contexts, where men, as affines, are associated with the woodland and with wild animals. This 'opposition', however, must not be construed as involving an attitude of control or dominion, still less one of technological mastery, over nature. It implies that humans and animals are essentially equals but in competition, the larger mammals, such as the buffalo, hippopotamus, lion and elephant (mammals which may embody the spirits of dead chiefs), are believed to have powers (*mphamvu*) superior to those of humans. It is noteworthy that humans and elephants are similar ecologically, sometimes competing for space in the Brachstegia woodland, and in the past the elephant often held the upper hand.

In contrast, the woodlands, and the mammals (and spirits) that are associated with them, are also seen by Malawians as a source of building materials, medicinal substances and life-generating powers. And, as we observed in the last chapter, in the hunting domain humans, especially affinal males, are fundamentally identified with wild mammals, the attitude towards them being almost one of sacramental equality.

Thus, a dialectical opposition – a 'unity-in-opposition' – between humans and mammals is pervasive in the culture and social practices of rural Malawians. This opposition reflects an ambivalent attitude towards the woodland, especially towards mammals. On the one hand, in terms of the village community and agriculture, wildlife from the woodlands is seen as fundamentally hostile and antagonistic to human endeavours. On the other hand, the woodland domain is seen as the external source of life-generating powers. Mammals are seen as prototypical of the woodland in this respect. They are regarded as the embodiment of 'power' and fierceness and are seen as essentially opposed to humans (as wild beasts or *chirombo*; but they are also seen as the source of meat (*nyama*), of activating medicines (*chizimba*) and, being closely identified with the spirits of the dead and affinal males, as the essential source of fertility and thus the continuity of the kin group (village). Wild animals, then, form a crucial part in the ongoing cyclical processes of life and of social reproduction. These processes are expressed in a complementary or dialectical opposition between two facets of Malawian social existence, the woodland and the village, hunting and agriculture, the in-marrying male affine and the kin-group focused around a core of matrilineally related women, and spirits and wild animals (which are closely identified) and living humans.

To facilitate the discussion to follow, this complementary dualism may be outlined in the following schema, though this should not be interpreted as some totalizing cosmology that systematizes all aspects of Malawian culture:

Woodland	Village
(thengo)	*(mudzi)*
hunting	agriculture
dry season	wet season
affinal males	matrilineal kin group
(semen)	(blood)
spirits of the dead	living humans
(*mizimu ya makolo*)	(*anthu*)
wild animals	domestic animals
(chirombo)	(*chiweto*)

This 'dialectical' attitude towards the woodland (nature) and towards mammals co-exists, of course, with very different attitudes and perspectives towards wildlife. Malawian attitudes towards mammals, and more generally towards the natural world, are, like those of people everywhere, diverse, complex and multi-dimensional. The idea of capturing this complexity by means of a single motif or metaphor seems to me to be reductive in the extreme. I discuss the various social attitudes that Malawian people have towards animals more fully in the next chapter and in a companion volume on Malawian rituals and religious life. In this chapter I focus specifically on folk classifications, but I want to preface my discussion with some reflections on the distinction between phenomenal or 'basic-level' categories and symbolic classifications.

The Power of Animals

In his famous but obscure work *The Critique of Pure Reason* (1781), the philosopher Immanuel Kant suggested that the human imagination took two forms – empirical and aesthetic. Empirical imagination mediated between sense perceptions and thought and made possible our knowledge of the phenomenal world. Through spontaneous synthesis, and linking with forms of intuition (time, space), our imagination provides us with an awareness, and intuition, of empirical objects or things. It is also a faculty through which mental representations (precepts, images) are ordered and unified to provide us with what Iris Murdoch describes as a 'sensuously bodied schemata of classes of empirical objects', bringing these schemata to conscious awareness (1992: 308). Drawing on Kant's insights and his theory of the imagination, Mark Johnson (1987) has proposed what he describes as a theory of 'semantics of understanding'. It is a theory that sets out to challenge 'objectivist' theories of language, such as those of the early Wittgenstein and many contemporary analytic philosophers, who tend to postulate a direct, one-to-one correspondence between language (concepts) and things in the world, as if language was a 'mirror of nature'. However, unlike many post-modernist anthropologists, Johnson does acknowledge the intrinsic importance of realism and the correspondence theory of truth (1987: 202–3). Like Hilary Putnam, whose work he cites, Johnson thus aims to steer the analysis between reductive materialism (objectivism) and cultural idealism, which tends to divorce language form the world entirely in a transcendental metaphysic (1987: 207, Putnam 1992). Johnson's essential thesis is that an adequate theory of meaning – and of rationality – can only be provided if a central place is given to embodied experience, and to the embodied and imaginative structures of understanding that arise out of this experience and through which we came to grasp and know the world. He thus suggests that through our basic human bodily experience – sense perception, interaction with things in the environment and our bodily movements – two basic forms of imaginative, and structured, understanding occurs: one alludes to 'the basic-level categories' that order specific domains and relate to 'natural kinds' and 'prototypes'; the other are the 'image schemata.' The latter are conceived as 'embodied understanding', i.e. the way we experience the world as an intelligible reality, as 'figurative processes of ordering' which are shared, meaningful, patterned and pervasive in human life. Through metaphor, metonymy and 'analogical reasoning' such schemata are given 'metaphorical extension', becoming what Lévi-Strauss and others have described as symbolic classifications. These link different domains of experience. Johnson discusses many different kinds of 'image schemata' – the container metaphor (in-out, boundaries), path, force, spatial metaphors (verticality, centre-periphery, near-far, horizons), process, cycles, balance schemata – arguing that they form both the basis of meaning and our conceptions of reason.

From Johnson's analysis and the general anthropological literature, it is evident that a distinction can be made between the classifications that order a specific domain, such as plants, fungi and animals, and the kind of ritual classifications – the image schemata – that link several domains of experience. In this chapter I shall focus on these classifications.

The chapter has four sections. In the first section I discuss the symbolic opposition, reflected in Malawian culture, between the woodland and the village. I emphasize that this opposition is complementary, as suggested above, and that it embodies an on-going cyclic process.

In the second section, as background material, I outline some of the recent debates within ethnobiology, focussing specifically on the seminal writings of Berlin, Atram and Ellen. As I have been involved in these debates over a number of years, I trust the discussion does not sound too self-referential. In the third section I outline life-form categories in Malawi, focussing particularly on the animal kingdom, and conclude the chapter with a detailed account of basic-level categories relating to mammals. Throughout these two sections, I stress the crucial importance of pragmatic concerns in the way Malawian people perceive and classify the natural world.

The Village and the Woodland

In the seminal writings of the phenomenologist Mircea Eliade, a contrast is drawn not only between the domains of the sacred and the profane, but between the primordial experience of 'formless expanse' (chaos) and the symbolic creation of a cosmic order through rituals which periodically re-enact the cosmogonic acts of the divinity. Rituals are thus merely the repetition of a primordial act which involves 'the transformation of chaos into cosmos by the divine act of creation' (1959: 31). This act of the divinities is thus not the creation of the material world *per se*, but of the structure and form of the world, as with Plato's demiurge. Such a dualistic formulation, reminiscent of Plato, leads Eliade to suggest a series of homologous oppositions:

chaos	cosmos
history	structure
becoming	being
profane	sacred
matter	form

Eliade thus conceives human life as consisting of two modalities of experience, and, like Plato, he views the sacred as preeminently the real, as an 'objective reality', 'at once power, efficacity, the source of life and fecundity' (ibid.: 28).

Vital power and fertility are thus seen as of spiritual origin, not as inherent in matter (chaos), and the sacred is essentially identified with the cosmic structure. Moreover, the primordial situation, the world of chaos and flux that preceded the creation of the cosmos (the world), is conflated with the profane world that stands opposed to the sacred. With regard to the present study, what is of interest is that the 'inhabited world' of humans, identified with the cosmos, with sacred space, is contrasted with the indeterminate space that surrounds it – chaotic space. As Eliade writes with reference to the celestial city and acts of settlement: 'All these wild, uncultivated regions and the like are assimilated to chaos; they still participate in the undifferentiated, formless modality of pre-creation' (1954: 9). Victor Turner has a similar dualistic vision, though he associates the sacred not with social or cosmic structures but with communitas and the 'seamlessness of process'. He suggests, like his contemporaries Leach (1964) and Douglas (1990), that humans experience reality as 'continuous', as a 'unitary form of experience', and that all structures, whether of language or society, and all systems of thought arise from a division of this 'undifferentiated reality'. Thus, like Eliade we have a division between a primordial ground of experience – linked by Turner to god and the sacred – and an ordered cosmos (1975: 1–23). Power and fertility for Turner seem essentially to relate to the former modality of experience. The contrasting perspective of these two religious anthropologists could well reflect their contrasting ethnographic experiences, Eliade in a North Indian ashram and Turner among the Ndembu of Zambia.

But what is important in the present context is that neither of these theoretical conceptions match the Malawian division between the woodland (*thengo*) and the village environs (*mudzi*). For Malawians – and I suspect for most African people – do not experience the natural world as an 'undifferentiated' flux, nor as 'unstructured'. On the contrary, as with Aristotle, the natural world is conceived as consisting of substances or things. Moreover, in the Malawian conception of being (*nthu*), such material entities (*chinthu*, thing) are seen as having inherent potentialities or powers. We shall return to this issue below in discussing folk classifications.

As in many other societies, people in Malawi make a fundamental distinction, which has both ecologicai and symbolic import, between the village (*mudzi*), the domain of living humans, and the Brachystegia woodland (*thengo*), the domain of wild animals (*nyama*) and of spirits of the dead. This kind of conceptual distinction has been widely discussed in the literature largely under the rubric of the opposition between 'culture' and 'nature'. Although this opposition has a deep resonance within European thought and science, given the dominance of the kind of dualistic metaphysic that stems from Cartesian philosophy, it has been subject to a plethora of meanings and interpretations. Long ago Lovejoy (1948) discussed the diversity of meanings of the concept of 'nature' even within the European literary tradition. He described the term as a 'verbal jack-of-all-trades', nature being at once the most sacred and the most protean of the concepts used during the Enlightenment period. However, the Greek distinction between *nomos* (custom) and *physis* (nature) can in no sense be equated with the kind of dualisms that were bequeathed to us by the Enlightenment tradition – culture/nature, society/individual, mind/body – although there are fundamental affinities between Plato and Descartes. For many Greeks, Aristotle in particular, *physis* (nature) was in an important sense animate, with latent potentialities.

Recent scholars who have discussed the nature/culture dichotomy have emphasized its problematic nature if applied uncritically as a cross-cultural conception (MacCormack and Strathern 1980; Croll and Parkin 1992). The dichotomy, along with its homology with gender categories, is reflected in much European thought (Ortner 1974; Merchant 1980), but the tendency to see this dichotomy as involving a Promethean ethic – the metaphor of 'man against nature', or of human (culture's) dominion over nature – has not been found to gell at all neatly with the cultural categories of pre-literate communities. Among the people of the New Guinea Highlands, for example, as Strathern (1980) has shown, although the distinction between the 'domestic' and the wild has a crucial significance, it is neither homologous with the gender division, nor can it be equated with the culture/nature division of Western thought. But what crucially emerges from much of the ethnographic literature on small-scale farming communities is that a pervasive symbolic dualism is evident which contrasts settlement or the domestic realm with that of the wild, even though its underlying cultural logic may be distinctive. It may indeed, as in New Guinea, not be seen as a rigid 'dualism' – in the neo-platonic or Cartesian sense – and may evoke quite different symbolic associations, the 'wild' or forest being associated with men and the spirits rather than with women (as it is in much Western thought; Gillison 1980).

In the African context the symbolic demarcation between domesticated space and the 'bush' or forest has been widely reported. In her classic and perceptive ethnographic writings on the Lele, Douglas (1954; 1975:

9–46) writes of the importance of what she calls their 'religious categories' and how these symbolically, even if implicitly, structure their thought. One fundamental distinction is that between the village and the forest, mediated by the grassland which is associated with women and the cultivation of groundnuts. By contrast the forest is seen as the abode of the spirits and animals and as the source of many of the essential necessities of life – maize, fish, meat, water, firewood, fertility. Likewise Jean Comaroff (1985: 54) writes of the distinction between the social or domesticated domain and the 'wild' or bush as the 'most fundamental' of all oppositions in the Tswana cosmos, even though the opposition is seen as being mediated by women and production. Recent ethnographic studies of the Dogon, Mende and Aouan of West Africa confirm this widespread articulation of an 'opposition' between the 'bush' and the 'village'. For the Dogon of Mali, the 'bush' is associated with the spirits and animals and with danger, yet at the same time it is considered the origin, the 'ultimate source' of everything that makes life possible: knowledge, wisdom, power, fertility, as well as life itself. The bush/village dichotomy thus implies an entropic system (van Beek and Banga 1992: 67–73). For the Aouan of the Ivory Coast, the forest forms an all-encompassing environment surrounding the village and contains the spirit beings that bestow life and rule over animals and plants. It is on the forest that the people depend for physical subsistence, and various taboos and rules exist to maintain the boundary between the two domains (van der Breemer 1992: 99).

There is, in Malawi, no widely used general category that could be considered equivalent to the English concept of 'environment', nor even to the more abstract category of 'space', although Malawians, like other Bantu speakers, have a highly developed spatial sense which is built into their language. The 'gaps' between things such as garden plants are referred to as *danga*, while the space between rocks and hills are denoted by the term *mpata*. A valley between hills, a mountain pass or a gorge is thus referred to by the latter term, and the famous gorge on the River Shire is named *mpatamanga* (*manga*, 'to make', 'bind').

The crucial spatial distinction for people in Malawi, however, is that between the Brachystegia woodland (together with the hill forests) and the villages and their cultivated environs. *Mudzi* means village, and the term has both an ecological and a social connotation, referring in rural areas to a cluster of huts – which may or may not form a discrete geographical unit – occupied by the core members of a matrilineal group. When Mitchell spoke of the village as a 'key concept in Yao thought' and as the 'fundamental unit' in their social structure (1956: 2–3) he was not exaggerating, and it is of interest that he entitled his study of the political and social structure of the Yao *The Yao Village*. The village head is a key figure in the day-to-day activities of the village and in the organization of rituals, even though his or her political standing in the wider community may be limited. When people refer to their own village or kin group, they commonly use the expression *kwathu* 'ours', which essentially means 'home' in both a geographical and a social sense, and the term carries connotations of intimacy. Within the village structure there are distinct households, focussed around a woman and her in-marrying spouse. The village environs include also the cultivated area (*munda*) which produces mainly maize, millet and cassava, together with pumpkins and beans which are planted inter-spaced.

Beyond the village cultivations are the Brachystegia or *miombo* wood-lands which, although they tend to look rather monotonous and uniform to an outsider, are in fact floristically rather complex, their nature and composition depending not only on specific local factors such as altitude, rainfall, drainage and soil type, but also on their past history. Many have stressed that such woodland is a plagio-climax, a plant community which has been formed and is maintained by continuous human agency (Morris 1970:155). The Malawian attitude to such woodland is essentially positive and contrasts markedly with that of Europeans. Even wildlife biologists who have spent long periods in Africa 'have little love for *miombo*'. The woodlands are described as a 'flat, monotonous stretch of trees' and as 'unchanging', and to travel through them one has to endure 'numbing boredom' (Adams and McShane 1992:123-4). Surprisingly, the woodland environment is hardly mentioned in Mandala's (1990) important account of the peasant economy of the Mang'anja of the Lower Shire. This environment, however, is a crucial source of essential subsistence goods: timber, string and thatching grass for building houses and granaries, mushrooms, fruits and wild vegetables, all kinds of medicine and, of course, wild animals, which provide an important source of relish. The woodland is also the primary source of energy in the form of firewood, which is often gathered by women far from the village.

Malawians refer to the woodland as *thengo* or *tchire*, and although the words are often used interchangeably, discussions with Malawians suggest that *tchire*, in contrast to *thengo*, is more often associated with regenerate Brachystegia woodland, where ample thatching grass and field-mice are to be found. In Malawi the firing of the woodland at the end of the dry season has both a pragmatic and a symbolic significance. In the past the right to initiate the burning of the woodland was vested in one of the senior chiefs (*mwini mzinda*), and it was a serious offence for anyone to burn the bush before the allotted time (Rangeley 1948:51). Formerly this was done late in the season and, as Schoffeleers (1971) has discussed, the burning of the bush had an important significance in the regeneration of the cosmic cycle and the subsequent coming of the rains. Burnt woodland is referred to as *lupsya*, the verb *ku-psya* meaning not only to cook, roast or burn, but also to be ripe.

The village environs are associated with what Fortes (1969) called the 'axiom of amity', with order, moral rectitude, structure and social well-being. But it would be misleading to equate the *mudzi/thengo* division with either a culture/nature dichotomy or a gender division. Although men are often associated with the woodland as hunters, it is not specifically the domain of men (*amuna*), but rather the domain of men as affines. Women too are associated with the woodland as gatherers of firewood and wild foods, while men are also identified with the village domain. Men are the people who clear the woodland of trees so that cultivation may be undertaken, they bring in woody material to construct the houses, they gather medicines from the woodland as well as meat, and most importantly it is from the woodland and from men (as affines/ spirits) that fertilizing power is derived for the procreation of children. Semen is called *ubwamuna* – the essence, as it were, of males as affines – and blood is referred to as *mwazi* or *magazi*, which is semantically close to the word for the female gender, *mkazi*. In essence, the procreation of a child consists concretely of the mixing of the semen of a man with the blood of a woman. Analogously, the most satisfying meal consists of a relish (*ndiwo* meat from the woodland) taken with maize porridge (*nsima* derived from women's activities in the village), and the most powerful medicines consist of plant substances (*mitengo* roots, leaves, bark of woody plants) activated by *chizimba* medicines, primarily the skins, tails and horns of animals from the woodland. It would be easy to construct an homologous series of complementary symbolic oppositions:

thengo	*mudzi*
woodland	village
hunting	cultivation
animals	plants
men	women

However, a structural analysis such as this tends to over-systemize the cultural reality (cf. Schoffeleers 1968: 231). The complementary opposition between the woodland and the human habitus reflects less the gender division than the opposition between affines and kin, for symbolically it is as affines that men are associated with the woodland and with the animals.

Although spirits of the dead/ancestors are also associated with the woodland, it would again be misleading to identify men specifically with these spirits. What essentially is expressed in Malawian culture with respect to the *thengo/mudzi* division is that whereas in the village environs a fundamental but complementary opposition is articulated between men and women, kin and affines, humans and wild animals, in the woodland there is a fundamental identity between these categories. In an important sense the spirits of the dead are collective ancestors, both men and women, kin and affines. In the woodland domain there is an essential identity between men and animals, and also between spirits and animals – and this is reflected in rituals. In the village, however, there is an opposition between humans and animals, which is also reflected in rituals.

In contrast to the village domain, the Brachystegia woodland is associated with medicines, wild animals and the spirits of the dead. Given a tradition of slash-and-burn agriculture and the essential nature of Brachystegia woodland itself, with its inherent ability to regenerate vegetatively, many areas of woodland represent old village sites. The site of a former village or an uninhabited area of woodland is referred to as *dzinja*, a term which also refers to the rainy season between December and March. Throughout Malawi, even in the heavily populated area of the Shire Highlands, areas of woodland are set aside as burial sites for the dead. These are known as *manda*, and the ancestors, or the dead, are collectively referred to as *amanda* (those of the woodland grave). In the Domasi district where I lived, almost every village had its own area of woodland where the dead were buried. These burial sites are in the nature of a sacred grove; no trapping or hunting of animals is allowed in them, and the area is protected from fire, for the site has to be kept 'cool'. It is also an offence against the spirits of the dead to collect firewood, medicines or thatching grass from the *manda*. In times of acute pressure on resources due to population increase, people may in fact gather firewood or grass from the *manda* woodlands, but this is not approved of. When I was in Ntcheu in the Central Region, many Chewa people I spoke to were very critical of the recent refugees from Mozambique who had gathered firewood from the nearby hill forests, forests which were particularly associated with the rain deities. Other than to attend funerals and make ritual offerings to their dead, people do not normally enter the *manda* woodlands. It is in these woodlands that the initiation site of the *Nyau* dancers is to be found. The *manda* woodlands thus essentially form a conservation area and refuge for wildlife. Even monkeys, when raiding the village gardens, act as though they feel safe in such environs.

The forests/woodlands associated with the graves of important chiefs or with the rain deities are of particular importance as ritual sites and may be entered only with the special permission of the ritual specialists associated with the spirits. The forest on almost every important hill in Malawi is associated with some particular rain spirit, and many of the lowland forests are important ecological sites because they have been untouched for many generations by either hoe or fire. In 1964 I was granted permission by the local priest to enter the relic forest on the loop of the Litchenya River, Mulanje (which is the graveyard of the ancestors of Chief Mabuka), in order to study the epiphytic orchids still to be found there. The forest is unique in being a remnant patch of the evergreen forest that once clothed the southeastern slopes of Mulanje Mountain but which was cleared in the early part of the century to make way for tea plantations (Chapman 1962: 16–17; see also Chapman 1988, Kath-amalo 1965, Schoffeleers 1992). Sacred forests associated with the spirits of the dead or with territorial rain deities are, however, to be found throughout Malawi.

An important distinction seems to be drawn between the *manda* wood-lands associated with the spirits of a particular local community and the forests to be found on particular hills or mountains, which are associated with various rain deities or with the original inhabitants of Malawi, the Batwa people. Mountains such as Michesi, Thyolo, Mulanje and the Nyika seem to be essentially seen as the abodes of spirits, and many people look upon these mountains with respect, awe, even with fear. One Lomwe writer has referred to Michesi mountain in southern Malawi as *malo otchuka a mizimu*, 'the famous place of spirits' (Soka 1953: 28–9)

Evidently in the Malawian context the complementary opposition between the woodland and the village is conceived as being homologous to that between the spirits of the dead and living people. This latter oppo-sition must, however, be seen in terms of a cyclical conception of life processes. There are specific ceremonies known as *manyumba* (*nyumba*, house), whereby individuals are seen – or rather witnessed – as undergoing a symbolic rebirth as the reincarnation of their grandparents. But this process is not a karma-like reincarnation of some immortal 'spirit', but rather a cycle of transformation implying a metamorphosis between the living and the dead, a cyclical transmutation. This process may be seen as an exchange of substances for people make offerings for their dead relatives, and on death a person becomes transmuted into an ancestral spirit. But essentially this is a cyclical process of life and death, or rather a process of life and its continuing renewal, activating agencies coming from the woodland.

As wild animals are associated with the woodland, they are identi-fied with the spirits and with affinal males, who are essentially seen as aggressive and sexual. This is why the inmarrying male affine is always conceptualized as a stranger (*mlendo*) and is symbolised by the cock and the hyena. *Nyau* and *chinyago* rituals among the Chewa, Mang'anja and Yao essentially involve the cultural creation of an affinal male, and the theriomorphic figures that are involved in such rites represent the spirits of the dead in animal form. This implies the identity – almost – of spirits, wild animals and affinal males. And such figures dance at the girls' initiation rites in opposition to the women, as a kin-group. Thus a clear distinction is made in Malawian culture between, on the one hand, the personality of a territorial chief and the affinal male (husband), who are conceptualized as outsiders and as hunters, and on the other hand, the village headman, who as a brother is identified with the collectivity of women who constitute the matrilineal core of the village community. Ideally he should be a male mother.

But in certain contexts, the woodland may also be seen as antagonistic to human endeavours, particularly to their endeavours as agriculturalists. Thus a perceptive observer of Malawian culture, Thomas Price, has written that to an ordinary villager, even trees may be seen as an 'enemy'. Price writes that when the trees are cleared away to make room for the gardens 'they sprouted up again, snagging hoes', and that when travelling between villages, people invariably carried a machete which they auto-matically used to slash back the growing saplings. He contended that the designation of forest reserves by the government was seen by local people as an intolerable interference with their movement and with settlement under shifting cultivation (cited in Potter 1987: 145). The point, of course, is that while in terms of medicine, energy, building materials and a supply of relish in the form of animal meat and mushrooms – and equally importantly, of human fertility via the spirits of the dead – the woodland is a crucial and indispensable provider of much that is central to human life, for the agriculturalist the woodland, and particularly the animals that are associated with it, are serious threats to livelihood. Hence their ambivalence towards this domain, and towards animals in particular.

I have outlined above the complementary opposition, based on the distinction between the domains of the woodland and the village, that is pervasive in Malawi cultural life, an opposition that is homologous to that between the dry and wet seasons – and thus fire *moto* and rain *mvula* – and between hunting and agriculture. Although Schoffeleers has perceptively explored this symbolic polarity – classification – with reference to Mang'anja religious culture (1968: 231), as I have suggested, it would be misleading to interpret this in some totalizing fashion, as a structural schema that integrates and systematizes all aspects of Malawi social life. It must be stressed too that this symbolic polarity is not a dualism, for the different modalities are interdependent, but reflects rather a cyclical *process*. But importantly, the woodland is *not* perceived as a 'wilderness' or as a 'wild' domain devoid of human significance. It is, in fact, the abode of the ancestral spirits, of past human life and of the mammals whose form the spirits often take, and thus a human world. Malawians' conception of the woodland and of the natural world is, therefore, one that sees it as 'humanized', as having human significance, even though, being associated with the spirits, the mountain forests are often treated with awe. The woodland/village dichotomy is not, then, a radical dualism. Nor is the woodland a wilderness, whether this is perceived as a place of fear, of elemental forces that need to be subdued to create a garden of Eden (as in the classical tradition) or as the symbol of a lost innocence, a nostalgic memory of a past golden age or a place unfrequented by humans (as in the romantic tradition and in the writings of the deep ecologists). The woodland for Malawians is not a human artefact, nor is it a pristine wilderness untouched by humans (cf. Short 1991: 5–28).

Like people everywhere – leaving aside certain academic philosophers and post-modernist anthropologists – Malawian people are realists and acknowledge the existence of a world beyond themselves. This world (*dziko*) is essentially viewed in material terms, as a country or land, and may be described as unsettled (*la uta*), peaceful (*la mphonje*) or open (*la tetete*) (Scott 1929: 116). But the land itself as a terrain is normally described as *dziko la pansi*, the world below (*pansi*, underneath, below, down). It thus contrasts with the heavens or firmament (*mlengalenga*) and the sky (*thambo*) which constitute the world above (*kumwamba, mwamba*, upwards, above). The firmament is associated with the creator spirit (*chiuta, mulungu*), a spiritual being which is closely identified with the rains, thunder and lightning. As we shall explore later, though a creator (*mlenga*), divinity is within the world, as are the ancestral spirits. Thus no radical dualism is conceived between the spiritual and material realms of existence. But importantly, as already noted, Malawian cosmology depicts a 'horizontal' world, the crucial division being between the village and woodland, rather than emphasizing the 'vertical' contrast between the heavens and the earth. Thus the sources of life and fertility are derived from the woodland, not from the 'vertical' locations of the sky and the earth. The 'horizontality' of folk models of fertility, as Jacobson-Widding and van Beek (1990: 27) describe it, is not therefore restricted to pastoral contexts, nor is the woodland conceived as the 'unstructured chaos of the wilderness', the locus of creative disorder, but rather as the domain of animals, medicines and the ancestral spirits, the ultimate source of fertility (see also Jackson 1989: 42).

I wish to turn now to Malawi folk classifications, particularly to their classification of mammals. But first, I will offer some reflections, as background material, on some recent debates within ethnobiology.

The Cognitive Foundations of Ethnobiological Classification

'The wealth of natural forms, in all their manifold configuration, is impoverished by the all-pervading power of thought, their vernal life and glowing colours die and fade away. The rustle of nature's life is silenced in the stillness of thought.'

So wrote Hegel in his *Encyclopaedia of the Philosophical Sciences* (1817). And he continues: 'In thinking things, we transform them into something universal: but things are singular and the lion as such does not exist' (Weiss 1974: 203).

Influenced by Kant, Hegel unfortunately tended to express himself in mind-boggling abstractions: thus one tends to forget that Hegel's whole tenor of thought is organic and holistic rather than mechanistic, and that the major influences on his philosophy were Aristotle and Goethe – both essentially biological thinkers. Yet in making a distinction between life and thought, Hegel, the objective idealist (as he called himself), never suggested that we experience the world as a formless continuum. This, however, seems to be the essential standpoint of many anthropologists who have written on animal symbolism, for they tend to take a rather cultural idealist perspective (e.g. Leach 1964, Turner 1975: 19).

In a more recent paper, Douglas has reiterated this viewpoint as a new approach to such symbolism, suggesting that 'similarity' is not an intrinsic quality of 'things' but rather is relative, variable, and culture dependent (1990: 26). Such relativism has been challenged by the studies of Atran (1990) and Berlin (1992), although neither writer seriously engages himself with the writings of Leach, Turner or Douglas. And it is equally significant that Douglas completely ignores the important work of Berlin and Atran. I will make no attempt to bring these two sides together, even though I think it is unhelpful to maintain a radical distinction between symbolism and cognition.

In this section I outline and offer some support for the theories of

Berlin and Atran, though questioning the extreme phenomenalism that is inherent in their work, suggesting that pragmatic and symbolic concerns do influence the way people classify the biological domain. I conclude the section with a review of the recent work of Roy Ellen (1993).

Some years ago (1976) I wrote a paper on the natural taxonomies of the Hill Pandaram, a South Indian foraging community. The paper was largely a critique of Lévi-Strauss and Douglas, stressing the need to distinguish clearly between symbolic and ethnobiological classifications, and emphasizing that Hill Pandaram classifications of animals and plants constitute a cultural domain that is largely independent of other aspects of their culture, thus lending little support to Douglas's theory of taboo. Although I stressed that these people, like all cultures, have a fairly detailed taxonomic system which orders the natural world, I also made a tentative contrast between their attitude towards folk classification and that of people in Malawi. In comparison with communities I knew well in Malawi, the Hill Pandaram had, it seemed, an unsystematic and uninterested approach towards biological taxonomy. The paper provoked the extreme ire of Brent Berlin, who wrote a long paper (1978) arguing that the Hill Pandaram have a structured system of ethnobiological classification that is identical in its main features with systems described elsewhere and that they utilize the same cognitive categories as other people in classifying the biological universe. I was quite taken aback by the stridency of this intellectual assault, for as a naturalist by disposition, I had never assumed otherwise. I found it rather puzzling that Berlin should think my article, and my speculative remarks, could be interpreted as a 'lesson' in extreme cultural relativism! Berlin's recent study *Ethnobiological Classification* (1992), which constitutes an important landmark in anthropological studies, has the same sense of urgency and the same essential theme, namely, the feeling that to admit that pragmatic and cultural factors have an influence (except in the most limited way) on the way people classify and name the natural world will lead us inevitably down a slippery slope into the seeming abyss of cultural relativism. Berlin's study therefore encapsulates, develops and re-affirms the 'universalist' approach to ethnobiology that he has been creatively exploring over the last two decades. Comparative in approach, the study nevertheless has an 'in-house' feel about it, and the 'utilitarian versus intellectualist' debate in ethnobiology, with Eugene Hunn being the main protagonist on the utilitarian side, runs like a silver thread throughout the whole book. Symbolic concerns are thus neglected, and surprisingly, apart from Kesby's (1986) work on the Rangi, there is no reference at all to African communities. As in several general accounts of religious culture (cf.

Campbell 1959, Eliade 1978), African culture is seemingly marginalized.

Berlin's basic argument is that the typological regularities that are found widely in systems of ethnobiological classification can best be 'explained' in terms of the 'perceptual and largely unconscious appreciations' of the natural affinities that exist between organisms in the environment. He makes a distinction between categorization and nomenclature, but in practice this distinction between morphotypes and named categories is somewhat redundant, as he sees an almost one-to-one relationship between them, the naming of categories being entirely (or almost entirely) motivated by biological considerations. To 'classify', for Berlin, thus has a double and a rather ambiguous meaning. People, he suggests, 'classify' or categorize only a certain 'subset' of the actual animals and plants that exist in a particular environment. This set is comprised of the most salient plant and animal species, where salience 'can be understood as a function of biological distinctiveness' (ibid.: 21). Such taxa form a hierarchical structure of categories with six ranks – kingdom (plant, animal), life-form (bird, herb, tree), intermediate taxa (often a covert grouping akin to the biological family), generic (the basic level), specific and varietal. The most numerous are those of generic rank (perch, dog, oak, buttercup), and empirical evidence seems to suggest that the number of folk generics in any system is around five to six hundred (hinted at by Lévi-Strauss), although my own studies of medicinal plants in Malawi suggest that the number of named plant categories in southern Malawi may be much higher than this 'magical' number (Morris 1996a). Berlin sggests that about 80 percent of generics are monotypic. Within each taxon there is often a prototypical member, which is usually seen by people as best representing the category, something that is confirmed by my own earlier studies of Chewa ethnobotany (1984: 51).

Berlin's naturalism leads him to suggest that the animal or plant that will be named by a community in a specific environment will be determined by its taxonomic distinctiveness (the degree to which it stands out from other organisms), its relative size, its prevalence in the area and the relative ease of observing it (ibid.: 263). Thus if a biologist goes into an area, making an inventory of all the animals and plants in it, he or she can predict, more or less precisely, what organisms will be given folk names. Such a system of names forms a general taxonomy that is prior to, and absolutely independent of, the utility or cultural significance of the organism. The largely 'unconscious appreciation of the inherent structure of biological reality' (ibid.: 8) is, then, for Berlin, directly reflected in language, in folk biological classification at the generic level.

Throughout the book, as already noted, there runs a dialogue between Berlin and those of his colleagues – particularly Hunn (1982) and Posey (1984) – whom he sees as taking a 'strict utilitarian approach' to ethnobiological classification and who argue, like Cesalpino and Mayr long ago, that only those natural species that have 'evident utility for man have been named' (Cesalpino in Atran 1990: 153, Mayr 1982). Seeing the issue in terms of an either/or position, cognition versus utility, Berlin strongly argues against what he constantly refers to as neo-Malinowskian functionalism. Linguistic recognition of animals and plants is not, he argues, based on either their utilitarian or cultural importance, but rather on their phenomenological salience. The reason, therefore, why folk biologists – Berlin always seems to refer to ordinary people as 'biologists' – tend to lump together many species of bats under a simple generic is, he suggests, because they are never seen until some zoologist comes along with his or her mist nets (ibid.: 81). Berlin brings forth plenty of evidence (and there is plenty i.e. Evans-Pritchard and Lévi-Strauss marshalled some many decades ago) to suggest that utility is not the primary factor in the naming of organisms. For example, more than half of the mammals given linguistic recognition by the Aguaruna Indians of Peru have no direct utility, either as food or for material goods (ibid.: 89).

I am in general agreement with much of Berlin's analysis, but in his anxiety to counter extreme cultural relativism and his emphasis on the universality and cognitive basis of folk taxonomic groupings, he (like, as we shall see, Atran) completely overstates his case. By doing so he sets up a series of rigid dualisms, nature/culture, theory/practice, science/symbolism, that are essentially a part of the Enlightenment tradition. Humans are, therefore, seen as essentially contemplative naturalists. Thus for Berlin functional concerns (as well as symbolism) are completely extraneous to folk biology, extra-taxonomic as it were, a part of 'second order' representation. He thus makes a rigid demarcation between general folk classifications that are purely phenomenal and biological, and special purpose classifications that relate to food, medicine, ritual and the like. Whether this rigid demarcation reflects the way that folk 'biologists' themselves relate to the world is questionable; but even if used as an analytical device, it would nonetheless be important to see how the various 'classifications' are related to each other. Yet like a true modernist anthropologist, Berlin seems to have little interest in these other classifications, even though they are of cultural importance in understanding the way humans classify and conceptualize animals and plants. On page 171 of the book there is a delightful picture of Berlin contemplating the taxonomy of the pangolin. The pangolin has great salience for many African communities, especially for Malawians, but the reason for this salience would never emerge from Berlin's general principles of ethnobiology, which completely marginalizes cultural factors.

While Cesalpino and Mayr (and it appears Hunn) see a simple relation between basic folk generics and usage, Berlin seems to go to the other extreme in seeing virtually no relationship at all. In response to Hunn and the utilitarians, he suggests that we must first recognize a 'species' phenomenologically before we can use it. This is true, but trite and misleading. It is equivalent in scope and as extreme as the opposite argument, which interprets utility so widely that it incorporates all interests. Surely we can incorporate the pragmatic and symbolic concerns of humans into the analysis without adopting either extreme?

Atran's (1990) seminal and important study of the cognitive foundations of natural history carries the same message. It consists of a refreshing, scholarly and informative journey through the history of biology, Atran's essential argument being that cognitive universals lie at the basis of biological knowledge. He thus suggests that human beings have an intuitive, psychologically prior disposition to structure the living world into discontinuous and separate 'species'. Such 'common-sense' or 'phenomenal' intuitions are seen as being reflected in basic-level folk taxonomies that are universal in scope. Although he specifically suggests that it is taxonomic 'categories' like folk generics and life-forms which are universal rather than folk taxa per se, his whole analysis, like Berlin's, assumes an almost one-to-one correspondence between phenomenological intuitions – the recognition of natural kinds (morphotypes) – and the basic named taxa of folk biology. He admits that there is an anthropocentric bias on the part of humans in their cognition of the world, but what they name is what has phenomenological salience – that is, the bias is cognitive and phenomenal and not pragmatic. Like Berlin, he therefore stridently refutes the utilitarian thesis of Cesalpino and Mayr. Utility is thus purely cultural. Atran offers an important discussion of folk biology, questioning the validity of Leach's (1964) cultural idealism and Rosch's (1978) theory of prototypes, in which respect he differs from Berlin. He also stresses the crucial distinction that people make between artefacts and living things, and the 'essentialist' nature of this thought as these are expressed in folk-biological taxonomies.

Atran's study, however, is less concerned with folk biology (or with natural history) than with the development of biology as a scientific discipline. What he concludes is that though this science has its foundations in common-sense intuitions, it is not simply a gradual refinement of common sense, nor does it represent an absolute rupture with it (as suggested by many philosophers of science); rather, it represents its development through highly specialized – and for Atran 'privileged' – cognitive programmes which 'transcend' common-sense intuitions. He thus sees basic cognitive dispositions, expressed in folk taxonomies, as psychologically prior; they represent, he feels, 'first-order' cognitive dispositions that have their basis in hominid evolution. Thus science, along with symbolism and pragmatic concerns, are second-order 'susceptibilities'. They have their anchorage in common-sense dispositions, but Atran considers them to be secondary cognitive elaborations. In a sense, science, symbolism and pragmatic interests are afterthoughts. As with Berlin, I am in general agreement with Atran's essential argument. More than a decade ago, in a critique of Douglas and Lévi-Strauss, I stressed the need to separate clearly folk-biological classification from symbolism and emphasized the intrinsic similarities between folk and scientific taxonomies. But I have also been concerned to explore the way in which symbolic and pragmatic concerns do influence taxonomic ordering at the generic and life-form level in an analysis of Navaho classification of insects (1979: 126) and in respect to Chewa ethnobotany and ethnomycology (Morris 1980, 1984, 1991, 1992, 1994a).

Ellen's study (1993) of Nuaula ethnozoology – the Nuaula being a small group of swidden cultivators living in the forests of south-central Seram – is essentially a sustained critique of the 'taxonomic' approach of Berlin and his associates. Although recognizing that his 'terminal' categories, which are roughly equivalent to Berlin's 'generics' and are the most specific and exclusive, are based on 'natural kinds' which reflect 'objective discontinuities' in nature, Ellen is highly sceptical of the notion that folk classifications are analogous to the phylogenetic models of biological taxonomists. He thus questions the hierarchical metaphor of taxonomic theory, with its emphasis on levels and inclusive higher categories. He notes that 28 percent of terminal categories of the Nuala are not classified into more inclusive groups. He emphasizes the fact that classifications are often overlapping, are inherently flexible, that they are based not simply on morphology, but on location, behaviour and cultural criteria, and that no clear division can be made between general purpose classifications – supposedly based on morphology and given priority – and more special-purpose classifications relating to pragmatic and cultural concerns. With much of this critique I can but concur, having criticized Berlin's taxonomic approach more than a decade ago, suggesting that folk taxonomic hierarchies are relatively shallow and something of a 'misnomer' when so many categories fall outside its reach, that folk classifications are inherently flexible with overlapping categories, and that functional criteria are intrinsically linked to taxonomic ordering. I also noted that both life-form categories and intermediate categories had an intrinsic functional bias and were not based on morphology (Morris 1984: 57; 1991, 1994a).

What is significant and important about Ellen's approach, however, is that he stresses that folk classifications can only be understood if situated in a cultural context, and with respect to diverse social practices. Like other ethnobiologists, he questions the notion of cultural idealists like Leach and Douglas that culture is simply an arbitrary grid that is imposed on an 'indifferentiated continuum' that is misleadingly seen as constituting the natural world (ibid.: 73). He is also critical of the distinctions between the 'literal' and the 'metaphorical', and between biological (technical) and symbolic (ritual) classifications, suggesting these are 'crude and pernicious' (ibid.: 165). In an earlier paper, cited by Ellen, I stressed the importance of making a *distinction* between folk-biological classifications, based on discontinuities in nature, that order a particular domain (fungi, plants, mammals) and the symbolic classifications that are often expressed in ritual contexts. These complex symbolic classifications or mythological systems were seen by many scholars as 'all-embracing' schemas that united into a totality, as an ideologic, the various *systems* of classification (1976: 542–3). I stressed the point that both Douglas (1966) and Lévi-Strauss (1966) had tended to *conflate* these different forms of classifications, as well as questioning the universality and totalizing nature – 'all embracing' – of these symbolic schemas. But stressing the *distinction* between these two types of classification, between the kind of 'symbolic' or metaphorical classification such as I have outlined above, and the folk biological classifications of the kind that interests Berlin and Atram, the 'basic-level' categories, did not imply that I was advocating a radical *dualistic* approach. My paper on Navaho taxonomy (1979) was devoted to exploring the links between these two forms of classification. Nor did my paper imply that these were the only forms of classification. As for the distinction between the literal and metaphorical, this is an essential distinction: it only becomes problematic if the distinction is expanded into a dualism between two realms of being. Human language is inherently metaphorical, particularly in relation to such intangible things as time and cultural phenomena – and the writings of ethnobiologists, with their concepts of 'domains', 'levels' and 'hierarchy', are replete with metaphors. Heidegger (1994) described the history of Western philosophy as if it was a game of 'hide and seek' in relation to being! But the distinction between the literal and the metaphorical is also intrinsic to human language, and irony and humour would not be possible without it. When a Malawian woman, in anger, calls her spouse a dog (*garu*), she is not suggesting that he might be useful as a hunting aid and has an acute sense of smell, only that her husband has behaved in a despicable way!

When Lakoff and Johnson – who, more than anyone, stress the pervasive nature of metaphor in everyday social life – define metaphor as 'the understanding and experiencing of one kind of thing in terms of another'(1980: 5), this presupposes a literal recognition of the things prior to their metaphorical linking. Johnson has stressed that although our conceptions of knowledge, language, rationality and morality are deeply and pervasively metaphoric, this does not imply that all our concepts and thinking are metaphorical, for conceptual systems are grounded in bodily experience and reflected in 'basic-level' categories (1993:61). Distinctions between cognition and belief, literal and metaphorical, mundane and sacred, biological and ritual classifications are only distinctions. And without making distinctions no thinking, let alone knowledge, is possible: they only become problematic if reified, or treated in a dualistic fashion. Ellen, of course, does not abandon the 'imputed' mundane-symbolic divide, he rather emphasizes the importance of explaining the similarities, the continuities and the 'mutual refractions' between them and the need for an understanding of how people classify the material world as a precondition for interpreting their symbolic schemas (1993: 185).

I turn now to exploring the folk classification of mammals in Malawi, examining first their life-form categories and then their classification of the *nyama/chirombo* complex.

Life-Form Categories

As with many other cultures, there are no terms in Malawi that can be considered equivalent to the English terms 'animal' and 'plant'. These terms both derive from Latin, and were not used widely in Britain until after the sixteenth century (cf. Morris 1980, Berlin 1992: 190). In the most general sense people speak of the natural world as having been created (*kulenga*) by the supreme spirit (*mulungu*) who is particularly associated with the rains (*mvula*). Thus created things can be described as *zolengedwa* ('that which is created'). But generally, Chewa speakers refer to 'things' as *chinthu*, and the root *nthu* seems to have the meaning of substance or being. *Nthuli* refers to a piece of meat, *kanthu* colloquially to 'anything' and *munthu* to a person (pl. *anthu*). *Nthawi*, which is derived from the same root, means 'time' and by extension 'space'. Although

Malawians do not clearly articulate the kind of ontological categories or modalities of experience as suggested by many theologically inclined scholars (Kagame 1956, Jahn 1961, cf. Mudimbe 1988: 147–8), the root *nthu is* close to Aristotle's concept of substance (*ousia*). Moreover, as with Aristotle and the pre-Socratics – and in contrast with Platonic philosophy – Malawians have a dynamic concept of being. But within the category of things or *chinthu*, Malawians make a clear distinction, again like Aristotle, between those aspects of the natural world that have 'life' (- *moyo)* and those things which do not (*zinthu zopanda moyo*). In conversations with people regarding what entities have life (*zili ndi moyo*) it is generally regarded that the following have life: *mtengo* (tree), *nyama* (animal), *njoka* (snake), spirit entities such as *napolo* (serpent spirit associated with mountains) and *mizimu* (souls of the dead), *bowa* (edible mushrooms), *mvula* (rain), *mbalame* (bird) and *nthaka* (soil).

Things without life are specified as *phiri* (mountains) and *mwala* (rock or stone). There is some ambiguity as to whether soil or rain have 'life', but what is clearly evident is that in the Malawian context, people clearly recognize a category of living things (*zamoyo*, 'that have life'), and thus make a distinction between animate and inanimate things. But it is important to note that for Malawians the ancestral spirits (*mizimu)* have life, and it is thus misleading to see the dead (*amanda*, 'those of the grave', almost always addressed in the plural form) as somehow in opposition to life. The claws, skin and horns of a dead mammal, which are of crucial importance in Malawi as medicine, are therefore not to be seen as the negation of life but rather as the essence and continuity of life, as Eliade long ago suggested (1960: 83). 'Spirits' of the dead should therefore not be viewed as lifeless or as lacking in vitality, as is often implied by anthropologists who advocate neo-Platonic interpretations of ritual concepts (e.g. Gyekye 1987, Bloch 1992), but rather as embodying life as a timeless dimension. For Malawians, the ancestors are immortals in the Greek sense of having eternal life. The important and perceptive interpreter of African religion and philosophy John Mbiti was therefore essentially correct in referring to the ancestral spirits as the 'living dead' (1969: 25). This is why ancestral spirits need to be 'fed', to be given beer or flour as an offering (*nsembe*) and to be kept always in communication with the living. And it is of interest when discussing 'life' with Malawians that a central focus tends to be put on food and on the difference between life and character. As one person said to me: *Moyo ndi kadya chifukwa kupanda kudya ndiye kuti sitingakhale ndi moyo ngakhalenso nyama*: 'Life is to eat because without food we do not live with life (health) and it is the same with animals.' Another remarked: *Nyama ziri ndi moyo ofanana koma mitima ndi yosiyana*: 'All animals have the same life, but their hearts (character) are different.' Life (*moyo*) for Malawians is therefore intrinsically linked with health and well-being. In fact *moyo* also means health as well as the principle of animate life. *Ali ndi moyo*, 's/he *is* with health', is a common expression of general well-being, not only in physical terms, but in relation to a sense of harmony with the social world around the individual.

Although Malawians do conceive of the spirits of the ancestors (*mzimu ya makolo*) as being associated with certain trees or animals, or even in certain circumstances taking the form of an animal (especially such animals as the snake, lion, leopard and hyena), it would be quite misleading to describe their world view as animistic. They do not conceive of the 'world' as animate, only certain aspects of it, and they clearly make a distinction between life and spirit or soul (*mzimu*), although these two notions are indeed closely associated, as life, human life in particular, is in a sense nourished or regenerated by the spirits of the dead. Ultimately, the supreme spirit (*mulungu*) sustains or nourishes all things. Malawian perceptions of the world are, then, not so much animistic (in a spiritual sense) but rather pan-vitalist implying a world view in which life is virtually 'co-extensive with being', as Hans Jonas perceptively describes the ontology of preliterate communities (1966: 19). Yet although Malawians see the ancestral spirits as having life and as forming a single community with their living kin, the ancestors (*makolo*) and the senior members of the matrilineal kin group (*akulu*) cannot be equated. The ancestors are conceived as having wider powers, and the term *mzimu* (spirit) belongs to the *mtengo* noun class, which includes such living beings as animals, trees and snakes as well as such things as diseases, stones and tools, and is quite distinct from living persons, who belong to the *munthu* noun class. This class includes all nouns that refer to people (gender and kin terms, herbalist, craftsman, as well as, as we shall see, some mammals; cf. Kopytoff 1971, Brain 1973).

While Malawians do not have terms for the two main categories of organisms (*za moyo*) i.e. plants and animals, they do, of course recognize clear distinctions between the two kingdoms, and this is reflected in language use. Plants are seen to grow and sprout (*ku-mera*) but to lack movement, and there is a host of terms referring to both plant morphology and plant use that would imply a distinction between plants and other organisms, but whether such distinctions warrant the label covert category is difficult to say (Brown 1974, Berlin 1992: 190–2).

Even though there is no distinct Chewa term for 'plant', literate speakers of the language often try to find or make one, and given the structure of Bantu languages this is easily done. Thus the term *chomera* or *chimerera* (derived from *ku-mera*) can be used to describe plants generally, but their focus is essentially on cultivated species, especially those, like sweet potato, which are propagated vegetatively. There are three basic terms in Chewa for what might loosely be described as the plant world: *mtengo*, a general concept for trees and woody plants; *maudzu*, grasses and grass-like herbs like the Anthericum lilies; and *bowa*, edible fungi. I have elsewhere discussed Chewa ethnobotany and ethnomycology at some length (Morris 1980, 1984, 1991, 1992), so little need be added here. But some reflections on the cognitive theory discussed above may be appropriate and indicate that functional criteria are not completely extraneous to general folk classifications. Take, for example, the Chewa concept of *bowa*, whose essential meaning is edible fungi. Interestingly, fungi hardly comes into the theoretical purview of either Berlin or Atran, although fungi constitutes a whole kingdom of organisms. Could this reflect the mycophobia of which Lévi-Strauss speaks and indicate that cultural concerns do influence the way we see the world – contrary to what both writers argue!

Atran indeed states in a general survey of his argument (1990: 56) that for all people 'every living kind is either a plant or animal'. This is not the case at all, for Malawians, like most people in the world, see *bowa* as different in kind from both animals and plants (*mtengo, maudzu*). But importantly, for the Chewa *bowa* essentially refers to edible fungi, and edibility is a defining characteristic. Other fungi, which do not have a generic name and are not seen as *bowa*, are conceptualized as useless and harmful organisms (*chirombo*). The Yao equivalents are *uwasi* and *chikoko*. Malawians, like other people, are clearly able to recognize many other species of fungi as morphotypes, and *Amanita muscaria* and *Russula deremsis* have as much phenomenal salience as *Amanita zambiana (utenga)* and *Russula schizoderma (chipindi)*, but for the Chewa only the latter have generic names and are considered *bowa*. Moreover, as we shall see, for the Chewa *chirombo* is not a residual category into which phenologically small and uninteresting species are lumped, but a key concept. Thus out of 362 species of macrofungi that I recorded in Malawi (1990), only a subset of around 60 edible species were named as folk generics and grouped under the life-form category *bowa*. This would suggest that functional criteria are important in defining this life-form (cf. Hunn 1982, Randall 1987, C.H. Brown 1992).

Similarly, utilitarian considerations are relevant within the life category *mtengo* and are important factors in plant classification, as I have described elsewhere (Morris 1984, 1991). Thus intermediate functional taxa such as *mwanawamphepo* (also a disease concept), *thelele* (a certain kind of relish) and *ulimbo* (bird lime) have salience as taxonomic groupings and are part of the general classification of plants rather than being some secondary classification of medicine or food. Malawians do not make a rigid demarcation between the mind and body, between the intellect and utility. Moreover, ecological criteria also play a part in the naming of plants, so that (for example) a generic term like *kalisachi* (to sit on one's own) may cover epiphytic plants like the orchid *Cytorchis arcuata* and *Loranthus* spp, as well as the fungus *Schizophyllum commune*. A phenomenalist approach is therefore not sufficient to explicate ethnobiological classifications.

Turning now to ethnozoological life-form categories, Malawians recognize the following:

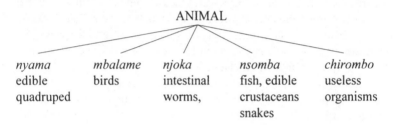

ANIMAL				
nyama	*mbalame*	*njoka*	*nsomba*	*chirombo*
edible	birds	intestinal	fish, edible	useless
quadruped		worms,	crustaceans	organisms
			snakes	

Mbalame (birds) form a largely morphological category and is used as a rubric to cover large flying creatures (*imauluka*), and so usually covers also bats, though not insects. But interestingly, the domestic duck (*bakha*) and the chicken (*nkhuku*) are not referred to as 'birds' (*mbalame*) but as domestic animals or *chiweto*. *Mbalame* covers several hundred named categories, and there seems to be a close correspondence between folk categories of birds and biological species, at least for the commoner species.

Birds are commonly trapped either by means of spring traps or by the use of bird lime. Those well liked as a relish include the wood doves *katundulu* (*Turtur* spp.), the red-necked Francolin *nkhwali* (*Francolinus afer*), the guinea fowl *Nkhanga (Numida meleagris)* and the wild pigeons (*Streptopelia* spp), as well as numerous small birds such as bulbuls, weavers, waxbills, flycatchers and sunbirds. Apart from feathers and bones, almost all parts of the bird are eaten (see Berry and Petty 1992, and my article on bird lime or *ulimbo*, Morris and Patel 1994). Table 3.1 lists some of the more common birds (see Benson 1953).

Njoka roughly corresponds to the snakes (order *Ophidia*), but it also includes intestinal worms *(njoka ya m'mimba,* snake of the stomach).

Folk Classifications

Table 3.1 Common birds (*mbalame*)

Chewa term	Common name	Scientific name
nkhwazi	fish eagle	*Haliaeetus vocifer*
chipweyo	white faced tree duck	*Dendrocygna viduata*
	fulvous tree duck	*Dendrocygna bicolor*
nkhwali	red necked francolin	*Francolinus afer*
khungubwe	pied crow	*Corvus albus*
ngalu	crowned crane	*Balearica pavonina*
mphamba	large hawks / buzzards / kites	*Buteo rufofuscus et al*
songwe	sunbirds	*Anthreptes sp*
		Nectarima senesalensis
kadzidzi	barn owl	*Tyto alba*
chikwangwala	white necked raven	*Corvus albicollis*
lumbe	nightjars	*Caprimulgus spp*
njiwa	doves	*Streptopelia spp*
nkhunda	green pigeon	*Treron australis*
mnang'omba	ground hornbill	*Bicorvus cafer*
tsekwe	spur-winged goose	*Plectropterus gambensis*
chinsoso	red-chested cuckoo	*Cuculus solitarius*
mkokafodya	european bee-eater	*Merops apiaster*
kakowa	egrets / herons	*Ardeola spp*
		Egretta spp
nanchengwa	hammerkop	*Scopus umbretta*
manchichi	eagle owl	*Bubo lacteus*
ntowitowi	pied wagtail	*Motacilla aguimp*
phwiti	firefinch	*Lagonosticta spp*
choli	lilac-breasted roller	*Coracias caudata*
kalanga	hottentot teal	*Anas hottentota*

Many snakes are ritually important, and the python, puff adder and file snake all have associations with the spirits. Over forty species of snakes have been recorded, and the main categories are listed in Table 3.2 (see Sweeney 1971).

Fish (*nsomba*) play a very important part in the economic life of Malawi, particularly with respect to those communities living along the lakeshore or in the Lower Shire Valley. Fish, fresh or dried, is an important food and widely traded as a market commodity. It forms an important relish, but is treated quite separately from meat, and fish are never referred to as *nyama*. It is beyond the scope of the present study to discuss the ecology and culture of fish or the fishing industry. Fish are caught by means of traps, nets, rod and line (often at night), hand scoops and fish poisons. Fish is either boiled (*-phika*) or roasted. I have records of around 300 different named categories of fish, the fish fauna of Lake Malawi and its rivers being extremely rich and varied (see Bertram *et al.* 1942, P.B.N. Jackson *et al.* 1963, Sweeney 1970/2: 1–6, Tweddle and Willoughby

Table 3.2 Common snakes (*njoka*)

Chewa term	Common Name	Scientific name
nthongo	blind burrowing snake	*Typhlops schlegelii*
biritsi		
mbitu		
nsato	python	*Python sebae*
chankusa	house snake	*Boaedon fuliginosus*
chirumi	water snake	*Lycodonomorphus rufulus*
njokandala	file snake	*Mehelya capensis*
chamasamba	green snake	*Philothamnus spp*
namasamba		
nalikukuti	vine snake	*Thelotornis capensis*
mbobo	boomslang	*Dispholidus typus*
chiwa	tiger snake	*Telescopus semiannulatus*
mamba	cobra	*Naja spp*
songwe	black mamba	*Dendroaspis polylepis*
songo		
kasambwe	night adder	*Causus rhombeatus*
mphiri	puff adder	*Bitis arietans*
chigonakusa	burrowing viper	*Atractaspis bibroni*

1979, for useful information). Table 3.3 lists some of the commonest species.

Nyama is a polysemic term referring both to meat and prototypically to any edible species of mammal. It can include edible reptiles and amphibians, but it excludes *nsomba* (fish and edible freshwater crustaceans), *mbalame* (birds) and *njoka* (snakes). *Nyama* has a complex meaning and in normal contexts it excludes the larger predatory mammals such as hyena, leopard and lion, as well as those smaller animals that are not usually eaten, like the hedgehog, pangolin, shrew and jackal. It also has great ritual significance to Malawians because of its association with hunting. Schoffeleers (1968: 406) suggests that besides meaning 'edible quadruped', it also refers to the spirit or power released by the blood of a slain person or animal, thus giving it a mystical quality. With respect to the Rangi of Tanzania, John Kesby (1979: 43) suggests that the term may be a recent borrowing from Swahili *wanyama*; this is certainly not the case with regard to Malawi, for the concept has indigenous roots (as indeed does the Swahili term). The concept *nyama* is thus widely used throughout Malawi by all the principal ethnic communities, Lomwe, Chewa, Yao, Mang'anja and Tumbuka. Indeed, Baumann (1950) found the term or its equivalent to be widespread throughout Africa and to denote mystical power, especially a kind of vengeance magic associated with the blood of the animal. This power was particularly evident in many

Table 3.3 Some common fish (*nsomba*)

Chewa term	Common Name	Scientific name
kampango	cat fish	*Bagrus meridionalis*
mlamba	common cat fish	*Clarius gariepinus*
mpasa	lake salmon	*Barilius microlepis*
mcheni	tiger fish	*Rhamphchromis spp*
		Hydrocynus vittatus
matemba	small fish	*Barbus spp*
chambo	bream	*Tilapia spp*
njolo	cornish jack	*Mormyrops anguiiloides*
nyanda		Mormyrops deliciosus
usipa	'sardine'	*Engravlicypris sardella*
ntchila	mudsucker	*Labeo mesops*
ntuwa		
mpanda	bottlenose	*Mormyrus longirostis*
kadyakolo	barb	*Barbus eurystonus*
nkomo	cat fish	*Bathyclarius nyasensis*
sapuwa		
mbuna	small coloured rock fish	*Labeotropheus and related cichlidae spp (many species)*
nkhungu	mottled eel	*Anguilla nebulosa*
utakia	–	*Haplochromis sp*
nyesi	electric catfish	*Malapterurus electricus*

large mammals such as the lion, leopard and eland. In Malawi there is a particular affliction, *chirope*, that affects hunters and which is associated with the vengeance power of the *nyama*; this was discussed fully in the last chapter. Significantly, the 'flesh' of a bird or snake or a vegetable substance tends to be referred to as *mnofu*, not *nyama*. By extension *nyama* can come to mean the essential substance of something like a tree or a piece of wood.

Although prototypically *nyama* refers to wild animals that constitute game, specifically such antelopes as duiker, kudu, klipspringer and buffalo, it is important to realize that it serves both as a taxonomic and as a functional category; thus its meaning can be extended in either direction. Taxonomically, *nyama* can be extended to cover carnivorous animals like mongoose and hyena and even humans (although, because it retains its 'edibility' criteria, people will be hesitant to do, as it implies that one is a witch). Thus the Lilongwe Nature Sanctuary is referred to as *nkhalango ndi nyama* (literally 'forest of animals') and carries the sign *Malo amene munguone nyama ndi mbalame* ('This is the place (where) you will see animals and birds'). And the *nyama* it lists to be found in the sanctuary includes the leopard (*kambulu)* and hyena (*fisi*), mammals which are never eaten as food. In contrast, functionally *nyama* can be extended to include mushrooms, birds and domestic animals, though taxonomically these would be held to be distinct life-forms (*bowa, mbalame* and *chiweto*). Women in Malawi often refer to mushrooms as *nyama*, and many generic terms of fungi indicate this: *manyame, kanyama, mnofu wa nkhuku* (flesh of the chicken) refer to species of *Cantherellus* and *Cymatoderma*. Likewise edible species of terrestrial orchids (*chanaka, Disa* spp) are often referred to as *nyama yapansi* (underground meat). As a category, *nyama* may even be extended to small invertebrates that are eaten, such as the termite in its flying stage (Yao, *ngumbi*).

Besides the four main life forms – to call them zoological drastically narrows their meaning – there is a kind of residual category, *chirombo*. This refers basically to any hostile wild animal, and the leopard and hyena are prototypical. Essentially, however, *chirombo* means any useless living thing and also includes weeds and most invertebrates. Like *nyama*, the term also has important symbolic connotations, being associated not only with wild animals of the bush, but also with evil spirits and with masked dancers (who impersonate spirits of the dead in the form of wild animals) at certain ceremonials. *Chirombo*, however, is a functional and not a residual taxonomic category, and although it includes most invertebrates and such animals as lizards and frogs, it does not correspond to the category of 'creeping things' of the authorized version of Genesis, nor to Brown's (1979) conception of 'wug' for small animals that are not incorporated into the categories of fish, bird or snake. The prototypical *chirombo*, as noted, are large mammals, the lion and hyena.

Although *chirombo* prototypically covers carnivorous mammals such as leopards, lions and hyenas as well as smaller carnivores like the civet, zorilla and domestic dog, and can be extended to cover the crocodile (*ng'ona*) and the monitor lizard (*ng'anzi*), I did not find any evidence in Malawi to suggest that it meant 'large creatures that bite' (Yoshida 1992:211). It essentially referred to any living thing that was harmful or useless. In this sense, it was used to cover a wide variety of animals – reptiles, amphibians, insects, millipedes, scorpions, spiders and crust-aceans – many of which were considered edible and thus not usually referred to as *chirombo*. Small animals that are considered useless or a pest may be described as *karombo*, or more frequently *kachirombo*. But it has to be noted that many small animals that are not considered *njoka, mbalame, nsomba* or *nyama* are generally felt to be unaffiliated to any life-form category. Thus edible insects like the cicada (*nyenje*), winged termite (*ngumbi*) or red locust (*dzombe*), while important as relish, are never described as *nyama*, nor are they usually thought of as *chirombo*, but rather as *cholengedwa basi*. They are simply created things. Needless to say, although *njoka* (snakes) is a clear life-form category, snakes are invariably referred to as *chirombo*. When Malawians use terms like *ndiwo* (relish), *nyama* (meat), and *chirombo* (useless/harmful) there is always an implicit pragmatic dimension. It must be noted too that Malawians do not make a categorical distinction between *chiweto* and *nyama*, for domestic animals are also considered *nyama* – of the village (*ya mudzi*), in contrast with those of the woodland (*ya tchire*) (cf Yoshida 1992: 210).

Table 3.4 lists the various animals that are usually described as *chirombo*, denoting those that are used as relish. Categories like *buluzi* (blue-headed agama lizard), *chule* (frog) and *birimankwe* (chameleon) are often described as consisting of several kinds (*mitundu*), even though these may not be named. (For useful studies of Malawi animal life, see Sweeney 1970, Stewart 1967, Hargreaves 1979.)

The life categories *nyama* and *chirombo* are thus prototypically functional categories, with, respectively, positive (as meat) and negative (as harmful) connotations. Together they are used quite flexibly and according to context. In many respects, they are akin to the early English concepts of 'game' and 'beast'. Both these terms were still widely used when I was a boy; indeed, books like Seton's *Lives of Game Animals* and Edward Step's *Beasts of the Field* were my companions during my teenage years. 'Mammal' had then – in the 1950s – still not come into the common language. Atran's suggestion (1990: 37) that folk-zoological life-forms correspond to scientific classes is highly debatable when it comes to ' mammals'. By no stretch of the imagination can either *nyama* or *chirombo* be classified as a life-form category that is equivalent to 'animal', 'vertebrate' or 'mammal'. Together, however, they roughly correspond to 'wild animal' and their inherent flexibility needs to be stressed. Thus, the kudu (*ngoma*) is prototypically *nyama*, as its meat is eaten by almost everybody. But because it lives in the bush (*tchire*) as a wild animal, it may be referred to as a *chirombo*. Conversely, the crocodile (*ng'ona*) is essentially a *chirombo* and much to be feared, but even if it is not normally eaten – except for medicinal purposes – it may be described as *nyama wa madzi* (water animal).

Within the covert category 'animal', a distinction is clearly made between wild and domestic species. Domestic animals are referred to as *chiweto* or *chifuyo*, derived from the verbs *ku-weta*, to tend, to keep, and *ku-fuya*, to tame. The former pair of terms includes chickens, ducks and dog, as well as the larger domestic livestock like sheep, goats and cattle (see Table 3.5). The division between wild and domestic is fairly clear cut. For example, *bakha* refers to the domestic duck, and besides being seen as outside the *mbalame* (bird) category, it is considered quite distinct

Table 3.4 Animals often characterized as *chirombo*

chule	frogs	*Rana angolensis*
		Ptychadena anchietae et al
mbululu	'tadpole	*Bufo regularis*
namtusi	toads	*Kinixis belliana*
kamba	tortoise	*Crocodylus niloticus*
fulu		
ng'ona	nile crocodile	*Chameleon melleri*
kalilombe	horned chameleon	*Chameleon dilepsis*
birimankwe	flap-necked chameleon	*Chameleon melleri*
nasikambe		
buluzi	agama lizards	*Agama spp*
dududu	spiny agama	*Agama hispida*
gondwa	monitor lizard	*Varanus niloticus*
guru	blue headed agama	*Agama mossambica*
nampopo		
kwawe	plated lizard	*Gerrhosaurus spp*
kwakwata		
nkhasi	turtle	*Cycloderma frenatum*
kamba wamadzi		
* *nyenje*	cicada	*Cicadae spp*
chiswambiya	praying mantis	*Mantidae spp*
* *nkhululu*	giant cricket	*Brachytrypes membranaceus*
* *dzombe*	red locust	*Nomadacris septemfasciata*
chiwala		
kafumbwe	wood-boring beetle weevils	*Bostrychoidea spp*
		Curculionidae spp
gulugufe	butterfly	*Many species*
kambalame	tsetse fly	*Glossina morsitans*
chiswe	termite	*Termitidae spp*
* *ngumbi inswa*	winged termite	*Termitidae spp*
tombolombo	dragonfly	*Many species*
nsabwe	common louse	*Pediculus humanus*
kafulifuli	ant lion	*Symmathetes moestus*
chitete	grasshopper	*Acrididae sp*
* *nkhungu*	lake fly	*Eucorethra edulis*
udzudzu	mosquito	*Anopheles sp*
nyerere	small black ants	*Pheidole spmals*
linthumbu	red ants	*Anomma sp*
kangaude	spiders	*Several species (araneae)*
kalizi	scorpion	*Scorpionidae*
* *nkhanu*	freshwater crab	*Potomonautes montivagus*
bongololo	millipede	*Diplopoda*
* edible		

from wild species such as *chipweyo*, the fulvous tree duck, and *kalanga*, the Hottentot teal. Europeans often use *bakha* as a generic term, but Chewa-speakers around Lake Chilwa were adamant that this term applied only to the domestic species. This conceptual demarcation is common

Table 3.5 The category *chiweto* (domestic livestock)

fowl	*nkhuku*
cock	*tambala*
goat	*mbuzi*
sheep	*nkhosa*
ram	*mphulu*
cattle	*ng'ombe*
duck	*bakha*
pig	*nkhumba*
guinea pig	*mbira*

among Malawians: *nkhumba* and *nguluwe*, for example, refer to the domestic and wild pig respectively, *nkhunda* and *njiwa* to the domestic and wild pigeon. Domestic animals may therefore be seen as *nyama* in a functional sense as meat, but conceptually they are grouped as *ziweto*, domestic livestock (which includes chickens), and are not *nyama*. As one person expressed it to me in discussing guinea-pigs (which share the same name *mbira* as the yellow-spotted hyrax), some animals are of the bush and are *nyama* (*zantchire ndi nyama*), and some are of the village and are domestic animals (*wina za mudzi ndi ziweto*). As we have already seen, the distinction between the village (*mudzi*) and the woodland (*thengo, tchire*) is indeed an important ecological and symbolic demarcation among Malawians, as it is for many other African communities (cf. Croll and Parkin 1992).

In an important sense, then, the two main animal life-form categories that are evident in Malawi, *chirombo* and *nyama*, cannot be understood simply as morphological categories: they have an important pragmatic dimension which suggests that folk taxonomies cannot be conceptually isolated as a domain from other aspects of Malawian culture. The polysemous nature of the main category *nyama* suggests, as Bulmer remarked, that such 'life-forms' 'may be defined as much by cultural evaluation as by their objective biological characteristics' (1974: 23).

Needless to say, in Chewa thought, people (*anthu*) form a separate and unique category. This, together with their highly pragmatic approach towards the natural world, suggests an anthropocentric world view. Indeed, both Kagame (1956) and Mbiti (1969) imply that the ontology underlying African religious philosophy is anthropocentric, in the sense that humans are placed at the centre of their ontology, the natural world the means of constituting their environment and means of existence. A radical opposition is implied between things (*chinthu*) and people. Although there is a tendency these days, especially among writers on ecological issues, and even some anthropologists, to identify whole

cultures or historical periods by a single ontological motif (anthropocentric, biocentric, mechanistic, holistic), the relationship of Malawians
to the animal world (like that of all cultures) is diverse and complex and
embodies several contrasting attitudes towards animals – pragmatic,
intellectual, aesthetic, symbolic, sacramental – that cannot be captured
by monolithic labels.

It is worth concluding this section with a brief note on the noun classes
as reflected in the Chewa language.

The noun classes themselves to some extent reflect a distinction
between animals and plants, and also serve as ontological categories.
Whereas many animals belong to the *munthu* (person) class (listed below),
most of the *mtengo* category, which includes the majority of the plants
known to Malawians, belong to the noun class typically referred to as
the *mtengo* (tree) category (trees such as *mkuyu, mkundi, msopa*, all taking
the plural prefix *mi-*). The other four noun classes refer mainly to objects
or abstract concepts. Some typical examples are given in the table below,
and although mammals may fall under any of the six classes, most come
under the 'person' noun class (one) or under the *nyumba* class (four),
the latter including many of the larger mammals and domestic animals
(see Table 3.6).

The Classification of Mammals

The Malawian conception of nature I earlier alluded to has certain affinities with that of the early Greeks as theorized by Aristotle. Malawians
are not animists: they do not conceive the world as 'animate', in the
classical anthropological sense, and such as we find among the Naulu,
among whom spirits inhabit every conceivable niche of the universe (Ellen
1993: 176). Nor do they have a theory of pan-psychism. What Malawians
convey instead is a sense in which the natural world – the earth, the fungi,
the plants, the animals – is believed to possess intrinsic powers and
potentialities. They conceive of nature in the Greek sense of *physis*, as
productive, self-unfolding, with latent powers that can be harnessed by
humans. These days *physis*, which is usually translated as 'nature', has
very physical or mechanistic associations. Physics is thus the science that
deals with the properties and inter-actions of matter and energy. It is,
however, important to remind ourselves that the word *physis* had very
different associations for the early Greeks. *Physis* is derived from the
Greek verb *phyto*, 'to grow', and *phyto* actually means 'plant'. Phyto-
therapy is a current synonym for herbalism. 'Nature', therefore, for
Aristotle and for the early Greek naturalists essentially had organic

Table 3.6 Noun Classes

class one mu-a} wa-a}	class two mu-mi} u-i}	class three u-ma} wa-a}	class four i-zi} ya-za}	class five chi-zi} cha-za}	class six li-zi} la-a}
munthu/anthu person	*mtengo-mitengo* tree	*uta-mauta* bow	*nyumba* house	*chinthu/zinthu* thing	*dzanja/manja* land
nyamata/anyamata young man	*mwendo/miyendo* leg	*ulendo/maulendo* journey	*nthawi* time	*chingwe/zingwe* string	*khasu/makasu* hoe
mlonda/alonda watchman	*mwala/miala* stone	*ufa* flour	*nyama* meat/animal	*chaka/zaka* year	*Banja/abanja* family/house
mwana/ana child	*mtima/mitima* heart	*ufumu* chieftainship	*nthaka* soil	*chiswe/ziswe* termite	*dimba/madimba* garden
sakhwi/asakhwi elephant shrew	*mbulu/mimbulu* wild dog		*mbuzi* goat	*chiuli/ziuli* ratel	*kholo/makolo* ancestors
nkhandwe/ankhandwe jackal	*mkango/mikango* lion		*ntchefu* eland	*chirombo/zirombo* wild animal	*khoswe/makoswe* back rat
njati/anjati buffalo	*msulu/misulu* banded mongoose		*njobvu* elephant	*chipembere/zipembere* rhinoceros	
changa/achanga bushbaby	*mleme/mileme* bats		*ngondo* hartebeest	*chiweto/ziweto* domestic animal	
njuzi/anjuzi serval	*mzimu/mizimu* soul of dead		*mvuu* hippopotamus		
mwili/amwili genet			*nyumbu* wildebeest		
fisi/afisi hyena			*ng'ombe* cattle		
boo/aboo nyala			*nchenzi* cane rat		
ngoma/angoma kudu			*nkhosa* sheep		
nyalugwe/anyalugwe leopard					
katumba/akatumba otter					
nungu/anungu porcupine					
kanyimbi/akanyimbi zorilla					
nguluwe/anguluwe wild pig					
nyani/anyani baboon					
kalulu/akalulu hare					

Table 3.6 Noun Classes (*continued*)

class one mu-a} wa-a}	class two mu-mi} u-i}	class three u-ma} wa-a}	class four i-zi} ya-za}	class five chi-zi} cha-za}	class six li-ma} la-a}
gwape/agwape grey duiker *pusi/apusi* vervet monkey *galu/agalu* domestic dog *namfuko/anamfuko* mole rat *sunche/asunche* shrew *gologolo/agologolo* bush squirrel *kamundi/akumundi* night ape			*mbidzi* zebra *nsato* python *mkumba* domestic pig *mbewa* rodent *mbalame* birds *ng'ona* crocodile *nkhuku* domestic fowl		

connotations: the world was seen as a living entity, not as inert matter that was activated by 'spirit'. The natural world was thus seen has having inherent powers and causal agency. This is very much how Malawians conceive the world. As Tempels expressed it in his study of African philosophy (1959), Africans have a dynamic conception of being.

But the Greeks also had another related conception, *zoe* (life), from which the terms zodiac (totemic) and zoology derive. *Zoe* was seen as *physis* intensified as self-emergence; it conveys what stands out and has an arresting quality among living things (Foltz 1995: 132–3). And of course, what is crucial about animals, particularly the larger mammals – what is indeed fundamental about them – is that they are 'things', substances, that have individuality. As active, mobile beings, possessing what Spinoza called *conatus*, the innate capacity for self-preservation, mammals are 'real unities' – as are human beings, in spite of what post-modernists say about the fragmentation of the psyche. In recent decades, philosophers have written much on the distinction between functional (that is human artefacts) and 'natural kinds' (Kripke 1972, Putnam 1975, Atran 1990; 71-80). Mammals are clearly recognized by Malawians as 'natural kinds', as living 'things', and as almost all mammals in Malawi have what ethnobiologists refer to as cultural 'salience', almost all are widely recognized and given names.

As with knowledge of plants and fungi, so knowledge of mammals – their names, ecology and behaviour – is highly variable, depending on a number of factors, age, gender, interests, occupation and where a person lives. The most knowledgeable people, with respect particularly to the larger mammals, tend to be men who are actively engaged in hunting or who work semi-professionally as herbalist/diviners (*sing'anga*). It was to such men that I mainly attached myself, although I also discussed mammalian life with many women.

A total of 187 species of mammals have been recorded from Malawi, belonging to 115 genera and 13 orders of mammals. Of these 132 species are terrestrial (see Table 3.7). Apart from the bats, which are usually categorized as *mbalame* (birds), and those species which are either rare or which have a local distribution (largely confined to montane forests) and are therefore unknown to most Malawians, almost all the mammals of Malawi are conceptually recognized by local people and have a generic name. Thus some 105 species of indigenous mammals are recognized and named, and these are detailed below. For the sake of exposition I have presented the material under four headings, relating to the carnivores, the ungulates, the category *mbewa* and 'other mammals' (see Tables 3.8–3.11). It should be noted, of course, that some mammals have a restricted

Table 3.7 Mammals of Malawi

order		number of species
Insectivora	hedgehog/shrews	10
Macroscelidae	elephant shrews	4
Chiroptera	bats	55
Primates	galogos, monkeys	6
Carnivora	cats, dogs, mongooses	27
Proboscidae	elephant	1
Perissodactyla	odd-toed ungulates	2
Hyracoidea	hyraxes	3
Tubulidenta	antbear	1
Pholidota	pangolin	1
Artiodactyla	even-toed ungulates	23
Rodentia	rats and mice	52
Lagomorpha	hares	2
totals: orders 13	general 15 species 187	

(After Ansell and Dowsett 1988)

distribution in Malawi and are thus not found in certain areas. They are therefore not known to ethnic communities living in these areas.

All these generics are covered by the *nyama/chirombo* complex, and it can be seen that almost all the mammal 'species' fall under a simple folk generic: there are virtually no specific folk taxa. Apart from the category *mbewa*, (discussed below) there are also no intermediate taxa. I have enumerated the folk taxa from the five major language groups found in Malawi, and it is evident that not only is there a close relationship between these different 'ethnic' categories, but that they correspond closely with the scientific taxa at the 'specific' level, thus confirming Atran's and Berlin's essential thesis. Within any one language group, the total number of generic taxa is around 91 (see Table 3.12).

Folk generics in Malawi are referred to as *mtundu,* which means kind or variety and not only covers different 'species' or kinds of plants or animals, but is also used widely to refer to different kinds of things, e.g. soils. Ethnic affiliation is described by the same term (pl. *mitundu*). The term *gulu* carries essentially the same meaning, though it tends to refer more to collectivities rather than to species. Although Malawians use the primary colours red (*fiira*), black (*kuda*) and white (*yera*) in describing mammals (as well as the term *tuwa,* ash or grey coloured),there is no implicit symbolic classification of mammals according to colour, nor any implicit division according to a triadic spatial division into sky, earth, underworld (waters) as suggested by Kesby with respect to the Rangi (1979: 392). But ecological criteria are important to Malawians in the

Folk Classifications

Table 3.8 Carnivores

	Chewa	Nyanja	Yao	Lomwe	Tumbuka
1. wild dog mphumphi *Lycaon pictus*	mbulu	mbinzi	lisogo	nanthara	
2. side-striped jackal *Canis adustrus*	nkhandwe	nkhandwe	likule	khatwe	kambwe
3. clawless otter *Aonyx capensis*	katumbu	katumbu	kausi	chumbu	chiwawu
spotted-necked otter *Hydrictis maculicollis*	"	"	"	"	"
4. ratel *Mellivora capensis*	chiuli	chiuli cheuli	mkuli	nyinga	chimbuli
5. african striped weasel *Poecilogale albinucha*	kanyimbi	kanyimbi			kanyimbi
6. zorilla *Ictonyx striatus*	kanyimbi	kanyimbi chinymbi	chinyeru	enyipi	kanyimbi
7. two-spotted palm civet *Nandinia binotata*	golopati pati	dengu			nkanganya
8. civet *Civettictis civetta*	chombwe	bvungo msenga	ungo	thugo	fungwe, fungo khalikhali
9. small spotted genet *Geneta rubignosa*	nsimba	mwili	mbendu ndendu	munyapa	himba mtolo
angola genet *Genetta angolensis*	"	"	"	"	"
10. Selous' mongoose *Paracynctis selousi*	nyenga	nyenga			
11. bushy tailed mongoose *Bdeogale crassicavda*	nyenga msangela	nyenga			khare dimbiri
12. egyptian mongoose *Herpestes ichneumon*	nyenga msalgela	nyenga	nyenga	likokwe myeka	lukoti jenga
13. slender mongoose kampumbu *Galarella sanguinea*	likongwe kanyenga	likongwe	kandini chindindi	nikongwe	
14. Meller's mongoose *Rhynchogale melleri*	kanyada	msunkunya nyenga	msunkunya		khare
15. white-tailed mongoose *Ichneumia albicauda*	nyenga	nyenga			khare kachewere
16. marsh mongoose *Atilax paludinosus*	khakhakha	khakhakha kaka	likhakhakha lipwisa	nikhatantau	

Table 3.8 Carnivores (*continued*)

	Chewa	Nyanja	Yao	Lomwe	Tumbuka
17. banded mongoose *Mungos mungo*	msulu	msulu	msulu *lisulu*	muthuri	msulwe *msuru*
18. dwarf mongoose kampumbu *Helegole parvula*	kasisibi				
19. spotted hyena *Crocuta crocuta*	mfisi fisi	mfisi fisi	litunu	khudupa	chimbwe
20. cheetah nkalamgonza *Aconyx jubatus*	kakwiyo kambulumbulu	kakwiyo			
21. leopard *Panthera pardus*	nyalugwe kambuku	nyalugwe	chisuwi	havara	nyalubwe
22. lion *Panthera leo*	mkango	mkango	lisimba	karamo	nkalamu
23. caracal nkaramungoza *Felis caracal*					
24. serval *Felis serval*	njuzi ndusi	njuzi	ndusi		njuzi
25. wild cat *Felis lybica*	bvumbwe	bvumbwe	chiulu	bvumbwe	zumbwe

grouping of mammals, which are frequently referred to in terms of habitat: *waphiri* (of mountains), *wamadzi* (of water), *wadambo* (of wetlands). In the categorization of *mbewa*, for example, the various species will typically be listed as either living in the wetlands, *zakhala m'dambo* – water rat (*nthukwi*), Angoni Vlei rat (*thiri*), creek rat (*mende*), pygmy mouse (*pido*), cane rat (*nchenzi*) – or as living in the uplands *zakhala mumtunda*, such as elephant shrew (*sakhwi*), bushveld gerbil (*phanya*), multimammate mouse (*kapuku*), pouched rat (*jugu*) and mole rat (*namfuko*).

When discussing the grouping or the relationship of mammals to each other – usually conceptualized in kinship terms (*mnzache*, its companion, *mbale wake*, its relative) – dietary habits (food) tend always to be uppermost in people's mind, besides morphology. And an anthropocentric bias is invariably evident. Thus in the grouping of animals, lion, hippopotamus, rhinoceros, crocodile, elephant, hyena and leopard will be invariably associated together as being fierce (*za ukali*) animals and as hostile to humans. The ungulates – zebra, klipspringer, duiker, impala, kudu, eland, bushbuck – will be associated as being edible (*nyama*) and as similar

Table 3.9 Ungulates

	Chewa	Nyanja	Yao	Lomwe	Tumbuka
26. elephant *Loxodonta africana*	njobvu	njobvu	ndembo	ethepo	zovu
27. black rhino *Diceros bicornis*	chipembere	chipembere	chipembere	pwethe echipembere	
28. Burchells zebra *Equus burchelli*	mbidzi	mbidzi	mbunda	epucha	boli
29. warthog *Pacochoerus aethiopicus*	kaphulika	njiri	mbango	epako	mnjiri
30. bushpig *Potamochoerus porcus*	nguluwe	nguluwe	liguluwe	ekuluwe	ngulube
31. hippopotamus *Hippotamus amphibius*	mvuu	mvuu	bokho ndomondo	chomocho mvuu	chigwere
32. blue wildebeest *Connochaetus taurinus*		nyumbu	sindi	okondo	
33. Lichtenstein's hartebeest *Sigmocerus lichtensteinii*	ngondo	ngondo	ngose	ekhosi	nkozi
34. red forest duiker *Cephalophus natalensis*	zombangoma kasese	insa, gwape kasenye			
35. blue duiker *Cephalophus monticola*	kadumba kaduma	kadumba insa		matupa	mtungwa
36. grey duiker *Sylvicapra grimmia*	gwape, gwapi insa	gwape	ngolombwe	nangwale nahe	nyiska nyisya
37. klipspringer *Oreotragus oreotragus*	chinkhoma	chinkhoma	chiwalama	khomache	mbuzi mawe
38. oribi *Ourebia ourebi*	chowe chosimbi	chowe	chilosimbi		
39. Sharpe's grysbok *Raphicerus sharpei*	kasenye	kasenye	kasenye	ekuputu	mtungwa
40. suni *Nesotragus moscha*	kadumba insa	kadumba			dukutu
41. impala *Aepyceros melampus*	nswala	nswala	nswala		nswala
42. roan *Hippotragus equinus*	chilembwe	chilembwe	mpalapala		mpherembe
43. sable *Hippotragus niger*	mpalapala nyambuzi	mpalapala	mbalapi	ephalavi	likudzi tonde
44. buffalo *Syncerus caffer*	njati	njati	njati	enari	njati
45. kudu *Tragelaphus strepsiceros*	ngoma	ngoma	ndandala	nangoma namukhoma	ntandala chipurupuru
46. nyala *Tragelaphus angasii*	boo	boo			

Table 3.9 Ungulates (*continued*)

	Chewa	Nyanja	Yao	Lomwe	Tumbuka
47. bushbuck *Tragelaphus scriptus*	mbawala	mbawala	mbawala	epaala	mpatu
48. eland *Taurotragus oryx*	ntchefu mpefu	ntchefu	mbunju		sefu
49. reedbuck *Redunga arundinum*	mphoyo	mphoyo	ndope	emphoyo	mkhamuka
50. waterbuck *Kobus ellipsiprymnus*	nakodzwe chuzu	nakodzwe	ndogolo	okhotwe	vulavula chuzu
51. puku *Kobus vardonii*	nsuela	nseula	nseula		seuli
giraffe *Giraffa camelopardalis*	nyamalikiti kadiyansonga				twiga

(*zofanana*) to either cattle (*ng'ombe*) or goats (*mbuzi*), depending on size. In Tumbuka the klipspringer is called 'hill goat'. Mammals with spines are all closely associated (hedgehog, porcupine and spiny mouse). The hedgehog is often called *kanungu* (*-ka* diminutive), and *soni* (or *chisoni*, meaning in Chewa pity or compassion) is a term that may describe all three animals, all of which, though not generally eaten, are widely used as medicine. Covert morphological groupings are also recognized. Thus the baboon and the blue and vervet monkeys, all common species, are grouped together and are seen as similar to humans, especially the baboon (*ufanana ndi munthu*). But although Malawians stress this affinity even more than Europeans, this does not necessarily imply that the baboon is tabooed as food (cf. Fiddes 1991: 135). In fact all three primates are eaten by many people.

Likewise the hyena, wild dog and jackal are seen as allied (*mzache*) to the domestic dog. Alternatively, animals may be grouped according to their dietary preferences: the wild cat, genes, civet, serval, zorilla and the mongooses may be grouped together as carnivores (*kadya mbewa*, they eat rats and mice), while the various species of antelope are put together as forest (*m'khalango*) animals who are herbivores (*amadya maudzu*, 'eat grass').

Although there are few explicit intermediate categories used in Malawi, several generic terms cover a number of mammal species. *Katumbu* covers both species of otter; *kanyimbi* although referring essentially to the zorilla, also refers to the African striped weasel, which is much less common and seldom encountered; *mwili* covers both species of genet. The generic taxa *nyenga* (derived from *ku-nyenga*, to cheat, deceive, a reference to

Folk Classifications

Table 3.10 The Category *Mbewa*

	Chewa	Nyanja	Yao	Lomwe	Tumbuka
52. four-toed elephant-shrew *Petrodromus tetradactylus*	sakwi zumbi sakhwi	sakhwi	namitumbi	muthavu	tondo
53. short-snouted elephant-shrew *Elephantulus brachyrhynchus*	zoro	zumbi deng'a	litawala	nanikata	zoro
54. Peter's elephant-shrew *Elephantulus fuscus*	sakwi sumbi	deng'a	litawala naliyeye	nanikata nadenga	
55. checkered elephant-shrew *Rhynchocyon cirnei*	sakhwi mbala sakhwinjobvu	sakhwi mbala	namitumbi		tondo wamawala
56. red musk shrew *Crocidura hirta*	sunche swiswili	sunche	sunje	mpuche ruje	mununka
57. grey musk shrew *Crocidura luna*	sunche	sunche			
58. cane rat *Thryonomys swinderianus*	nchenzi nchezi	nchenzi	ngungusi	ethechi	chilima sezi
59. lesser cane rat *Thryonomys gregorianus*	nchenzi	nchenzi	ngungusi	etechi	sezi
60. silvery mole-rat *Heliophobius argentocinereus*	mfuko	namfuko	uko	nahuwo	thunku
61. common mole-rat *Cryptomys hottentotus*	mfuko				kamizumi
62. angoni vlei rat *Otomys angoniensis*	thiri	thiri	liulukusi	ntwiri	chauuko
63 bushveld gerbil *Tatera leucogaster*	dondwe tong'ondo dowole	tong'ondo phanya	upanya	nivala ndolu	mphundu
64. Boehm's gerbil *Tatera boehmi*	nsatanjira nsakanjira tchaswala				
65. giant rat *Cricetomys gambianus*	bwampini kunda gundani	bwampini	ngwime	nivolowa nawili kuve	likupi
66. pouched rat *Saccostomus campestris*	chi tute tsambe	dugu jugu	takula	nahurama napuso	chatuta
67. long tailed pouched mouse *Beamys hindei*	chidiubaya			yungurukuve	
68. lesser climbing mouse *Dendromus mystacalis*	nambalala kamkoko	nambalala kapamzimbi		sonthe wang'on mungole	

- 161 -

Table 3.10 The Category *Mbewa* (*continued*)

	Chewa	Nyanja	Yao	Lomwe	Tumbuka
69. fat mouse *Steatomys pratensis*	nsana, kafula kapeta kabwanda	kachesi	chingowe	gwede laphe, lambe	kabwira
70. spiny mouse *Acomys spinosissimus*	sakachenzi kachenzi	sakachenzi chikuzubweya chinyerere chisoni	kasengula chanasa	tarakali	kasena
71. creek rat *Pelomys fallax*	mende	bvumbe	lilende	nihumbe pholochi	mbuku- mulima
72. single-striped mouse *Lemniscomys rosalia*	lingwere mphinzu	mphera	ngwawi	nyima muliwki	julungwere jungwele
73. four-striped mouse *Rhabdomys pumilio*		mphera		nyima	
74. water rat *Dasymys incomtus*	nthukwi chitukwi	nthukwi		kiraswa	
75. long-tailed forest mouse *Grammomys dolichorus*	jelela sontho	sonthe sontho	uchambiri	chinkoli mulele	sontho kokota
76. grey-bellied pygmy mouse *Mus triton*	pido chantanga	tsibwi		chigadada	
77. Ppgmy mouse *Mus minutoides*	pinji pido	pinji tilonje	katolo	nangwandu chigadada nantikwa	kabwira
78. rudd's mouse *Uranomus ruddi*		sakachenzi			
79. brush-furred rat *Cophuromys flavopunctatus*		sithwa chitwa kundwelu	liulwa	etwa	
80. mulanje rat *Praomys delectorum*		chitwa		jikagada namakupha	
81. multimammate mouse *Mastomys natalensis*	mpuku mbewa nthika	kapuku mbewa	lipuku liwondo	mtoro	mbewa
82. black-tailed tree rat *Thallomys paedulcus*	sontho		lipuku		
83. red veld rat *Aethomys chrysophilus*	mphakadzi mphutsa	chiradzulu mphokosi		likwetu	nthantha
84. black rat *Rattus rattus*	khoswe	khoswe	likoswe	nikhule	
85. dormouse *Graphiurus microtis*	kadyam- kwikwi kadyamlamu	kadyamlamu	kasepembe mbembe	mpandari	

Folk Classifications

Table 3.11 Other Mammals

	Chewa	Nyanja	Yao	Lomwe	Tumbuka
86. hedgehog *Atelerix albiventris*	chisoni kanungu	chisoni kanungu	chanasa	echisoni	soni lupem- phezi
87. fruit bats *Epomophorus crypturus* *Eidolon helvum* *Rousettus aegyptiacua*	mleme msanasana	mleme	lichinji		
88. insect-eating bats (generally) *Taphozous mauritianus* *Nycteris thebaica* *Rhinolophus blasii* *Hipposideros caffer* *H. Commersoni* *Scotophilius dinganii* *Pipistrellus africanus* *Tadarida condylura* *Tadarida pumila*	nampsipsi namzeze ndemiya mnalimpsimbi mnamsinsi chuchu	nanthuthu	liputiputi chiputiputi		
89. bushbaby *Otelemur crassicaudatus*	changa	changa	likomba	echanoa	changa
90. night ape *Galago moholi*	kamundi	kamundi	chipimbi kapimbi	neko matache	kaundi
91. yellow babboon *Papio cynocephalus*	nyani mkhwere	nyani	lijani	okole	mkhwere
92. vervet monkey *Cercopithecus pygerythrus*	pusi	pusi	chitumbiri	nachama	mbwengu
93. blue monkey Cercopithecus albogularis	nchima	nchima	lichiru	nkhwonde nsimwe	nchima
chimpanzee *Pan satyrus*	chiyendaweka				
colobus monkey *Colobus angolensis*			mbenga		nchoma
94. rock hyrax *Procavia capensis*	mbira nkhonkho nkhonkho	zumba nkhonkho	ngangawila tundugulu	nthupa	
95. yellow-spotted hyrax *Heterohyrax brucei*	mbira	mbira	njechele	epila	mpyayi mpimbi
tree hyrax *Dendrohyrax arboreus*					
96. antbear *Orycteropus afer*	dzimba nengo	nkumba- kumba nsele	mbawe		godi
97. pangolin *Manis temminckii*	ngaka nkaka	ngaka	ngaka	ekaya	ngaka

Table 3.11 Other Mammals (*continued*)

	Chewa	Nyanja	Yao	Lomwe	Tumbuka
98. sun squirrel *Heliosciurus mutabilis*	gologolo ngorogoro	gologolo	gologolo		belama
99. black and red squirrel *Paraxerus lucifer*	kasira				
100. bush squirrel *Paraxerus cepapi*	tsinde gologolo	gologolo kalikongwe	kandindi gologolo chisapembe	nchelela	benga peremende
101. red squirrel *Paraxerus palliatus*	gologolo	kalikongwe	kaleje		
102. flying squirrel *Anomalurus derbianus*		imbeta	liseu		mbininini
103. porcupine *Hystrix africaeaustralis*	nungu	nungu	ndinu	nasinuku	chinungu soni
104. scrub hare *Lepus saxatilis*	nkalulu kalulu	kalulu kalambwe	kalungu sungula	walulu	kalulu
105. red rock hare *Prondolagus rupestris*	kafumbwe	kajolombwe			

Table 3.12 Number of Folk Generics

Order	Biological species	Number of species recognized	Folk genera
Insectivora	10	3	3
Macroscelidae	4	4	2
Chiroptera	55	2	3
Primates	6	5	5
Carnivora	27	25	19
Proboscidae	1	1	1
Perissodactyla	2	2	2
Hyracoidea	3	2	2
Tubulidenta	1	1	1
Pholidota	1	1	1
Artiodactyla	23	23	22
Rodentia	52	34	28
Lagomorpha	2	2	2
totals	187	105	91

the animal's habit of raiding chicken pens) prototypically refers to the large Egyptian mongoose, but it also covers all the other medium to large mongooses, most of which are either local in distribution or secretive and thus rarely seen. It tends not to cover the slender, marsh or banded mongooses, all of which are common. Interestingly, Malawians see a very close relationship between the slender mongoose and the bush squirrel, which are often described by the same term, *likongwe*. Both are ubiquitous, often frequenting gardens even in urban areas; they look similar and have similar habits in spite of belonging to distinct zoological orders.

Among the ungulates likewise there are no intermediate taxa, and although Scott (1929: 279) suggests that the term *mbawala* may be used generically for 'antelope', I never heard it used in this way. It always had a specific reference, namely the common and widespread bushbuck. Uncommon and rather local species of small antelope like the suni, blue duiker and red forest duiker are frequently conjoined when it comes to naming or referred to as *gwape* (grey duiker) or *kasenye* (Sharpe's grysbok), the two common species of small antelope. For almost all the larger ungulates, the males are distinguished by a different term, which is especially applicable to the lone bull. Examples are (in Chewa):

nkhwinyimbi	(elephant)
nawanga	(warthog)
mpangwe	(hippopotamus)
nabudzi	(sable)
lambwe	(buffalo)
mpoto	(kudu, bushbuck, eland)
mphangala	(waterbuck)

The baboon (*nyani*) also has terms that are specific: for old, solitary males (*mchimbo, chiyendaweka*, 'it walks alone', a term also used by people to describe chimpanzees that are seen on films, although this species is in fact a sociable animal); for those baboons who act as sentinels keeping guard while the other baboons steal the garden produce, *kanjema, kauuzi* (cf. Marks 1976: 94–5).

There are 55 species of bat to be found in Malawi; many of these are rare or have a local distribution, but several species (listed in Table 3.11) are widespread and common. As some species roost in houses or in banana groves, they are well known to Malawians and thus have a phenomenal salience that is certainly as great as that of the many species of *mbewa*, most of which live in burrows and are nocturnal in habit. But whereas the *mbewa* are widely eaten throughout Malawi as *nyama* (meat), none of the bats are eaten apart from one species, the cave-dwelling *Rousettus aegypticus*. Significantly this species has a generic name, *msanasana*, and many suggest it is not a *mleme*. Bats, which as already noted are usually categorized as 'birds' (*mbalame*), are referred to generically as *mleme*, which prototypically refers only to the larger fruit-eating bats.

The small species, however, are referred to by a variety of terms, including the term *namzeze*, which includes swifts and swallows. As with the Rangi (Kesby 1979: 43), Malawians do not make a strict demarcation between bats and those birds which often make their nests among rocks, although they recognize their distinctiveness, and many people eat the nestlings of rock swallows.

The only intermediate category widely recognized in Malawi is that of *mbewa*. This is a general category widely used among the Chewa to describe rats, mice, shrews and elephant shrews. In Yao the equivalent term is *lipuku*, in Lomwe *mtoro*. The terms are general categories covering around 34 species of mammals (see Table 3.10), but they have as their prototype the ubiquitous multimammate mouse, *kapuku (Mastomys natalensis)*. Thus *mbewa* (C), *mtoro* (L) and *Lipuku* (Y) are not only used as a general intermediate category, but are also often used specifically to describe the multimammate mouse.

Although *mbewa* includes shrews and elephant shrews, and may at times be used to cover also the bush squirrel *gorogoro (Paraxerus)*, the category essentially refers to rats and mice, almost all of which, apart from the house rat and dormouse, are eaten as food. This group of mammals has great cultural significance for many rural Malawians, and many proverbs refer to *mbewa* species. It excludes, however, the hedgehog and the porcupine, so *mbewa* is by no means coterminous with any zoological order (see Figure 3.1). Again, with the *mbewa* category, several generic

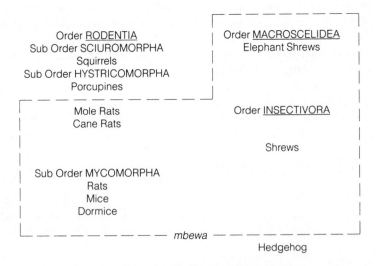

Figure 3.1 The Category *mbewa*

terms cover more than one mammal species; *sunche* refers to all the common shrews; *nchenzi* to the two species of cane rat; *mfuko* the two common mole rats; and *chitwa*, which essentially refers to the brush-furred rat, is also extended to the *mlanje* rat, both being montane species.

The high degree of differentiation among the *mbewa*, which are eaten, and the lack of differentiation among the various species of *mleme* (bat), which are not, is significant. And it is of interest that while I recorded Tumbuka terms for several species of rodents from one individual, almost all Tumbuka speakers with whom I discussed rats and mice, even among people who were extremely knowledgeable about wildlife generally, seemed only to recognize three categories: *fukuzani*, the mole rat, *sezi*, the cane rat, and *mbewa*, which seems to cover all the other species of rats and mice, including the black rat. Significantly, of course, unlike other ethnic communities in Malawi, the Tumbuka do not eat rats and mice, an observation which again would suggest that pragmatic concerns do influence folk classification.

I have outlined above the folk classification of mammals in Malawi. This data essentially confirms the phenomenalist perspective of Berlin and Atran and suggests that similarities between living organisms are universally recognized cross-culturally, certainly between biologists and the various ethnic communities in Malawi. The kind of cultural idealism suggested by Leach and Douglas cannot therefore br sustained, at least at the level of folk biological taxonomies. But my studies also indicate that pragmatic and cultural concerns are not extraneous to phenomeno-logical classifications, that they do influence the way ordinary people in Malawi classify the natural world. Some engagement between the 'symbolists' and the 'ethnobiologists' is therefore still called for.

−4−

Attitudes to Nature

Introduction

In the last two chapters, on hunting traditions and folk classifications, both empirical and symbolic, I have indicated some of the contrasting ways in which Malawian people acknowledge the nature of human–mammal interactions. I have thus indicated that Malawian attitudes towards mammals and to the natural world generally are diverse, complex and multi-faceted. We may, to facilitate the discussion, distinguish between the following eight social perspectives towards nature and towards mammals in particular.

- A *phenomenal* attitude, expressed in the 'intuitive' – imaginative and psychological – recognition of the discontinuities of nature. This is reflected in 'basic-level' categories and corresponds to what Heidegger refers to as *Vorhandenheit*, things 'present-at-hand' (1962:106), an orientation towards the world that Heidegger misleadingly *conflates*, in a distorting fashion, with other very different attitudes towards nature. This is nature as *phenomena*. I have discussed this phenomenal attitude fully in the last chapter.
- A *realist* attitude, the acknowledgement that the natural world, mammals especially, have intrinsic value and inherent powers, properties and potentialities that are independent of humans. This is similar to the Greek notion of nature as *physis*. This acknowledgement of a 'real' world independent of human cognition is not a 'positivist notion', and the conflation of realism with positivism by interpretative anthropologists and post-modern philosophy is obfuscating (Riesman 1986: 112; see Bhaskar 1989, Collier 1994). It has affinities to what Bruce Foltz, following Heidegger, calls the 'primordial sense' of nature (1995: 37–51). This attitude is reflected in the use of animals as medicine.
- A *theoretical* attitude, expressed in terms of theoretical knowledge, a perspective that is akin to what the Greeks referred to a *theoria*, looking at the natural world in terms of rational contemplation. As Aristotle

suggested in the first line of his *Metaphysics*, 'All men by nature desire to know' (Ackrill 1987: 255). But how this knowledge is expressed is, of course, extremely variable, ranging from everyday empirical knowledge (based on experience) through to Plato's idealist metaphysic and modern science. It includes what Kellert describes as the ecologistic and scientistic (i.e. positivist) attitudes towards animals (1988: 139–43).

– A *pragmatic* attitude, which Heidegger refers to as *Zuhandenheit*, things 'ready-to-hand' (1962: 102–5), which is similar to what the Greeks referred to *techne*. In Malawi, this is particularly reflected in the use of mammals as food and medicine, which I shall discuss later in this chapter. The fundamental concern of the pragmatic or utilitarian attitude is the practical and material value of nature, which needs to be distinguished from that of 'dominion' (Kellert 1988: 143).

– A *practical* or socially engaged attitude, reflected in both the friendship (*chibwenzi*) which is expressed towards domestic animals – especially cats and dogs – and the strong empathy that is experienced between humans and the hunted mammal and which, as noted in the last chapter, seems to have been widespread among hunter-gatherers. This socially engaged attitude recognizes the fundamental affinities between humans and mammals as living beings who share a common world and are often in competition. It is particularly reflected in the 'dialectical' attitude towards nature that I discussed in the last chapter. Such a perspective combines the 'humanistic' and 'moralistic' attitudes discussed by Kellert (1988: 142) and is akin to what the Greeks described as *praxis*. It involves an intrinsically social attitude towards the world and includes not only a practical (productive) engagement but also a moral one. It may be recalled that the Greek notion of 'practice' was a social concept, including what we would now describe as 'politics' and 'morals'.

– An *aesthetic* attitude, expressed not simply in the aesthetic (romantic) conception of nature as landscape, but rather in the role that animals play in ritual symbolism, as cultural metaphors, and in moral education through folk tales, proverbs and art forms. It combines what Kellert describes as the naturalistic and aesthetic attitudes to wildlife (1988: 139–43). The role of mammals in Malawian aesthetic forms and in ritual will be discussed in this chapter and in a companion volume.

– A *sacramental* attitude, which is expressed in certain contexts in which a fundamental close affinity or interrelationship is expressed between humans and animals. This is not one simply of social engagement, but rather of spiritual affinity, alluding to the fact that humans and animals are both created beings (*-lengedwa*), and that the spirits of the dead (*mizimu*) and the divinity may take the form of animals. This is also discussed more fully in a companion volume.

– An attitude of *dominion*, which is particularly reflected in the technological mastery of nature. This attitude was evidently present in Malawi in the commercial hunting of elephant – mimed in certain Nyau rituals by the Jere hunters – but generally speaking an attitude of conquest or dominion over nature is not emphasized in Malawi culture. As suggested in Chapter Two, hunting in Malawi, like meat-eating (discussed below), cannot simply be read as a symbolic expression of the human control and mastery of nature. Indeed the *conflation* of 'control' over nature, expressed in hunting and in the pragmatic attitude towards nature, with 'dominion' over nature by Heidegger, critical theorists like Marcuse and deep ecologists is highly misleading (see O'Neill 1993: 154–5). This attitude of dominion over nature is symbolically expressed not by subsistence hunting, but by big game 'trophy' hunting and by such sporting spectacles as bullfighting and rodeos. In these contexts, animals are valued in a ritual drama which presents them as challenging opponents to be conquered and subdued. It gives opportunities for humans – specifically aristocrats or men – to demonstrate their power, strength, skill and masculinity. It represents a symbolic conquest over nature and the archetypal 'wild'. The importance of the 'man on horseback', reflecting the qualities of dominance, pride, independence, heroic striving and superiority, is crucially related to the attitude of dominion over nature. Such spectacles are not found in Malawi (see Lawrence 1982, 1990).

Each of these social perspectives towards nature – mammals – is implicitly recognized in Malawi. Thus a mammal may be recognized as a species or folk generic (*-zindikira*), its habits and ecology known (*-dziwa*), its uses (*ntchito*) expressed, and people may see the animal in terms of friendship (*chibwenzi*), affinity (*ngati munthu*), or hostility and opposition (as *chirombo*). Equally, the mammal may be seen as a created being (*wolengedwa*), or a spirit may be held to have transformed (*-sanduka*) itself into mammal form. Mammals find their place too in traditions, folktales (*nthano*) and proverbs (*chisimo*), as well as playing a significant role in rituals. But these diverse ways in which Malawians relate to mammals, expressing different perspectives are not all radically separated: rather, they express overlapping attitudes towards nature and towards mammals in particular.

One historian has remarked that historically African people have always lived 'cheek-by-jowl' with nature and wild animals. He writes:

> Animals have been feared and admired, worshipped and detested. They have
> been sought after as an important resource in the re-creation of human life or
> sought out as a threat to its preservation. They have been hunted for sport and
> recreation in the spirit of adventure, and they have been killed in deadly earnest
> as a matter of survival (Steinhart 1989: 247).

Although it leaves out the aesthetic and theoretical attitudes towards
wildlife, this passage indicates the diverse attitudes that people may have
towards animals. However, it must be pointed out that Malawians do not
'worship' animals – it is questionable whether anybody does – though
their attitude to mammals may be a sacramental one, particularly as they
are seen as 'hierophanies' of spiritual beings, to use a term of Mircea
Eliade (1958: 11).

All these various social attitudes towards nature, and towards animals
in particular, are encompassed within what Roy Willis has described as a
'structural complementarity' recognized by all human cultures. It is thus
important to note, he writes, that all people '*Simultaneously* recognize
a *duality* that divides each cultural group's world view or cosmology
while also recognizing some *underlying commonality or continuity* between the opposed constituents' (1990: 7). This implies a complementary
opposition between the principles of separation (metaphor) and continuity
(metonymy), a 'co-existent unity and duality' between the two domains,
specifically nature/culture, animals/humans, however these may be
expressed in different cultures. Willis cites Tambiah's classic article on
the classification of animals in Thailand. The Thai recognize three classes
of animals, *sad baan* (animals of the house/village), *sad paa* (animals of
the forest) and *sad naam* (water animals). But in an important discussion
of Lévi-Strauss's theory of totemism, Tambiah concludes that 'the Thai
villagers' relation to the animal world shows a similar complexity which
expresses neither a sense of affinity with animals alone nor a clear-cut
distinction and separation from them, but rather a co-existence of both
attitudes in varying intensities which create a perpetual tension [1969
(1973): 163].

This sort of dialectical tension has resonance in Malawi, as I have
described in the last chapter with regard to the cosmological dualism
between village and woodland. But it must be noted that symbolic complementary dualisms, though widespread, particularly in the African context
(see Needham (1973), are not all-embracing, and within a culture, they
often co-exist with other metaphorical schemata, or incorporated within

a more complex symbolism (see my discussion of symbolic classifications, Morris 1987: 291–6).

Willis notes that the 'disjuntive bias' of Cartesian – mechanistic philosophy, with its *radical* dualism of humans and nature, has tended to obscure the structural 'complementarity' that is expressed by the majority of human communities (see my critique of mechanistic philosophy, Morris 1981).

In an earlier path-breaking study *Man and Beast* (1974), Willis noted that animals, because of their 'self-acting' propensities, were apt symbols for representing both the existential and normative aspects of human experience. Animals lend themselves, he wrote, 'to the expression of two primary and polar modes of human thought, the metonymic and the metaphoric' (1974: 128). Although proclaimed as a 'structuralist' analysis and employing structuralist terminology, Willis's study, as I have commented elsewhere, is a far cry from the formal analyses of Lévi-Strauss and Leach (Morris 1987: 224). Indeed, it has an existentialist–phenomenological bias, with its focus on the life-world (*Lebenswelt*) of three African communities. What Willis thus sought to explore from a comparative perspective was human–animal relationships in three communities, the Nuer, Lele and Fipa. Their underlying cosmological assumptions of how they perceived the world were, according to Willis, very different, and is lucidly summarized in the following passage:

> The Nuer sense of distance from and equality with the counterposed world of nature contrasted markedly with the Lele sense of the dependence and moral inferiority of the village in relation to the forest, and again with the Fipa sense of the village's properly dominant role in relation to the surrounding bush (1974: 8).

But rather than exploring the rich and complex symbolism that each of these cultures express with regard to their relationship with the world of nature, Willis suggests that their ultimate value – the 'meaning of life' within these communities – is expressed by a single animal, as a theriomorphic theme. Thus, he writes, each culture has one symbolically dominate animal: the *ox* in the case of the Nuer, whose cosmology is eptomizes by a sense of 'balanced opposition' pervading all dimensions of their universe; the *pangolin* for the Lele, who emphasize the primacy of the forest which is associated with men and the spirits; and the *python* for the Fipa, whom Willis describes as 'unashamedly pragmatic' in their evaluation of the natural world and who stress the priority of humanistic values associated with the village community. Willis notes that for the

Fipa hunting is very much a solitary and utilitarian activity, in contrast to the communal hunts of the Lele, which have a spiritual significance (1974: 47).

Malawian attitudes towards the natural world, specifically towards the woodland (*thengo*) and the mammals (*nyama*) associated with it, appear to fall midway between those of the Lele and Fipa. There is thus an underlying balanced complementarity between humans and the woodland domain, but as I have earlier intimated, people's relationship with mammalian life and the attitudes they express are very much contextual. As subsistence agriculturists, and in symbolically identifying mammals with the male affine, an opposition is expressed between the village (humans) and the woodland (mammals) – the paradigmatic dimension – while in other contexts the affinity and interdependence of humans and animals is highlighted. The syntagmatic dimension is therefore highly pronounced, it being recognized that humans (*anthu*) and animals (*nyama/chirombo*) share many qualities, attributes and sentiments. But it would be very difficult in Malawi to highlight any mammal as the prime exemplar; a metaphor, of their 'ultimate values' (and I emphasize the plural).

In this chapter I will focus the discussion essentially on two social attitudes towards mammals: the aesthetic and the pragmatic. I will thus explore the role of mammals in Malawian oral traditions and their use as food and medicine.

Animals in Oral Literature

As many colonial writers seem to suggest that Malawian people were deficient in moral sentiments, so it was also suggested that they lacked any aesthetic sense. Thus the administrator Hector Duff wrote:

> The sense of beauty is, of course, very defective in Central Africans . . .. The sublimest scenery leaves them totally unmoved. The most brilliant flowers are without any attraction for them and are neither cultivated in their gardens nor plucked in the wild state from the woods. Nothing in the beauty of animate creatures touches them . . .. The truth is that the point of view of pure aesthetics is unintelligible to these natives (Duff 1903: 281–2).

But as Steve Chimombo points out in his pioneering study of Malawian oral literature (1988), Duff's own account is contradictory, for he unwittingly acknowledges the decorative and aesthetic quality of Malawian pottery and metalwork. All people, of course, have an aesthetic dimension to their lives, and Malawian people are no exception. Chimombo has attempted to outline the main parameters of an integrated aesthetic theory for Malawi, which he terms *ulimbaso*, a concept it seems of his own devising, derived from *-ula*, to divine, reveal something, and *-omba*, to beat drum, *-ombeza* to divine, *chamba*, dance. At least I never heard this term spoken, and none of my friends knew its meaning.

Malawians recognize many different art forms: dance and ritual drama (*gule* or *chamba*), songs (*nyimbo*), ceramics or pottery (*choumba*), drawing and decorative arts (*cholemba*) and painting (*chojambula*), as well as different craft industries, basketry, metalwork, weaving. And there is a term for recreational games or play, namely *sewero* (*ku-sewera*, to play), which has come to be used for any drama or theatrical performance. *Mwambo* (pl. *miyambo*) is another general concept essentially meaning 'custom' and covering songs, proverbs, folk tales and riddles, as well as important behavioural norms, particularly those relating to sexual matters, which are part of the instructions given during the initiation rites. *Mwambo* is restricted by Chimombo to factual spoken narrative (*zoona*, true, factual), including *mbiri* (historical narrative), *nkhani* (reports, news), *madawi* or *chilape* (riddles) and *chisimo* (proverbs). In contrast, *mwambi* is used for oral narratives that are functional (*zopeka* is the term he coins), and this includes narratives that are sung, namely the folk tales (*nthano*) and narratives without song (*nthanthi*). Many of these Chewa terms, like *mwambo*, and *chisimo*, which Chimombo defines in a restrictive sense, have a wide meaning and are in fact polysemic. Chimombo notes that there are many Chewa terms to express aesthetic appreciation – *-bwino* (good), *-sangalala* (to make happy or glad), *-komba* (to be pleasing), *-kongola* (to be beautiful), *kaso* (excellence, beauty, pleasure) and *-kondwa*, (to be pleased).

I want here to focus on the folk tales that depict animals and to centre the discussion on an analysis of more than fifty folk tales collected by early scholars who were both sympathetic to the local culture and knew the local language well (MacDonald 1882, 1938, Rattray and Hetherwick 1907, Stannus 1922, Young 1931). There are problems with these early collections of oral traditions – they are incomplete, written down out of context and often not recorded in the local language (although the above scholars did so) – and some of the informants may have been unreliable (Chimombo 1988: 37–59). In its proper setting, as a public performance at night, folk tales are sung (*kuyimba nthano*), as Alice Werner noted (1906: 230), and include, in their enactment, other oral traditions: songs, riddles, proverbs, dance and gestures. The audience are participants in the performance (for an outline of one such performance, see Chimombo 1988: 83–129).

Mention may be made of the folk tales written by Geraldine Elliot (Margaret Metcalfe), which are based on Malawian oral traditions and are focussed around animals. Her four books, *The Long Grass Whispers* (1939), *Where the Leopard Passes* (1949), *The Hunters Cave* (1951) and *The Singing Chameleon* (1957), have become bestsellers and have given immense pleasure to generations of English-speaking children. In a rather ungenerous review of her work, Chimombo demonstrates what is patently self-evident, namely that these are stories meant to be read by English speakers, not Malawians. (When her books were published, only a minority of Malawians were literate, and few spoke English). Chimombo also chides Elliot for misspelling some Nyanja names, e.g. *nadzikambe* instead of *namdzikambe*. Two points need to be made. One is that Elliot clearly anglicized the Nyanja terms, which is acceptable. Nobody chides Malawians – or Chimombo – for spelling church as chalichi or register as lejisitala. The other point is that anyone who has undertaken enthno-biological studies recognizes that in oral cultures – and rural Malawi is still largely an oral culture – there are wide variations not only in the names used, but also in their pronunciation. The civet cat has thus been described to me as *vungo*, *fungo* and *ungo* – and is mistakenly termed *mmwiri* in the Zambezi Mission dictionary, this being the name of the genet, which is usually pronounced *mwiri*. Whether a mammal term carries as a prefix *mn-* or *n-* or is dropped completely depends on the prolivities of the speaker, who is not bound by literacy and academic conventions, with their analytic bias. Surprisingly, Chimombo himself refers to the tree *Sterculia appendiculalia* as *njala* (ibid.: 151), when it is usually described as *m/njale*, and accepts uncritically the early translations of missionaries, which allude to lemurs, ostriches, moles and gazelles, none of which occur in Malawi. But the important point of Chimombo's critique of Elliot's writings, is that these 'twice retold' tales involve considerable embellishment and literary licence, such that the character of the animals depicted is often very different from what it is in the Malawian oral tradition. The chameleon, for example, is transformed in Elliot's writings into an artist, a poet or 'singer of tales' (Chimombo 1988: 212). But though Elliot's books have ethnographic limitations they are nonetheless, like the writings of Rudyard Kipling and Joel Chandler Harris, valuable contributions to literature.

In her useful discussion of Malawian folk-stories, Werner wrote that local people do 'not recognize such a clear distinction between animals and human beings as we do', and she noted the widespread belief that certain human beings were able to transform themselves into animals (1906: 233–4). In the animal tales, animals take the form of human beings and are referred to by their generic term, *mkango* (lion), *fisi* (hyena), *kalulu* (hare), with the prefix of politeness *che-* usually being added. Early writers often misidentified the local animal names: thus *nsimba* (c) and *mbendu*(y) (genet) is mistranslated as 'wild cat', *sungula* (y) and *kalulu* (n) (hare) as either 'rabbit' or 'fox', *ngungusi* (y) and *nchenzi* (c) as either 'buck' or 'marsh pig', *nyani* (c) (baboon) as 'monkey', *kamundi* (night-ape) as 'lemur'. Described as if they were human beings, the animals in the stories live in villages, certain of them, especially crocodile, leopard and lion, are considered chiefs (*mfumu*), and they engage in human activities. They clear the woodland for gardens and cultivate them, dig wells for water, collect honey, and are especially engaged in hunting and in trapping other animals by means of either spring (*msampha*) or pit-fall traps (*mbuna*). Humans are frequently part of the story, sometimes a main participant, invariably so in the role of the hunter, out with his dogs (*agaru*) in the woodland (*kuthengo*) to hunt game (*kusaka nyama*). The animals are related to each other in terms of kinship, especially in terms of the in-marrying male affine (*chikamwini*), as well as through friendship (*chibwenzi*). The central animal characters are often described as if they were males, with a spouse (*mkazi wache*). As already noted, hunting and trapping are central motifs in many of the stories. The animals speak like humans, and the tales have an earthy quality; spirits of the dead are rarely mentioned, and the capturing, killing and eating of one animal by another is an important theme throughout the tales. So too is the 'skinning' of an animal, the skins (*chikopa*) being detachable from the animal and often being taken off as if they were 'clothes' or worn by another animal as a disguise. This motif of a detachable skin, as Chimombo notes (1988: 137), has analogies with the masks and animal structures of the Nyau and Chinambande rituals which we discuss in a companion volume.

Although the animals in the folk tales have human characteristics and human desires – they eat porridge and chicken, have a fondness for honey, salt and meat, and depict human personalities, with their foibles, idio-syncrasies, longings and behaviour – the animals are also sometimes depicted in terms of their own natural propensities. Bushpig thus raid gardens for cassava, lions are fierce predators, elephants have strength and tortoises have difficulty in climbing trees. Many of the stories convey a sense that in the past humans and all the animals lived together in relative harmony, and, as in the creation myths, this primordial unity is sub-sequently shattered through quarrels. Thus enmity prevails between humans and certain animals, especially elephant, lion and crocodile.

In the fifty or so folk tales recorded by the early ethnographers, more than thirty different animals are mentioned. Some are only mentioned briefly or in passing in one particular tale, but six animals are key figures in many of the stories: these are the leopard, lion, hyena, hare, elephant and tortoise. The animals mentioned are as follows:

Table 4. Frequency of Appearance of Animal Species in Folk Tales

Animal		Number of Tales in which mentioned	
Hare	24	Eland	2
Lion	14	Bushbuck	2
Elephant	11	Cane Rat	2
Hyena	10	Dog	2
Tortoise	9	Genet	2
Leopard	8	Monitor Lizard	2
Baboon	5	Sable	1
Buffalo	4	Water Mongoose	1
Grey Duiker	4	Waterbuck	1
Cock	3	Rhinoceros	1
Kudu	3	Night Ape	1
Bushpig	3	Reedbuck	1
Crocodile	3	Civet	1
Python	3	Hippopotamus	1
Zebra	3	Vervet Monkey	1
		Pangolin	1

The key animal, mentioned in around half the tales, is the common hare, *kalulu*, who is invariably described as a trickster figure. 'Brer Rabbit' of the North American Uncle Remus Stories is evidently derived from African tales that focussed around the hare. In Malawi the Scrub Hare is common and widespread and is regularly hunted by groups of men or boys with dogs, armed with bows and arrows, knobkerries and spears. It is considered a wily creature, for it is well camouflaged and is reputed to sleep with its eyes open. Every one speaks of the hare as being very clever (*chenjera kwambiri*), and this attribute is depicted in the folk tales. In common parlance *kalulu* is the term for a clever and deceptive person (Chimombo 1988: 176). In the stories the hare, as a trickster figure, is always outwitting and deceiving the other animals. Here are some typical tales:

> The hare looks after the six cubs of the lion, the great hunter. He kills the cubs one by one, keeping their skins. He blames it on some wild beast, expressing great remorse. He then tricks some zebra into singing 'We ate the cubs of the lion' in exchange for charcoal. The lion, hearing the song, in anger kills the zebra, and the hare then plays a trick on the lion and kills him too (T.C. Young 1931: 201–7).

In the past animals lived and ate together. They collected bananas and had put them in a pit to ripen. They then went off hunting together. The hare stole the bananas, expressed great indignation at their loss and suggested the culprit was some wild beast who could be recognized by the large size of its dung. The elephant was thus accused by the other animals and killed, and the clever hare went around singing songs (Singano and Roscoe 1980: 31–2).

The hare separately challenged the elephant and hippo to a tug of war, tricked them both, and got them to exhaust themselves by pulling against each other. He thus won the wager (Stannus 1922: 334–5).

A man planted his garden with beans, which were continually ravaged by wild animals. So he set a spring trap. It caught a leopard. A bushbuck came upon the trap, took pity on the leopard and let him go. The leopard was invited back to bushbuck's home, where he demanded the bushbuck's children as food. The bushbuck did not like to refuse. Having eaten his children and his wife, the leopard expressed his desire to eat the bushbuck himself. Frightened, the bushbuck ran to the woods and there asked the advice of the elephant, buffalo and the other animals as to what he should do. They all suggested that he give himself up to the leopard. Then along came the hare to adjudicate the dispute between the bushbuck and leopard. He cajoled the leopard into showing him how he had got himself caught in the spring trap. This done, the leopard was left caught in the trap to die of hunger (Stannus 1922: 332–3).

But the hare does not always get the better of other animals, even though he is often depicted as helping them to overcome powerful predators like the leopard. The tortoise (*fulu, kamba*), who resembles the hare in many ways, often outwits him, though the tortoise gains the upper hand more by simplicity than by cunning and deceit. The well-known story 'The Hare and the Well', of which there are many different versions, runs roughly as follows:

In the olden days there was a severe drought. The elephant, who was chief, called a meeting. It was decided to dig a well (*chitsime*). Every animal in turn came to dig (*kuponda*, stamp) but failed to reach water. The hare did not help, as the work was too tiring. Eventually they obtained water. The elephant put a watchman (*mlonda*) on the well to stop the hare drinking there. The various watchmen, hyena, baboon, kudu, were each tricked in turn by the offer of honey, the hare taking water and leaving his tracks. Then the tortoise was made watchman. He put wax on his back, and pretended to be stone. The hare came again to the well for water, sat on the tortoise and became stuck. He was thus captured. He pleaded with the chief that he would be properly punished if held by his tail. The hare thus escaped and ran back to the woods (Rattray and Hetherwick 1907: 139–42, Singano and Roscoe 1980: 28–30).

The tortoise is an important figure in Malawian folklore, and like the hare is widely used in medicine, as well as being eaten. People always speak of the reptile as being a very shy creature, and as having a great liking for mushrooms (*bowa*). In the tales the tortoise is depicted as outwitting the baboon who had stolen his bag of fish; of getting his friends to form a line, and thus beating the grey duiker (*gwape*) in a race; and, after giving the leopard and zebra their beautiful markings, tricking the conceited hyena, who thus became one of the most depised of animals. One tale is worth recalling in more detail.

> The tortoise and the night ape (*kamundi*) are both in-marrying affines (*mkamwini*) in a certain village. Their mother-in-law asks them to clear the bush and hoe a garden. The night ape does this task easily, but the tortoise finds it difficult. He asked the genet (*nsimba*) to do it for him, and the new garden pleases the mother-in-law greatly. When the old chief dies *nsimba* has his heart set on being the new chief. To return the favour the tortoise hides in the graveyard and speaks from the grave in support of genet as the new chief. Once installed, genet invites the tortoise for a drink of beer (Rattray and Hetherwick 1907: 146–9).

In the folk tales the lion is usually depicted as a chief and as owner of the country, over which it asserts its authority. The lion is indeed often termed *mwini thengo*, owner of the woodland. In terms of folk knowledge the lion is greatly to be feared and is often associated with the spirits of dead chiefs or other spirit agencies (*nyama za ziwanda*). At night its eyes are said to be very red (*ofiira kwambiri*), and it is reputed not to eat the heads of humans, though lions in Malawi have a long-standing reputation as 'man-eaters' (see Morris 1995). This reputation is carried over into the folk tales, but the lion's power and authority are often usurped or ridiculed. Humans and lions are often depicted as enemies; it is with the hare that humans find friendship. One story runs:

> One day a man goes out hunting with four dogs, and they kill five cane rats (*nchenzi*). They meet a lion, who says: 'Let the dogs eat the cane rats, you eat the dogs, and I'll eat you'. Not agreeing with this suggestion, a quarrel ensues between the man and the lion. A hare comes along. The lion insists on his proposal as he is owner of the bush. The hare tricks the lion into entering a pit-fall trap (*mbuna*), and while helpless there, suggests to the men that he bring fire. Thus the lion was killed, and ever since humans and the hare have been eternal friends (*ubwenzi wosatha*) (MacDonald 1882: 339–40).

Frequently in the folk tales the hare gets the better of the lion; helping to dry the lion's meat while he is out hunting, he kills the lion's cubs, and frequently the hare uses the lion's skin to hoodwink the hyena.

The leopard has a similar role to that of the lion: frequently depicted as a chief, it is nevertheless often duped by the hare (or in one Tumbuka tale, the mouse *mbewa*) to re-enter a spring trap and thus be killed. In one Yao hunting tale a leopard kills a man, and when it is shot it is burned on a fire as a witch (*msawi*) (MacDonald 1938:203).

But the animal that lays the main role as a dupe in the animal tales is the hyena (*fisi*). In real life the hyena is seen as anything but a dupe, for it is greatly feared and despised. Most Malawians view the spotted hyena with a mixture of fear, awe, disgust and contempt, both as a living animal and as the embodiment of all that is anti-social. Hyenas are thus seen as full of deceit and cunning, and are not simply associated with witchcraft, but witches (*mfiti*) are believed to be able to transform themselves into this animal in order to take livestock or to kill humans. The brain, tail and genitals of the hyena are greatly esteemed in medicine. In August 1995 a big hyena was killed by a truck on a road near Ntcheu. Early in the morning a young man cut off some of the parts of the hyena, especially the brain, to take them to his uncle who was a practising herbalist. Within minutes an angry crowd had gathered, intent on beating up the young man, who had to take refuge in the local police station. The reason was that during that month marauding hyenas had been 'terrorising' the people of the Ntcheu district and had taken the lives of several women and young children. And there was a strong feeling among people in the area that the hyenas were witches or that they had been 'sent' by people using medicines (*Daily Times*, 18 August 1995).

However, in the folk tales the hyena is a very different character, continually being deceived or tricked by the wily hare and beset with problems because of its insatiable greed. The following is a Yao tale:

> One day a hyena begged some meat from the lion, who was the chief and he gave him some. The next day he begged for more meat and was refused. Some days later the lion asked the water mongoose (*likakaka*) to fetch the hyena. He also called the kudu (*ndandala*). He suggested to the kudu that he climb a tree so that his shadow would be cast on the water. When the hyena came, they pointed to the kudu's reflection in the water, and said to him 'there, O chief is your meat'. The hyena, in his greed, plunged into the water, got caught up in the mud and died. (MacDonald 1938: 265).

Although Malawian folk tales depict a time when animals and humans lived together, when the animals talked and lived like humans, the humans remain essentially true to type, and the world depicted is not a vegetarian paradise, but one where animals and humans are constantly trapping, hunting, killing and eating each other. This is the case even though many of the animals depicted, like the kudu and hare, are in fact herbivores. This is completely opposite to the Christian myth, in which the lamb lies down with the lion: here all the animals go hunting, and the hare, a herbivore, traps, kills and often eats the lion. Meat (*nyama*) is a central motif in many of the stories, and as already noted, humans are invariably depicted as hunters. Realizing that every animal is potential meat to every other animal – the hyena in one story offers humans (the 'meat without hair') to the lion – animals are also depicted as attempting to avoid being eaten as meat. One story will illustrate this point:

Two men were close friends, one man had a tame baboon and the other a tame kudu. One day they visited each other. They each remarked to the other that their tame animal could be meat. The animals overhead this and ran off into the woodland. A dispute arose between the two men, but it was amicably settled and they shared beer together (MacDonald 1938: 271).

But what the tales also reflect is a constant dialectic between being friends and killing each other, with nothing in between. A grey duiker constructs a spring trap, catches a leopard, has pity on the leopard and takes him back to his village in friendship to nurse his children. A dispute arises: the leopard complains that he has been trapped, the grey duiker that his children have been eaten. The case is resolved by the wily hare (or some other trickster figure), who entices the leopard to re-enter the trap and is thus killed. Another tale illustrates this constant dialectic between friendship and emnity (and being eaten).

In the past animals and humans were all friends together. One day a person came upon a honey guide bird, *nsadzu* or *soro*, (*Indicator spp*), who called him to extract honey. The man followed the bird and in turn met and was joined by the civet, cock, grey duiker, leopard, eland, lion and elephant. After guiding this party to the bees' nest, the honey was extracted. It was shared out on four plates, one for the civet and cock, one for the grey duiker and leopard, one for the eland and lion, and one for the elephant and the human. But trouble broke out, and the cock, grey duiker, eland and elephant were all killed by their partners. The lion then said, 'We have spoiled the land, and will live in emnity from now on', and the three predators fled into the woodland (T.C. Young 1931: 255–9).

Apart from the dog, who is an aide to hunting, domestic animals play a minor role in the folk tales. But the dog itself is greatly esteemed. One tale records a man going hunting for a cane rat with his dogs. He goes into a swamp and is caught by a crocodile, who takes him to a cavern below the reeds. The villagers mourn the loss of the man, but four days later his dogs discover him alive. He returns to the village joyfully, and everybody in the village then acquire dogs (MacDonald 1938: 273).

The significance of animal folk tales, variations of which are found throughout Africa, particularly in relation to the hare as a trickster figure, have been widely discussed. Some have seen oral literature as 'treasure boxes of Africa's past'; others have seen the stories as moral tales, which teach young people the values of generosity, co-operation, the importance of living in harmony together and showing respect to the elders and compassion towards those in difficult circumstances. Others have suggested that the principles that the animal tales extol often contrast sharply with the normative values expressed in everyday life and indicate that it is not easy to draw a line between actions to be emulated and actions to be decried. Others again have suggested that folk tales give one scope for individual self-expression or simply provide an explanation for certain things (Marwick 1965: 230–1 Singano and Roscoe 1980: foreword). There is, perhaps, some truth in all of these suggestions, and there is no doubt that the hare as a 'trickster figure' provides a kind of 'mirror image' of respectable human society, but as Ruth Finnegan puts out what is crucial to these folk tales is that they have great entertainment value. They also convey important empirical knowledge about animal life, rooted as people are in the practicalities of human life in Malawi, with depredations of humans and crops, and trapping and hunting being important dimensions of social life (for a general account of animal tales in Africa, see Finnegan 1970: 344–53).

I turn now to examining the role of mammals in other art forms, although it is worth noting that in a recent short novel by Joseph Banda, *The Startling Revelation* (1991), all the human characters bear the names of animals or birds: *kambuku* (leopard), *kadzidzi* (owl), *kalulu* (hare) – the central character – *nyani* (baboon), *njati* (buffalo) and *njoka* (snake).

Mammals and other Art Forms

Riddles (*ndawi*) and proverbs (*chisimo*) play an important part in Malawian social life and are widely used. Many of these refer to mammals, whose behavioural characteristics are thus employed to reflect on human actions and motivations. Although the proverbs are used in everyday speech, they often include archaic words or expressions, and their meaning is often metaphoric or somewhat esoteric, difficult to understand if one does not know the culture or the habits of the mammals to which they allude. Thus the common proverb: *Wakwatira mende waleka chitute*

'He married the creek rat and left the pouched mouse', only makes sense if one realizes that the creek rat has an iridescent fur and is easily caught in a bamboo trap, while the pouched mouse lives in a deep burrow and stores much food, bringing it back to its burrow in its cheek pouches. Thus the proverb suggests that someone is being foolish in being carried away by outward appearances. Several hundred proverbs have been recorded from Malawi, and a large number of these refer to animals, focusing around those that have particular salience for Malawians: the *mbewa* (rats and mice), hare (*kalulu*), hyena (*fisi*), baboon (*nyani*) and dog (*garu*). I will simply give a selection of these proverbs as reflections of *nzeru za kale* (the wisdom of old times), as Kumakanga entitles his booklet (see Appendix; for important collections, see Johnson 1922, T.C. Young 1931: 265–84, Gray 1944, Kumakanga 1975, Salaun 1978: 100–10, van Kessel 1989).

Riddles are equally important in Malawi social life, and many are taught during intiation rites as part of the instructions in 'traditional wisdom' (*mwambo*). A few may be noted, like these related to mammals:

Q. *Anyamata akwathu buleki ndi pachulu.* A young man from our village breaks at the termite mound
A. *Insa*, grey duiker, which slows on climbing a hill.
Q. *Amnzake ayenda usiku, iye ayenda masana.* His relatives move at night, he at midday.
A. *Zolo*, elephant shrew, which is diurnal unlike other *mbewa*.
Q. *Kayenda ndi mipaliro m'nthiti.* It travels with arrows on its ribs.
A. *Nungu*, porcupine.
Q. *Anyamata akwathu ayenda ndi zikoti.* Young men from the village go around with whips.
A. *Ng'ombe*, cattle, their tails chasing away flies.
Q. *Khalidwe langa lonyenga lokhalokha.* My character is very deceptive.
A. *Birimankhwe*, chameleon.
Q. *Ndidzayera nditadzafa.* I'll be clean (white) after death.
A. *Nkumba*, domestic pig.
Q. *Ndinapita kwa bwenzi langa, koma moni andipatsila ku njira.* I went to my friends, but they greeted me on the path.
A. *Garu*, dog
Q. *Mwana wa mfumu abvala ndi zokongola, koma sabvuula, angogona nazo.* The child of the chief wears beautiful (clothes) but does not undress; he sleeps in them.
A. *Kamba*, tortoise.

Riddles, of course, like other aspects of culture, are not simply static repositories of past traditions but, like proverbs, are actively used in everyday social practice, and their creation often plays a crucial part in political struggles. (Chimombo 1988: 217–54); for useful collections of riddles, see Gray 1939, Singano and Roscoe 1980: 84–106).

Both the proverbs and the riddles indicate a wealth of empirical knowledge about the ecology and behaviour of mammals, which is then used metaphorically to affirm what are considered to be important social values: to share and not to be greedy or selfish, to respect elders, to persevere in a task in spite of difficulties, to listen to others and be attentive to their well-being, to be patient and show discretion, and, above all, to use one's common sense. Importantly the proverbs tend to focus around a number of animals that have particular cultural salience for Malawians, including, the lion, elephant, hyena, bushpig, *mbewa* (as a general category), bushbuck, hippopotamus, grey duiker, baboon, crocodile, tortoise, hare and python. I found it of great interest that at the annual convention of the Malawi Congress Party held in October 1990, four animals were put on display by the Department of National Parks and Wildlife for the benefit of the delegates. Significantly, these were the hyena (*fisi*), hare (*kalulu*), python (*nsato*) and crocodile (*ng'ona*). It had also been hoped to display an elephant and lion, but no live animals could be obtained. It may be noted that the magazine of the wildlife clubs organized by the Wildlife Society of Malawi is called *Kamba* (tortoise).

This focus on animals that are seen as having a certain cultural salience – and are thus depicted regularly in Malawian folk tales and proverbs – is also indicated in contemporary children's drawings and essays. A group of children at one primary school made some drawings for me, and the animals they depicted were the lion, elephant, leopard, zebra, hare, crocodile, rock hyrax, dog and rhinoceros, even though the children had no direct experience with most of them. In an essay competition organized by the Wildlife Society of Malawi on the 'Wild Animal I would most like to see' (1985), essays from the children in the Lilongwe District were on the following animals:

Animal	Number of essays
baboon/monkey	7
antelope	6
hyena	12
leopard	5
elephant	23
lion	21
hare	12
zebra	10
buffalo	2
crocodile	5
tortoise	3

with single essays on the rhino, mouse, python, chameleon and cobra. This gives some idea of the animals that have cultural salience for young people. What is striking in reading these essays is their realism and the emphasis on hunting – one young boy graphically described hunting baboons with dogs and spears – on crop depredations, and on the eating habits of the various animals. One thirteen-year-old boy described in great detail the 'favourable food' of the tortoise – which included termites, snail, mushroom and the fruits of the *masuku* (*uapaca*) and *nkhuyu* (*Ficus*) trees – as well as giving a vivid account of how the ground hornbill (*nang'omba*) captures and eats the tortoise. He also notes that the tortoise 'is edible by some people'. Another young girl wrote as a lion: 'I am a very powerful animal', she wrote. She concluded the page with the words 'Between me and people there is no relationship'. To give the flavour and substance of these essays, I give one below by a twelve-year-old boy on the 'hare'. I give it verbatim, without being patronizing. The boy writes better English than my written Chewa.

> 'Hare is animal which have short legs, but it runs well much. Some time when a dog want to caugh it. It can run very far that the dog cannot caugh it. When it had children it doesn't run far from the place where is the children. This animal eats classes and stems. It meet is good when you eat. But a male hare is small while a female is big and fat on its size. Long ago with my grandfather we went to bush with dogs, bows, allows, and also traps. My grandfather told me how to put the traps. And when we recher at the place whey he put the traps, we find a hare and a bird in the traps and he told me how to take off from the traps. After that we went home. This animal is friendly because it doesn't eat people or any animal, but some animals eats hare. Mostly I like this animal because it doesn't eat any person and it is also meet.

Many of the children expressed their liking for an animal or described it in terms of its being 'wonderful' or 'beautiful'. Thus although Malawians tend to have a very pragmatic attitude towards animals and will hunt them down with apparent glee – especially if they are harmful, like the baboon, monkey or bushpig – I found little evidence that people are wantonly cruel towards them, or 'completely indifferent to the suffering of animals', as one early administrator suggested (Coudenhove 1925: 36). Even so, Malawians tend not to be sentimental about animals, and express both affection and friendship towards one, like the young boy above with regard to the hare, while at the same time hunting them for meat. Many men express affection for their dogs and describe them as 'friends' (*bwenzi*), while at the same time considering them unclean and using the term *garu* as an 'epithet' of abuse. Such meanings are, of course, contextual.

I now turn to the practical uses of mammals, specifically in relation to their uses (*ntchito yache*) as food and medicine.

Animals as Food

In recent years, with the rise of vegetarianism, there has been an increasing interest in the sociology of meat-eating. Two texts in particular (Adams 1990, Fiddes 1991) have been especially noteworthy, as they have both been concerned to emphasize the 'barbarity' of meat eating and have been the recipient of glowing reviews in academic journals (but cf. my critique, Morris 1994b).

The studies of both Adams and Fiddes are well researched and provide stimulating reading. Their focus is largely on the European context, yet they both tend to make generalizations about meat-eating that are seen as having a wider cross-cultural relevance. Three of these generalizations are specifically, if implicitly, addressed below when I attempt to counter them with reference to Malawian ethnography.

The first is the notion that meat eating is a 'barbaric' custom that plays only an insignificant role in clan-based or pre-literate countries. I indicate that meat-eating is important in Malawi and carries no such negative connotations; 'meat' is seen in a positive sense as an essential and important ingredient in food intake, one that is conducive to health and well-being.

Secondly, in stressing the role of meat as a 'symbol' of male power, Adams suggests that meat-eating is the prerogative of men. I argue that among Malawians, meat is as important to women as it is to men, even though there is a symbolic association of men with animals, and men tend to be given more than their fair share of meat, as well as of other foodstuffs.

Finally, I question whether meat-eating simply reflects the Enlightenment ethic of 'power over nature', as this ethic is far from universal and is certainly not articulated in the Malawian context. I am extremely loathe to follow the lamentable tendency of many anthropologists and radical ecologists to describe cultures, or even entire epochs, in terms of a single motif or paradigm, for cultures are complex, often indicating diverse and contrasting ontologies. Malawian culture is no exception: social attitudes towards animal life in Malawi are, as I have suggested throughout this study, complex, diverse, and multi-dimensional.

Suffice it to say that meat-eating in Malawi reflects not an attitude of opposition to or control over nature: on the contrary, it implies the incorporation of the intrinsic powers of nature. Such powers are associated with the Brachystegia woodland (*thengo*), with men as an affinal category and with animals, but the harnessing of these powers, through food, medicine and ritual, is seen as essential for human well-being, both individual and social. In presenting the ethnographic material on meat-eating in Malawi, I shall focus first on the role of meat as food and then on the nature of the various food taboos relating to wild animals.

Throughout Malawi the term for food, *chakudya* (from the verb *ku-dya*, to eat), implies only one thing: a solid meal consisting of a thick porridge (*nsima*) and a savoury side dish or relish (*ndiwo*). A basic meal consisting of a thick porridge accompanied by a relish dish is, of course, common throughout much of south-central Africa. Both constituents of the meal are deemed to be essential (cf. Richards 1939: 46–8). The porridge is made of fine white flour (*ufa*), the most widely used being maize flour (*chimanga*), but other cereals such as finger millet (*mawere*), sorghum (*mapira*) and rice (*mpunga*) may also be eaten. The stiff maize porridge is 'the staff of life of every Malawian', as the recent cookbook of the Chitukuko Cha Amayi M'Malawi (the national women's organiz-ation) puts it (CCAM 1992). Unless Malawians get a meal of *nsima* at least once a day, they will not consider that they have been properly fed. They may have eaten large quantities of such filling foods as sweet potatoes (*mbatata*) or green maize (*mundokwa*), but they may still feel unsatisfied and say, 'I shall sleep with hunger' (*ndigona ndi njala*). However, if a person has eaten sufficient porridge they will declare themselves full or satisfied (*wakhuta*). The expression *wakhuta* has a deep emotional resonance, indicating a feeling of well-being; only someone whose own life is focussed around basic subsistence can fully appreciate its meaning. The term can also refer to a general satisfaction of heart or mind, or to a pregnant woman (*ali ndi mimba*, 'she is with stomach', is the more familiar expression).

Malawians in rural areas usually eat two meals a day, around midday and at sunset, though snacks are also taken. Surveys have shown that many households have only one meal a day (Burgess and Wheeler 1970). What makes a meal satisfying is that enough porridge is eaten to feel really full. This is possible only if there is an adequate and appetising side dish. The role of the side dish is therefore a crucial component of the meal. The pounding of the maize and the preparation of the meal is undertaken by women with the help of young girls, and in an area in the Thyolo district where I lived for four years (1958–61), it was estimated that about a third of a woman's day was spent on domestic tasks (Bieze 1971). A meal is usually eaten communally, as a family, or according to gender or age. A group of people will sit around a bowl or basket of porridge and one or more side dishes. Each in turn will break off a lump of porridge, roll it in the fingers to form a small ball and then dip it into one of the relishes. If the *ndiwo* is a poor one, owing perhaps to its bitter flavour or to a lack of groundnuts or taste, then there will be little enjoyment in the meal; little porridge will be eaten and there will be no real satisfaction.

For a Malawian the ideal relish should be well seasoned and of a good flavour, neither insipid nor bitter. It should contain a certain amount of liquid or gravy and be of a soft consistency, so that it will attach itself to the lumps of porridge dipped into it. Groundnut flour (*nsinjiro*) is important in this respect. Not only is it very rich in oil, it forms a sauce that is very appetising when mixed with leaves or mushrooms. The flavour of the relish depends very largely upon adding the right amount of salt (*mchere*), usually bought locally. But failing this, women will resort to salt (potashes) (*chidulo*) derived from plant ashes, while if neither is available, tomatoes take their place in providing flavour. A side dish without salt is said to be *za madzi* (of water) and is scorned by everyone. The principal plants used in the making of vegetable salt (*chidulo*) are *Canthium huilense (chisunkunthu), Cyperus alternifolius (chesa), Cyperus articulatus (mdulu)* and *Pistia stratiotes (kakombwe)*.

In her truly pioneering studies of nutrition in Malawi, Jessie Williamson (1942, 1972, 1975) outlined in detail the various foodplants that are used as a relish. It is important to realize, however, that not all vegetables are suitable as side dishes. While, for example, yams and sweet potatoes constitute important snacks between meals, they are not used as relish. There are four main kinds of vegetables that are used as ingredients in the relish dish, namely:

Leafy vegetables. The green leaves of certain plants, both cultivated and wild, when cooked form a relish dish. Important among these are the leaves of Chinese cabbage (*mpiru*), cassava (*chinangwa*), pumpkin (*dzangu*), sweet potato (*mbatata*) and various Amaranthes (*bonongwe*). Usually the leaves are referred to by a different name than that given to the plant itself. Thus, as with animals, so with plants there is often a distancing, an 'absent referent', as Adams (1990) calls it, between the vegetable and the plants from which the leaves are taken. One particularly important group of leafy vegetables is *thelele* (Y. *linyololo*). This term is derived from the verb *ku-terera*, to be slippery, and consists of plants whose leaves are mucilaginous when cooked, usually with the help of potashes. The cultivated herb okra (*Abelmoschus esculentus*) is the principal herb used. What is of interest about *thelele* is that it is associated primarily with women and young children. *Thelele* is seen as a strengthening food. The leaves are thus usually the first *ndiwo* to be given with porridge to a young child. Men, in contrast, have a general disdain for this form of relish.

Legumes. Pulses play an important part in the diet of Malawians and provide a welcome change from the almost daily side dish of leaves. Though groundnuts are of almost daily significance, if available, beans and peas are not usually eaten more than two or three times a week. Many people feel that if eaten in large quantities, they lead to digestive disorders. The most popular kinds eaten are the pigeon pea (*nandolo*), cow pea (*khobwe*, and its smaller variety *nseula*), kidney bean (*mbwanda*) – the most popular bean relish – and the hyacinth bean (*mthungadzu*) (see Williamson 1943). In one nutrition survey pulses were eaten on 27 per cent of the family/days enumerated (Burgess and Wheeler 1970).

Edible fungi (bowa) constitute an important relish during the rainy season (December-February), and many varieties are gathered by local women. They are usually cooked with a little potash and groundnut flour and as a relish are closely identified with meat (*nyama*). Many fungi names indicate this association: *manyame (Cantharellus cibarius), mnofu wa nkhuku* (flesh of the chicken, *Cantharellus longiporus), mphamfa* (liver, the Bolete *Phlebopus colossus), kanyama (Cymatoderma dendriticum)* (see Morris 1984, 1987).

Several species of ground orchid (chanaka, chikande, Disa or Satyrium spp.) are also cooked as ndiwo. Like the mushrooms, they are often cooked with potashes and are associated with meat being referred to as *nyama yapansi* (underground meat).

Although fish (*nsomba*) and insects (particularly locusts, *dzombe*, and flying termites, *inswa*) are almost universally liked and form a regular constituent of many side dishes, to a Malawian the relish *par excellence* is meat. But before turning to the role of meat as a relish dish, two points are worth noting. The first is that there are seasonal variations in the availability of food, and that during the early part of the rainy season in rural areas there is often a severe food shortage. This is often described as a time of hunger (*njala*). Williamson, in 1940–41, observed that children in villages showed a consistent loss of weight from December to February, due to a shortage of staple food (1942: 13).

Secondly, although women are owners of the granary and have a good deal of autonomy in domestic affairs, the distribution of food within the family is by no means equal. In a normal year there will be enough maize porridge for all, but there always is a very unequal distribution of relish. Men, as well as older women, invariably get more than their fair share of meat, and women are publicly frowned upon for openly showing an enjoyment of meat. This undoubtedly reflects the public affirmation of the supremacy of the affinal male in Malawian society. But it is as well to bear in mind that men also are given more of the valued plant food – it would be deemed very unseemly if a man ate a porridge that included bran (*gaga*), which is commonly eaten by women when there is a shortage of maize – and that meat-eating, specifically of the bat and chicken, forms an essential component of the girls' initiation rite (*chinamwali*), which is entirely under the auspices of women. When a woman is serving out the food, she will thus invariably send the lion's share of the side dish to the men, keeping back only a small amount for herself and the young children. In the case of meat or fish, she will invariably see to it that the men of the household not only get a larger share, but often the choicest morsels. Consequently women, as well as girls and younger boys, on the whole eat many more snacks. Williamson (1942: 16) observed that it was young boys between 8 and 14 years old who probably fared worst with regard to food. Not old enough to work or earn money, not yet strong enough to force or entice their mothers to give them food, young boys are left very much to their own devices, spending an inordinate amount of time searching the bush for food morsels, gathering fruit and wild foods, digging up mice and collecting insects. I have spent several hours of the day with young boys engaged in such subsistence activities. Fish and meat are undoubtedly the most popular kinds of relish, and Williamson suggested that if the supply were sufficient they would willingly be eaten daily (1941: 14). Many early observers spoke of the craving that Malawians have for meat. Lt. E.D. Young, who led the Livingstone Search expedition (1875–6), wrote:

> If there is one thing more than another which makes a light-hearted African forget his woes and cast care to the winds it is the prospect of meat – meat, no matter what animal forthcoming, or in what state, so long as it does not happen to be the particular beast held as unclean by his tribe (1877: 55).

He goes on the describe how the expedition came across the carcass of an eland lying on the rocks on a bend of the Shire River above Chikwawa, and how the sight of the animal brought their journey to a standstill. Even though in an advanced state of decomposition, the eland was eagerly retrieved from the river by his porters and eaten. I have myself been present on numerous occasions when the sudden appearance of an elephant shrew or a hare has caused several hundred tea planters, both men and women, to down their baskets and eagerly chase the animal, hurling a maelstrom of rocks, sticks and knobkerries.

A decade after Young another Scottish traveller, Professor Henry Drummond, also remarked, though in a rather patronizing manner, that Africans would do 'anything for flesh in whatever form'. He describes one incident in which he shot a bushbaby with the aid of a Winchester rifle. The ball ripped the animal apart but left some of its viscera on the higher branches of the tree. This, to his surprise, was immediately retrieved by his African companion, Moolu, and within a few minutes it had been 'cooked and eaten' (1889: 13, 115–16). As in other African communities, Malawians have an eagerness and craving for meat and see it as the *ndiwo par excellence* (cf. Richards 1939: 56 on the related Bemba of Zambia). Carol Adams's suggestion that 'on an emotional level everyone has some discomfort with the eating of animals' (1990: 66) is certainly not borne out by the Malawi data. Her notion that meat-eating is a white male prerogative indicates a rather dismissive and prejudicial attitude towards African people, for the evidence suggests that they value meat-eating highly. Although hunting and animals are associated with men – and correlatively agriculture and plants with women – both men and women in Malawi eat and enjoy meat. Malawians use the terms *nkhuli* and *nkhwiru* specifically to refer to this craving for meat.

The suggestion by the same author (1990: 40–1) that concepts used to describe meat deny that such food is derived from living animals is certainly not true of Malawi. The concept *nyama* is a polysemic term meaning both meat and edible quadruped. *Nyama* covers all mammals that are eaten as food, and by extension also to fungi and the roots of certain orchids, which are seen as having a similar texture and taste to that of meat. The term has a functional contrast in the concept of *chirombo*, which covers the carnivores – lion and hyena are prototypical – and all animal organisms that are useless, noxious or dangerous to humans. Again, by extension, *chirombo* covers weeds and inedible fungi. The term *nyama* is not used to cover domestic fowls (*nkhuku*) nor the many wild birds (*mbalame*) that are eaten, nor does it cover fish.

Williamson remarks that 'more or less anything in the way of animal flesh is eaten' (1942: 8). This is to some extent true, as there is hardly a creature great or small that may not be eaten, but as we shall see, there are wide variations in what mammals are eaten in Malawi, reflecting a variety of factors, both cultural and personal. Although it is considered unseemly for women to show any eagerness for meat, for animals are intrinsically connected with male virility (seen, however, as essential for societal well being), women do in fact eat meat. There appear to be no food taboos relating to animals that are specifically gender-linked, although there are certain circumstances when the eating of specific animals is prohibited to women.

Meat, as already noted, is the side dish *par excellence.* Almost all parts of the animal or bird are eaten and practically nothing is wasted, except for the bones, which are too hard to be chewed. Meat may be eaten, whatever the state of decay. Early writers invariably commented upon the fact that meat was often eaten in an advanced state of putrefaction (MacDonald 1882: 27, Coudenhove 1925: 44). From my own personal experience, this is still the case.

The meat is invariably boiled until the flesh is very soft and comes away easily from the bones. The pot may be refilled many times during the cooking, depending on the toughness of the meat. Salt is always added, and sufficient liquid is always left to form a gravy. In urban areas meat tends to be fried initially in cooking oil and then casseroled together with onions and tomatoes (Williamson 1942: 62, CCAM 1992: 175). In the preparation and cooking of mice, I can do no better than quote verbatim an extract from a school essay written by a young lad from the Lilongwe district.

> When we were digging with my friend I saw a mice jumping in our school garden and I told my friend that there was a mice and we ran away and I started to run fast that everyone could not reach it. And fortunately we reached it and it entered its hole and we went to our class and took the hoe and we started to dug the hole and after dug we saw it jumping on my left foot and I was huppy and it was beside me. I took a big stick and hit on its back and after hitting it I saw that it was died and when it was died I took it and put in my big pocket and go to our class. And when the teacher said we can go home, I ran away with my friend and took a smallest stick and I started to remove its hair and after that I remove all the wastes in its stomachache and I went and throw them in our pit. And I went to the tap and I pulled water from the pot and I started to washed it and when it was clean I took it and put in the pot and I went again to the tap and pulled water from the pot and I started to cook it and cooked it side by side and when it was well cooked I took it from the pot and put in between two sticks called *mpani* in Chichewa. And I ate it with a good good called *msima*, I was with my uncle, my sister, my aunt and my father and I cut it into four parts and I divided it from them. We were happy because we have a good super at that time.

This extract indicates how well liked mice are as a source of relish among Malawians, and in discussions I have had with some Malawians they have become quite lyrical about their taste – and it is their taste, rather than the amount of meat that they provide, that is of crucial importance in their role as relish source.

Apart from the Ngoni and the Nkhonde of the northern region, none of the Malawian people has a pastoral economy. Goats and domestic fowl are the principal domestic livestock, though sheep, cattle and pigs are also found in certain areas. In a survey I made of a hundred families in the Mulanje and Zomba districts (see Table 5), hens and goats were the principal domestic animals, with a few families owning pigs, sheep and cattle. All the families were essentially subsistence agriculturists, describing themselves as *alimi* (cultivators) but augmenting their incomes through various trades and occupations. Although hens are owned by a majority of families, though not all, only a minority of households possess domestic animals, 12 percent of families have cattle, 35 percent goats, 4 percent sheep and 4 percent pigs. No pigs are owned in the Zomba district, where Islam is practised by Yao-speakers, who form a high percentage of the population. Since, like most parts of Malawi, wild mammals are confined to wooded hillsides in both areas, they are only infrequently captured as food, even though trapping and hunting are widely practised. The principal animals captured are monkeys, duikers, hyraxes and various species of field mice. In rural areas, domestic animals and poultry are

Table 5. Domestic animals among families in Mulanje and Zomba districts

	Mulanje		Zomba		Totals	
	Number of families	Number of domestic animals	Number of families	Number of domestic animals	Number of families	Number of domestic animals
livestock						
cattle	10	65	2	14	12	79
goats	26	115	9	60	35	175
sheep	–	–	4	15	4	15
pigs	4	16	–	–	4	16
rabbits	5	15	2	15	7	30
guinea pigs	1	2	–	–	1	2
cats	35	41	14	15	49	56
dogs	7	17	12	18	19	35
doves	7	108	5	14	12	122
hens	44	267	30	221	74	488
ducks	3	10	1	6	4	16

Total number of families = 100

rarely killed for food, unless there is good reason, such as a feast for a wedding or funeral, or to honour an important visitor with good *ndiwo*. Whenever I stayed in a village with friends, a hen was always automatically killed for my benefit, even though I did not wish it. The suggestion of many vegetarians that nobody would eat animals if they had to kill them themselves receives no support at all from the Malawian context. People who kill animals invariably eat them. But it is worth reiterating that meat is only infrequently taken as *ndiwo*, even though highly valued. Nutrition surveys indicate that meat (goat, hens or wild animals) forms only a small percentage of the dietary intake of most Malawians, about 15 percent of the family/days on which food was used, amounting on average to between 8 and 15 gms per person per day. Meat-eating is no higher in urban areas (Burgess and Wheeler 1970, Williamson 1972). Cattle (*ng'ombe*) and goats (*mbuzi*) are the most popular as meat relishes, although the latter can often have a strong unpleasant smell. Mutton is not so well-liked: it is said to be lacking in taste (*ku-zizira*) and not to have as good a smell as the other two meats. But in Moslem areas, among Yaos, it seems to some extent to take the place of goat flesh in popularity. Among the Ngoni, there are elaborate rules in the distribution of meat of cattle (*nyama ya ng'ombe*), and some of the choicest parts, which are considered delicacies, are reserved for men or for the owner of the beast. These include the heart (*mama*), kidneys (*mpsyo*), head (*mutu*) and tongue (*lilime*). The intestines (*matumbo*) of domestic animals are very popular and eaten by both sexes, young and old. On market stalls, it is often sold rolled around meat ready for cooking (*ntumbwana*). Chicken is universally eaten in Malawi and well liked. The hens are usually killed only when there is some occasion to celebrate. The greatest welcome you can give to a visitor, suggests the CCAM cookbook, 'is to produce a whole chicken deliciously prepared' (1992: 161). All parts are eaten except for the feathers and those bones that are too hard to chew. Liver, kidneys and gizzard, which are considered delicacies, are usually cooked with the rest of the bird. The intestines, head and feet are given to the children. The choicest morsel, however, is the parson's nose (*chinyophilo*), which is usually claimed by the bird's owner. Eggs (*mazira*) were traditionally never eaten, certainly not by women. Young women are told not to eat eggs lest they have difficulties in childbirth, while boys are informed that eggs may diminish their sexual potency. Williamson notes (1942: 12) that eggs were given to young children when recovering from illness. The reluctance to eat eggs is usually attributed to the social attitude that the resulting bird is more valuable than the egg. It is worth noting too that traditionally Yao people did not drink milk, whether cow's or goat's, nor take dairy produce of any kind. Stannus noted that 'milk is never consumed in any form. They say "What a disgusting habit, to suck the juice of an animal while it is still alive"' (Stannus 1922: 348, MacDonald 1882: 27). Eggs and milk are nowadays widely consumed, particularly in urban areas. In the past, when large game animals such as elephant, hippopotamus and eland were more plentiful and often obtained by hunting, meat was frequently dried for further use. It was usually cut into strips, roasted over the fire for a short period and then hung in the smoke of the hut. These days, only mice are dried for further use, although one can occasionally find the dried meat of small game in the huts of local hunters.

Throughout Malawi, there are wide variations in the wild animals that are eaten as food and the species that are specifically prohibited. But generally speaking, because animal food is seen as energy-giving (in modern parlance), as conducive to the activation of 'heat' (*otentha*), meat-eating, like sex, is seen as potentially harmful in certain contexts. Thus a menstruating or pregnant woman will not eat meat during these vulnerable periods, particularly meat of animals that are seen as highly 'potent, such as bushpig, hippopotamus and elephant (Mikochi 1938: 21). All rites of passage (*chinamwali*) have similar restrictions, as do occasions involving the administration of medicines (*mankhwala*) or the making of offerings (*nsembe*) to the spirits of the dead or to rain deities. Food taboos relating to animal life were frequently remarked upon by early missionaries and administrators, particularly those who had ethnological interests. In a discussion of prohibited meat (*nyama zosala*), the Blantyre missionary David Clement Scott wrote:

> Certain people, and varying duties, are supposed to require to abstain (*ku-sala*) from certain meats. Hence those who offer sacrifice don't eat rats (rats are supposed to be specially uncanny); girls are a particular age won't eat eggs or drink milk; the Yao mostly abstain from milk and eggs; each tribe or family has its particular abstinence from certain foods . . .. Hence a great many refuse swine's flesh; very few eat crocodile; still fewer eat fox (jackal), leopard, lion, hyena; a good many eat zebra, hippopotamus; most eat mice, elephant; almost no one refuses buffalo, fish and game of all kinds; though some few actually do not eat fowl (1929: 492–3).

Scott lived mainly among the Mang'anja of the Blantyre area. Hugh Stannus, on the other hand, spent many years as a medical officer at Zomba, working among Yao-speakers. He was a man of wide interests and sympathetic in his approach to local culture. In his important study of the Yao, Stannus wrote regarding their food prohibitions:

The flesh of all the antelopes, of oxen, sheep and goats is eaten greedily; only bushbuck is avoided by some people as it is said to cause a skin eruption. Elephant is shunned by many on account of its rough skin, also rhinoceros because of the ulcers which it often has on its body, and hippopotamus on account of its marks on its back which are often thought to be akin to leprosy. People eating the flesh of these animals are supposed often to sicken with leprosy . . .. Few will eat pig or warthog on account of the digging habits of these animals. It is thought they may sometimes grub up bodies from graves. These flesh taboos may be due to Mohammedan influence. The lion, hyena and fox (jackal) no one would touch, as they are supposed to be connected with *usawi* (*ufiti*, witchcraft), but the heart of the lion might be eaten to acquire courage. Few will touch leopard flesh . . .. All will eat the flesh of the serval cat but very few of the common wild cat. The rock rabbit (*hyrax*), *ngangawira* (*mbira*), is refused by most Yao as it is a 'beast without shame' having no tail to hide what should in decency be hid. Very few will partake of the baboon, but monkey is acceptable to many. A few reject porcupine, supposing they will break out in spots, while the zebra may cause stripes and none will touch the skunk (*zorilla*). No one eats *sunje*, a mouse (shrew) that is believed to die if it crosses a path. All kinds of rats are eaten, but the shrew-rat (elephant shrew) and cane rat only by boys. Snakes no one will touch. With the exception of carrion birds such as the crow and hawk, most birds are considered fit to eat (1922: 347–8).

These early accounts indicate selectivity and variability in the kinds of animals that are eaten by Malawians. They counter the crude stereotype, reflected in the writings of one colonial administrator, that local people have a palate so 'absolutely devoid of taste' that they eat anything left by the raven and hyena and have a bill of fare so extensive that they eat 'everything that breathes', though Coudenhove noted that Yaos did not eat birds of prey or the ground hornbill (1925: 42–3).

Oral traditions confirm the early observations of Scott and Stannus (cf. Nkondiwa *et al.* 1977) and suggest that religious, totemic and personal factors all play a part in determining food prohibitions relating to animal life. To obtain more exact information on this issue, a hundred people in the Zomba and Mulanje districts were interviewed with regard to their dietary preferences, as these specifically related to sixty-four of the commoner or better known mammal species. The people interviewed had religious and ethnic affiliations as shown in Table 6. What these interviews indicated with respect to the edibility of wild animals can be summed up in the following observations:

First, there were a number of animals that were not generally known to the people. These included the night ape (*kamundi*), the roan antelope

Table 6. Ethnic and Religious Affiliations

	Male (57)				Female (43)			Total
	Yao	Ngoni	Lomwe	Nyanja	Yao	Lomwe	Nyanja	
Protestant Churches (C.C.AT., Anglican)	8	1	14	10	12	3	12	60
Roman Catholic	1	–	4	1	–	2	1	9
African Independent Churches (P.I.M., Topia Church, Faith in Action)	–	–	8	3	–	6	–	17
Islam	5	–	–	2	6	–	1	14
Totals	14	1	26	16	18	11	14	100

(*chilembwe*) and the dormouse (*kadyamlamu*), all of which have a limited or local distribution.

Secondly, there are many species outside the *mbewa* category (discussed separately below) that are widely recognized as food (see Table 7). What is of interest is that although antelopes are widely recognized as meat, and mammals such as buffalo, common duiker and kudu are eaten by almost everyone, in all categories there are a significant number of people who do not eat such meat. As we explore below, there may be several reasons for this. It is also noteworthy that the hyrax, hare and bushbuck, which are mentioned in the literature as being animals of ill-omen, are, it seems, eaten by the majority of people. The bushbuck is of particular interest. A beautiful creature with a spotted coat, the eating of its meat is often associated with the skin disease *chiwengo*. Yet in spite of this, all those we interviewed indicated that they consumed its meat.

Though a shy animal, plenty still survive even near populated areas, and I have many records of it being hunted on all the hills of the Shire Highlands. Both Duff (1903: 268) and Stannus (1910: 323) suggest that the bushbuck is not eaten because it is said to frequent graveyards. The woodland thickets that constitute such protected graveyards (*manda*) are, however, frequented by a variety of mammals, giant rats, duikers, hares, all of which are regularly eaten, though never hunted in the *manda* itself. In my discussions, almost all respondents indicated that they used

Table 7. Animals generally recognized as food

Species	not known	eaten	not eaten	% people
Ungulates				
elephant *njobvu*	6	72	22	77
rhino *chipembere*	12	67	21	76
zebra *mbidzi*	24	63	13	83
hippo *mvau*	6	74	20	78
warthog *njiri*	14	69	17	80
bushpig *nguluwe*	1	82	17	84
hartebeest *ngondo*	48	37	15	71
red duiker *kadumba*	66	26	8	76
impala *nswala*	23	43	34	56
waterbuck *nakodzwe*	55	35	10	78
duiker *gwape*	1	97	2	98
klipspnnger *chinkoma*	12	80	8	91
sable *mphalapala*	7	87	6	94
buffalo *njati*	7	90	3	97
kudu *ngoma*	11	87	2	98
bushbuck *mbawala*	2	98	–	100
eland *ntchefu*	12	87	1	99
reedbuck *mphoyo*	22	71	7	91
Non-ungulate				
rock hyrax *zumba*	10	79	11	88
yellow-spotted hyrax *mbira*	–	93	7	93
hare *kalulu*	–	98	2	98
serval *njuzi*	25	65	10	87
antbear *nkumbakumba*	39	45	16	74
civet cat *chombwe*	23	47	30	61
genet *mwili*	4	71	25	74
grey mongoose *nyenga*	2	66	32	67

bushbuck meat as *ndiwo*, even though it is one of the mammals widely associated with the ailment *chiwengo*. Elephant, impala, hippopotamus, bushpig and several other species also have the same association and are thus not eaten, on personal grounds, by a large number of people. Both bushpig and warthog are generally not eaten by Moslems, the men tending to be more strict in the observance of this dietary restriction, as Table 8 indicates.

Thirdly, around sixteen species of mammals are not eaten as a relish by the majority of people (see Table 9). This rather dispels Coudenhove's suggestion that the people of southern Malawi eat all forms of animal life. None of the larger carnivores are eaten, and this includes the cheetah (*kakwio*), which has a very limited distribution in Malawi. Several of the smaller carnivores are, however, eaten such as genet, civet cat, grey

Table 8. Edibility of bushpig and warthog

| | Male | | Female | | |
	Islam	Christian	Islam	Christian	Total
Bushpig					
eaten	–	46	3	33	82
not eaten	7	4	4	2	17
not known	–	–	–	1	1
Total	7	50	7	36	100
Warthog					
eaten	–	42	4	23	69
not eaten	7	3	1	6	17
not known	–	5	2	7	14
Total	7	50	7	36	100

Table 9. Animals not eaten

	Not known	Eaten	Not eaten
Non-carnivores			
shrew *sunche*	2	–	98
hedgehog *chisoni*	–	1	99
fruit bat *mleme*	–	2	98
insectivorous bat *nanzeze*	–	17	83
banana bat *chuchu*	18	2	80
pangolin *ngaka*	50	11	39
black rat *khoswe*	–	7	93
Carnivores			
jackal *nkhandwe*	–	3	97
zorilla *kanyimbi*	4	3	93
hyena *fisi*	–	10	90
leopard *nyalugwe*	–	4	96
lion *mkango*	–	3	97
wild dog *mbulu*	21	5	74
water mongoose *nkhakhakha*	44	21	35
banded mongoose *msulu*	29	11	60
wild cat *bvambwe*	29	16	45

mongoose and serval, and the latter is, in fact, considered a delicacy by some, *ndiwo yabwino* (good relish). None of the animal species associated with witchcraft (*ufiti*) are eaten. Besides the jackal and hyena, this includes snakes and various species of owls (*kadzidzi*). Although the civet cat is considered to have a bad smell (*kununkha*) and its meat to give rise to headaches, it is nonetheless eaten by about 60 percent of people. Many of the animals that are not considered sources of relish are widely used as medicine (*mankhwala*). The civet cat, hyena and zorilla are typical examples.

Fourthly, there is an important category of animals, the *mbewa* (rats, mice, shrews and elephant shrews), which consists largely of edible species. In many rural areas they constitute an important source of relish, and in the latter part of the dry season are sold by young boys, dried on sticks to passing motorists. In this category only the shrew (*sunche*) and the black rat (*khoswe*) are not eaten, the first because of its offensive smell (*kununkha*), the second because of its association with human habitations (see Table 10).

Finally, there is a group of mammals with a rather ambiguous status (see Table 11), eaten by many, but not by others. These include the primates, along with the otter, bush squirrel and porcupine. All these animals have important uses as medicine. Thus as a general prospectus, we have the following:

Widely recognized as food

Ungulates	18
Non-ungulates	8
Mbewa category	12
Not eaten as food	16
Ambiguous status as food	7
Total number of species	61

We can turn now to consider three factors that may be relevant in guiding dietary prohibitions: gender, ethnicity and religious affiliation. The edibility of two species, the giant rat (*bwampini*) and baboon (*nyani*), is indicated in detail in Tables 12 and 13. It can be seen that neither gender nor ethnicity are crucial factors in determining what animals are eaten as *ndiwo*, though women are less inclined to eat baboon meat.

Table 10. Edible *mbewa* species

Species	Not known	Eaten	Not eaten	% people
elephant shrew *sakhwi*	4	64	32	66
mole rat *namfuko*	1	64	35	67
vlei rat *thiri*	36	51	13	80
giant rat *bwampini*	–	74+	26	74
gerbil *phanya*	–	83	17	83
pouched rat *jugu*	–	82	18	82
long-tailed forest mouse *sonthe*	21	51	28	65
single-striped rat *mphera*	22	63	15	81
creek rat *mende*	14	69	17	80
spiny mouse *chinyerere*	4	74	22	77
fat mouse *kapeta*	–	82	18	82
cane rat *nchenzi*	–	93	7	93

Table 11. Edibility of ambiguous animal categories

Species	Not known	Eaten	Not eaten	% people
otter *katumbu*	8	46	46	50
bush squirrel *gologolo*	3	38	59	39
porcupine *nungu*	1	66	33	66
baboon *nyani*	–	57	43	57
vervet monkey *pusi*	–	57	43	57
black monkey *nchima*	8	57	35	62
bushbaby *changa*	5	51	44	57

Table 12. Edibility of giant rat, *bwampini*

		Male	Female	Total
Ethnicity				
Yao and others	eaten	10	14	24
	not eaten	5	4	9
Lomwe	eaten	20	8	28
	not eaten	6	3	9
Nyanja	eaten	12	10	22
	not eaten	4	4	8
	Totals	57	43	100
Religious affiliations				
Protestant Churches	eaten	28	23	51
	not eaten	5	4	9
Roman Catholic	eaten	6	3	9
	not eaten	0	0	0
African Independent	eaten	7	4	11
Churches	not eaten	4	2	6
Islam	eaten	1	2	3
	not eaten	6	5	11
	Totals	57	43	100
	Totals eaten	42	32	74
	% eaten	74	74	

Baboons are widely recognized as being like humans, both in the care of their young and in their use of medicines, and it is widely believed that the males may have forced sexual relations with Malawian women. Nevertheless many people will eat them as food. Although throughout Malawi, Yao and Chewa speakers tend to suggest that Lomwe people

Table 13. Edibility of baboon, *nyani*

		Male	Female	Total
Ethnicity				
Yao and others	eaten	7	7	14
	not eaten	8	11	19
Lomwe	eaten	21	6	27
	not eaten	5	5	10
Nyanja	eaten	7	9	16
	not eaten	9	5	14
	Totals	57	43	100
Religious affiliations				
Protestant Churches	eaten	23	16	39
	not eaten	10	11	21
Roman Catholic	eaten	6	2	8
	not eaten	–	1	1
African Independent	eaten	6	1	7
Churches	not eaten	5	5	10
Islam	eaten	–	3	3
	not eaten	7	4	11
	Totals	57	43	100
	Totals eaten	35	22	57
	% eaten	61	51	

eat anything, from leopard and snakes to field mice (*Lomwe amadya*, 'the Lomwe eat them', is a common phrase that comes out spontaneously in many discussions about food), my studies indicated that there was not a great deal of difference in the dietary preferences of the different ethnic groups. Lomwe people, like other people in Malawi, do not normally eat hedgehog, pangolin, shrews, leopard, jackals or wild dog, and the giant rat and field mice more generally are eaten and are well liked not only by the Lomwe, but by all ethnic communities in Malawi. Of the seven people who admitted that they ate the black rat, only three were Lomwe-speakers. Religious affiliation, however, is an important factor in dietary attitudes. Moslems (particularly men) and members of Independent African Churches such as Topia Church and Providence Industrial Mission (particularly women) refrain from eating the *mbewa* category and such mammals as baboons, monkeys, squirrels and the smaller carnivores (which may be eaten by other people). It is of interest that none of the Moslems interviewed owned a domestic dog. Chakanza (1980: 4) noted that bushpig and mice were not eaten by members of the African Full Gospel Church, who also reject traditional medicine and beer-drinking.

As elsewhere in Africa, Moslems (*Asilamu*) in Malawi have elaborate rites relating to meat-eating, clearly distinguishing between edible and non edible animals. Any animal that dies of its own accord (*nyama yukufa yokha*) is not eaten, and only animals whose throat has been cut by an Islamic teacher (*mwalimu*) or someone recognized by him can be eaten. It is stressed that the individual performing the slaughter must be circumcized (*wodulidwa nsonga ya mbolo yake*) and never to have been bitten on the body by either a dog or a snake. When undertaking the ritual slaughter, the *mwalimu* must have ritually bathed his body beforehand and to be barefoot though wearing his cap (*chisoti*). When the throat is cut, a prayer is said praising God (*Mulungu*) and asking for his compassion. God is referred to as great (*wamkulu*) and as grandfather (*ambuye*). 'There is nothing to fear, but only you God' (*Palibe wina woyenera kumiiuopa koma inu Mulungu*), is one prayer used when a cock (*tambala*) is killed. Animals that are considered by most Moslems to be unclean (*haramu*), which are referred to as *nyama zo detsedwa* (dark to soiled animal), include elephant, hyrax, the category *mbewa* (rats, mice and elephant shrews), hare, monkeys, baboon, bushpig and warthog, jackal, hippopotamus and caterpillars (*mphalabungu*). Two other factors are important in determining what animals are not eaten as food: clan affiliation and personal dietary preferences.

In pre-colonial times, the many African communities living north of the Zambezi constituted essentially a clan-based society. Social identity focussed less on the local politics – the various Maravi states – or on ethnic categories than on clan membership. In the early period ethnicity was primarily related to language and to bioregional criteria: it had little political or even cultured significance. The area was, as many early writers have hinted, characterized by an underlying cultural unity. Antonio Gamitto, who accompanied the 1831–32 expedition from Tete to Chief Kazembe, recorded in his narrative the names of the various people living north of the Zambezi – Chewa, Mang'anja, Makua, Bororo, Nsenga, Yao – but suggested that 'it is beyond dispute' that they belong essentially to the same Marave people in having the same habits, customs and language (Gamitto 1960: 64). It is of interest that in Linden's essay on Nyau societies in the Mua area, which specifically emphasizes 'Chewa' identity, a local headman, Njoro, when asked to what tribe he belonged, identified himself not as a Chewa but as belonging to the Banda clan (1975: 36).

In Malawi the term *mtundu* is a general category meaning variety, kind or tribe. It is akin *to* the concept of *guru*, which means grouping, assembly or type. Different kinds of plants and animals are referred to by these terms. If a person is asked what *mtundu* he or she belongs to, they will often respond with an ethnic category, Nyanja, Chipeta, Yao or Chewa. These terms have essentially a geographical connotation or refer to place of origin: they tend to be terms used more by neighbouring people, and often have pejorative associations (Nurse 1978: 16). In the past, however, it was clan affiliation that was of more social significance, and although clan membership is still recognized by many people – and reflected in their use as surnames – it is nowadays socially less important. Among the matrilineal people of Malawi, clan membership is inherited through the mother. The terms usually employed to describe clan affiliations are *pfuko* (pl.*mafuko*) or *mfunda* (Yao *lutosyo*) which is distinguished from the praise-name (*chiwongo*), which is inherited patrilineally (Mwale 1948: 33–4, Mitchell 1956: 184, Nurse 1978: 25). Clans in Malawi do not have any corporate functions either economically or ritually, nor do they carry out communal tasks. In the past they were strictly exogamous units, and a person was not allowed to marry (*saloledwa kukwatira*) anyone of the same clan, as they were viewed as kin (*mbale wake*). Discussions with local people suggest that clan exogamy these days seems to be less strictly observed. As one woman said: *Masiku ano anthu amangolwatira mfunda uliwonse*, 'These days people may marry (someone) from any clan'. What was important about clan membership in the past was that it enabled people to establish substantive relationships, interpreted as kinship, with people in distant places. It thus facilitated the movement of populations. Over a wide area either clan names are the same, or those of the different ethnic groups are identified or given the same meaning (Soka 1953: 35–6, Mitchell 1956: 73, White 1987: 98–9).

In the present context, what is significant is that clans have totemic associations. Many are in fact named after animals. These we may list: *nguluwe* (bushpig), *mbawala* (bushbuck), *chitolo* (multimammate mouse), *nchima* (blue monkey), *nchenzi* (cane rat), *njuzi* (serval), *njobvu* (elephant), *ngoma* (kudu), *chinkoma* (klipspringer), *ng'ombe* (cattle) and *kunda* (giant rat). All have dietary restrictions with respect to the clan 'totem'. Lévi-Strauss's suggestion (1966) that there is no connection between totemic clans and food taboos is certainly not borne out by the Malawian data. The term *nyama* itself is in fact a clan name (Mwale 1948: 35). Nurse's suggestion that the Lomwe do not observe any totemic clan avoidances was not confirmed by my own researches in the Phalombe area, but throughout Malawi many people these days are rather vague about the specific dietary restrictions associated with clan membership. Detailed below are some of the more important clans among the matrilineal peoples of Malawi and their associated totemic (animal) avoidances.

Phiri. This is one of the most important clans in Malawi, to which belonged the early Maravi rulers. The term means 'hill' and is said to derive from the early migrants to Malawi who slept on top of a large hill. Clan members are forbidden to eat the animals that are associated with the hills, such as baboon, porcupine, klipspringer and hyrax. The genet cat and zebra (associated with the Ngoni clan Tembo) were also noted as prohibited categories.

Zimbiri. This clan is seen in the Mulanje district to be related to the Phiri in terms of cross-cousinship (*chisawani*), having long ago been their domestic slaves and iron workers. The usual meaning of *zimbiri* is 'rust'. Bushpig, chameleon, *nthonga* (the blind burrowing snake) and porcupine are noted as not being eaten by members of this clan. Stannus (1910: 308) notes the meaning of the clan name as puff adder (Yao *lipili*, Nyanja *mphiri*).

Banda. This clan is also related to the Phiri clan in terms of cross-cousinship (*usuwani*), and together they constitute a implicit moiety system that is basic to Marave culture. The Banda are, in oral traditions, seen as the original inhabitants of the country; they are thus closely associated with the land and are credited with rain-making powers (Marwick 1963: 378). Associated in tradition with the country at the foot of the hill, their name is said to derive from the fact that they had to level the grass (*ku-wanda*, to beat down grass) (Ntara 1973: 6, Hodgson 1933: 144). Apart from the common duiker, no food taboos were recorded relating to this clan.

Mwale (Ngondo). This clan is said to derive from a group of people who went out hunting (*kukasaka nyama*). They picked up a dead hartebeest (*ngondo*), cut it up and shared the meat amongst themselves. But they disagreed about the brain (*ulembe*). Because of the fighting that occurred they were nicknamed thereafter Mwale (from *ku-mwalira*, to die), as well as being known as hartebeest (Ntara 1973: 6). This animal is therefore not eaten by members of the clan, nor is the bushpig.

Nkhoma. This clan, according to Lomwe people, is named after a flat-topped mountain, also referred to as Nakumwe. Members are not allowed to eat the zorilla (*kanyimbi*). Hodgson (1933: 144) notes that the term refers to a root eaten by baboons – it is the yam bean (*Sphenostylis marginata*) that is also eaten by humans – which is therefore not to be eaten by members of the clan.

Mbewe.   According to Ntara (1973: 7) people belonging to this clan are called Mbewe because their work was to hunt mice (*kusaka mbewa*). Accordingly they are not allowed to eat this category of mammals, which includes elephant shrews as well as rats and mice. Nor are bushpig eaten by the Mbewe (Phiri *et al.* 1977: 70).

The patrilineal clans of the Ngoni (*Isibongo*) are even more explicitly linked with totemic animals than are those of the matrilineal people. Table 14 indicates some of the Ngoni clans and their associated food taboos as these relate specifically to animals.

Among the Tumbuka, members of the Gondwe clan will not eat its totem, the monitor lizard (*gondwe*) (Fraser 1910).

Many clan names are the names of animals or an archaic name, such as *soko* for nyani (baboon), *nyaji* for *njati* (buffalo). It is of interest that

Table 14. Ngoni clan totems

Mvuu	hippopotamus
Shumba	lion, zebra, and all members of the cat family
Mbizi (Mbidzi)	zebra
Moyo	(heart); Members of the clan do not eat the heart or liver (both associated with life) of the animal
Manyoni	common duiker (*nyiska*), field mice (*mbewa*)
Chirwa	porcupine
Nkosi	zebra
Ndlovu (Njobvu)	elephant
Jere	(literally bangle), domestic pigeon, elephant
Mkandawire	hippopotamus
Kurnwenda	hippopotamus
Maseko	(literally pebble), elephant, domestic fowl, rhinoceros
Ngulube	bushpig
Soko	baboon, bushpig, monkeys
Nungu	porcupine
Newa	lion, genes, wild cat, leopard
Honde	hippopotamus
Nqumayo	hippopotamus
Hara	zebra
Nyangulu	python
Shaba (shawa)	eland, buffalo
Shonga	buffalo
Tembo	zebra
Nyati	buffalo

(Rangeley Papers V1/2. Chipeta et al. 1977).

few of the totemic species are carnivores. Generally speaking, the taboo (*ku-sala*) not only implies that the animal must not be eaten, but a person should not harm the animal in any way, nor wear its skin, nor eat the roots associated with a particular species like the baboon or bushpig. Eating the meat of the tabooed animal, whether intentionally or unintentionally, is said to cause the disease *chiwengo*.

The term *chiwengo* refers to an ailment that is brought about by eating certain kinds of meat. It is derived from the verb *ku-wenga*, to bring out in spots. Although Scott (1929: 411) notes that it covers also nettle rash and eczema, it is essentially associated with meat-eating and as a disease (*nthenda*) is usually distinguished from scabies (*mphere*), leprosy (*khate*), sores (*mphere*) and smallpox (*nthomba*). The suggestion made in Yao oral traditions (N. Khondiwa *et al.* 1977) that the eating of porcupine will cause leprosy was not confirmed by my researches, but it is thought that it may lead to the skin disease *chiwengo*. But although this disease is specifically associated with animals that are tabooed on religious grounds or in terms of clan affiliations (*nyama zosala*, prohibited meat) – and such animals as bushpig, porcupine, bushbuck and domestic ducks (*bakha*) are frequently mentioned in this connection – there is also the belief that a skin rash (*chiwengo*) may result from eating any animal whose meat does not accord with a person's own physical constitution. As one woman put it, *Zimawenga malinga ndi thupi lamunthu* 'You develop spots or skin eruptions according to the body of the person'. A game guard expressed it in similar fashion: *Nyama kapena ndi nyani sanagwirizana ndi thupi lache apezeka agwira matenda achiwengo, ndiye chiwengo chimakhala chakutiumu mutuluka timibulu-mbulu tachonchi ndiye pokhanda pakhonza kamatuluka magazi* 'Meat/animal, perhaps a baboon that doesn't accord with their body, they contract the disease *chiwengo*, then spots (sores) come out and if scratched will cause much bleeding'.

It may be noted that the wild hunting dog is called *mbulu*. It has a spotted, patchy coat and is eaten by very few people. Medicinal herbs are mainly used to treat *chiwengo*, but the meat and skins of certain animals are also thought to be a cure for this skin ailment. These include the buffalo, the spiny mouse and fat mouse.

I have reviewed above some empirical data relating to meat-eating (as food) in Malawi. The evidence suggests that not only is meat-eating important to Malawians, but, contrary to what Adams implies, it is eaten and enjoyed by both men and women. Although cultural representations in Malawi symbolically associate men, or rather affinal males, with mammals, and both with the Brachystegia woodland, the eating of meat was by no means restricted to men. Such categories (woodland, animals, affinal males) essentially form a complementary opposition to the domain of the village, the cultivations (*munda*) and matrilineal kinship (for in an important sense in Malawi kinship subsumes and takes priority over the gender categories). There is thus an essential kinship expressed between male affines and wild mammals, and in the ritual context they are virtually identified. In terms of their symbolic logic, therefore, and consonant with Fiddes own mode of reasoning, men – the affinal males – ought not to eat meat. But of course they do, as well as eating the porridge that derives from the domain of matrilineal kinship (agriculture). It follows, therefore, that there is a symbolic opposition expressed between women (kinship, agriculture) and animals (male affines, hunting). In Malawi the in-marrying affine is frequently referred to not only as *tambala* (cock), but also as a hyena, the prototypical wild animal. What one finds in the Malawian cultural context, therefore, is a series of symbolic equations which can be presented in summary fashion as follows:

earth	+	rain	=	agricultural	
substance		'fertilizing' agency		productivity	
agriculture	+	hunting	=	communal	
		(fishing)		life	
blood	+	semen	=	human	
substance		activating		child	
		form			
herbs	+	activating	=	curative	
(*mitengo*)		animal		medicines	
		substances		(*mankhwala*)	
		(*chizimba*)			
kinship	+	affines	=	collectivity	
banda		phiri		of	
ancestral		clan		spirits	
clan					
(*mizimu*)					
village	+	wooded	=	country	
(*mudzi*)		hills		(*dziko*)	
		(*thengo*)			

These are not radical but complementary, oppositions, and human life and well-being involves the sustaining and harmonious union of the two contrasting domains. Thus it is – following the same cultural logic – that the ideal basic meal consists of two distinct components, namely the porridge (*nsima*), which is derived from agricultural work focussed around a group of matrilineally related women (kin), and a relish (*ndiwo*). The latter ideally consists of meat (*nyama*) obtained from an affinal male through hunting in the woodland. Neither *nsima* nor *ndiwo*, on their own, constitute a 'meal' (*chakudya*) by Malawian reckoning. Both are necessary and both men and women need the two constituents for health and well-being, the porridge giving the sustenance or the substance to a meal, the meat relish supplying its strengthening quality. The term *nyama*, in fact, besides meaning meat or wild animal, also refers to vital energy or to the essential property of a thing. Given a gender hierarchy, implicit even within a matrilineal context, men are invariably given prominence in the distribution of the valued relish, but it would be misleading to see meat-eating as simply reflecting 'male power'. Nor can meat-eating be viewed as simply reflecting a Promethean ethic or a social attitude of domination over nature. It does indeed reflect a philosophy of power, for it is through meat-eating – as well as, alternatively, through animal medicines and rituals – that humans, both men and women, are able to harness the powers inherent in wild nature: the woodland, the abode of both wild animals and the ancestral spirits. Ultimately it is from the woodland that fertility is derived, whether in the form of rain or semen, which are, in Malawi, symbolically associated.

With respect to food prohibitions relating to meat, I also tried to indicate that these are subject to wide individual variation and are not specifically related to either gender or ethnicity. Religious affiliation, however, is a important factor, as are totemic associations; and the eating of meat of a totemic species is thought to give rise to the skin disease *chiwengo*, even though this ailment is also seen in terms of an individual's physical constitution. Given the wide variations in individual dietary preference – although I did not meet any Malawian who was a vegetarian – the explanation of dietary prohibitions simply in terms of cosmological or classificatory schemes is clearly inadequate.

I turn now to the use of animals in medicines.

Animals as Medicine

In June 1991 the national newspaper of Malawi, the *Daily Times*, carried a news item with the heading, 'Scramble for Hyena's Brain'. It reported on the 'pandemonium' that had broken out at Nthalire trading centre. Apparently a hyena had been killed by the Karonga/Chitipa bus near Changoloma Hill. The driver had picked up the animal and had taken it to the trading centre for viewing. When the news got around of the hyena's demise, crowds of people soon rushed to the scene, brandishing knives and axes. Within minutes, one eyewitness, Mathews Kamphambe reported, 'People started hacking the hyena's head for its brain while other jostled for the tail and its other parts'. The Malawi news agency concluded the article with the words: 'The brain and tail of the hyena are believed to be potent magical medicines'.

The same month the *Daily Times* carried another news item entitled 'Guarding Dead Hyena'. It gave a brief report of how personnel from the Wildlife Department had to stand guard over a hyena that had been hit by a car early one morning near Lingadzi Inn in the city of Lilongwe. This was to stop people from hacking off certain parts of it which were said 'to be useful in making charms' (*Daily Times*, 6 June 1991).

These reports indicate the passion many Malawians have to acquire certain animals for medicinal purposes – and the hyena is not alone in this regard. Yet, rather surprisingly, animals (as medicine) are hardly mentioned in Janzen's (1992) important study of 'cults of affliction' in central and southern Africa. He notes that the sacrifice of chickens and goats is one of the core features of these rituals, but he sees such sacrifices simply in terms of atonement and exchange and has nothing to say about animals as medicine nor even on the close relationship, evident in a world-wide context, that seems to exist between animals and spirits of the dead. Indeed, he has a rather theological approach to African therapeutic systems, seeing all medical traditions and practices as essentially focused around spirit-healing, around 'rituals of affliction', which he sees as a pan-Bantu institution. He titles this institution *ngoma*, a word that prototypically means 'drum' throughout Africa. But like the cognate term 'dance', it may come to have a wider meaning, covering not only communal rituals of affliction, but also initiations and secular entertainment. While, in his early study, Janzen (1978) was concerned to emphasize the diverse and pluralistic nature of the 'quest for therapy' in Lower Zaire, the institution *ngoma*, focussed as it is on 'spirit rituals', has a rather totalizing quality, subsuming all other 'medical' beliefs and practices. Janzen makes some important criticisms of the tendency of scholars to conflate what he calls the 'spirit hypothesis' with spirit possession *per se*, and he recognizes that there is an important practical and empirical dimension to the rituals, but his essential thesis is that the 'spirit' rituals provide the major framework that sets up and legitimizes as an 'institution' 'many kinds of perspectives and theories' (ibid.: 176). It is hardly surprising, then, that witches and spirits of the dead tend to be virtually equated, all being part of the same world view, and the herbalist and the 'secular cosmological' traditions – the latter relating to conceptions of colour, blood and a 'balance' between hot and cold in the maintenance of health – becomes completely marginalized, or is seen simply as an adjunct to a ritual process that is essentially 'spiritual'. Bewailing the fact that other anthropologists have been preoccupied and fixated on exotic trance and possession (ibid.), Janzen himself seems equally obsessed with the 'spirit hypothesis' and its associated 'performance ritual' and discourse, although he is alive to the need to situate such 'rituals of affliction' in a social and historical context. My misgivings about Janzen's study are thus not with the content of the study itself, focussed as it is on 'cults of affliction'. The study is exemplary. It is rather on what is left out – the empirical dimension to African thought. Herbalism, used in its widest sense to include animal substances – which is how people in Malawi use the concept of medicine, *mankhwala* – is as much a pan-Bantu 'institution', with its own theories and practices, as are 'cults of affliction': and both, of course, have wide cross cultural reference that extends beyond the Bantu context.

Having 'broken down', as Janzen puts it (1992: 4), the division between religion and healing, the latter is now verily equated with religion, with spirit-healing. It is indeed described as the 'classical' healing system of central and southern Africa (ibid.: 9). Some time ago Kwasi Wiredu (1981) remarked that one of the ways in which African culture was continuously being misunderstood was through the 'exaggeration' of the role of religion in African life, to the neglect of its empirical aspects. Contrary to the ethos that Janzen portrays, African culture, it seems to me, is less concerned with 'spirit' than with life; it is pantheistic or biocentric rather than theocentric. Although Janzen has a central focus on 'health', especially on its 'social reproduction', he nowhere examines the indigenous concepts of life, even though the book is essentially concerned with a lexical exploration of proto-Bantu concepts. In Malawi, *moyo* (life) is not only the principle of animate life but also the generally recognized term for health and well-being in its widest meaning. In an important sense, therefore, African thought is closer to that of Aristotle than to the Judeo-Christian tradition, with its dualistic Neoplatonic emphasis 'god' being seen as outside the world and material existence as being in essence 'unreal' or 'lifeless', plant and animal substances only having efficacy if 'activated' by cultural metaphors, eidos or spirit. For Janzen 'metaphors' have 'active agency', 'power', and 'efficacy' because of their association with the 'spirits', but seemingly plants and animals do not: they are, it seems, 'lifeless', without intrinsic efficacy or power. Medicines only become powerful, he writes, if the ancestors are invoked (1992: 67).

This Neoplatonic kind of interpretation is similar to that of Maurice Bloch (1992), who, in a recent analysis of ritual, sees the 'spirits' as the antithesis of life and vitality. Becoming a spirit is to become dry, bone-like, lifeless. But as Eliade (1960: 83) long ago recognized, the bones and skins of animals – and animal life is intrinsically connected with the spirits of the dead – do not represent the antithesis of life, but rather its essence, life that does not die. This belief in 'life' as an ongoing process via immaterial spirits is, however, by no means restricted to the Bantu context. It represents an episteme or world view quite different from that of Neoplatonism and the Judeo-Christian tradition, with, its radical dualism of spirit and vital matter, a dualism that was inherited and developed by the mechanistic philosophers of the seventeenth century. Carlo Ginzberg (1991), attempting to unearth the folkloric roots of Indo-European culture, has stressed its shamanistic origins, involving the close identity between spirits and animal life reflected in the use of animal bones and skins. He writes of the 'profound identification' of animals with the dead (ibid.: 262), and the same may be said of the Malawian context. 'Spirit', for Malawians, is the essence of life, not its negation or antithesis. So are skins and hairs and tails – which is why they have medicinal value.

It is of interest that, while many contemporary scholars give a very theological or Neoplatonic interpretation of African culture (cf. Idowu 1973; Gyekye 1987), the founders of African ethnophilosophy were much more inclined towards Aristotle, whose philosophy, as Mayr (1988: 59) suggested, can only be fully understood if Aristotle is seen for what he is – fundamentally a biological thinker. Thus Tempels (1959), in a famous text, argued that the key to Bantu thought was the idea of 'vital force'. He wrote,

> In the minds of Bantus, all beings in the universe posses a vital force of their own: human, animal, vegetable, or inanimate. Each being has been endowed by God with a certain force, capable of strengthening the vital energy of the strongest beings of all creation . . . .. (the) Bantu speak, act, live, as if, for them, beings were forces (1959: 32–5).

He thus argues that there is a fundamental difference between Western thought – which allegedly has static conception of being (he evidently has Plato in mind) – and that of the Bantu, who have a dynamic conception of being. There has been a welter of criticism levelled at Tempel's thesis, but his general approach has affinities with that of Alexis Kagame (1956), who continually evokes Aristotle and has I think some substance (for useful discussions of these writers, see Mbiti 1969: 10–11; Hountondjii 1983: 38–44 – who suggests that Bantu philosophy is a myth – and Mudimbe 1988: 50, 145–52). For the central concept, *ntu* does not mean (as Janzen suggests, 1992: 58) 'person', but is a much wider category, meaning, in Malawi at least, 'being' or 'substance'.

Chinthu in Chichewa refers to 'things', *kanthu* colloquially to 'anything' and *munthu* to a person (pl. *anthu*). *Nthawi*, which is derived from the same root, means 'time', and by extension, 'space'. Although Malawians do not explicitly articulate the kind of ontological categories suggested by writers like Kagame (1956), the root *nthu* certainly has close affinities with Aristotle's concept of substance (*ousia*). For, like Aristotle and the pre-Socratics – and in contrast to the Neoplatonists – Malawians have a dynamic conception of being. The material world is conceived as an active substance with potentiality. God is not a being outside the world but a shaper, the nourisher and the ultimate source of life within the world. Malawians make a clear distinction, again like Aristotle, between those aspects of the natural world that have life (*moyo*) and those things that do not (*zinthu zopanda moyo*). In conversations with people regarding what entities have life (*zili ndi moyo*), it is generally regarded that the following have life: *mtengo* (tree), *mbalame* (birds), *nyama* (animal), *njoka* (snakes), *bowa* (edible mushrooms) and spirit entities such as *napolo* (a serpent-spirit associated with the mountain) and *mizimu* (spirits or souls of the dead). There is ambiguity as to whether or not soil (*thaka*) and water (*madzi*) have life, but neither *phiri* (mountains) and rocks (*mwala*) are considered to have life. It is thus clearly evident that Malawians recognize a category of living things (*zamoyo*). It is important to note that for Malawians, ancestral spirits (*mizimu*) are a part of the world and have life; and it is thus misleading to see the dead (*amanda*, 'those of the grave', almost always addressed in plural form) as somehow in opposition to or as the negation of life. Life in a sense is an ongoing process that includes the living and the dead. The skins, horns and claws of a dead mammal are thus like the spirit: they are not dead but represent the essence of life as an ongoing process and, with regard to certain mammals, they have intrinsic efficacy as medicine. In a sense it is not animals that are associated with spirits but dead animals: in life there is a fundamental opposition in a dialectical sense between humans and animals; in death (and ritual) humans (as spirits) and animals are united, even equated. John Mbiti was, therefore, essentially correct when he referred to the spirits of the dead as the 'living dead' (1969: 25).

Although Malawians, conceive of the spirits of the ancestors (*mzimu ya makolo*) as being symbolically associated with certain animals and trees or even in certain circumstances taking the form of animals, it would be quite misleading to describe their world view as spiritual or animistic. They do not conceive of the whole world as animate (any more than did Aristotle), only certain aspects of it, and although they make a distinction between *moyo* (life) and *mzimu* (spirit of the dead), specifically associating the latter with humans only, the two notions are closely identified, since life, human life in particular, is nourished and regenerated by the spirits of the dead. Because mammals more than any other aspect of the material world embody life and power, and because the essence of life is essentially conceived as residing in the outer coverings, as it were, of the mammal, substances such as skins, horns, teeth, bones and tails are believed to have intrinsic power and efficacy, power that may be used, of course, for diverse ends.

In my studies of comparative medical systems (1986b, 1989a, 1989b), I tried to indicate that a clear distinction could be drawn between three medical traditions that coexisted throughout the world. These were: an empirical herbalist tradition, based on a belief in the intrinsic efficacy of certain plant and animal substances; a cosmological tradition, which saw the human subject as a microcosm of the world and in which health was seen as restoring a balance or mix between certain vital 'humours' or principles; and a tradition that was focused on 'communal rituals of affliction' and involved spirit healing. Although these traditions often overlapped and the use of herbal medicine was often – but not always – a component of all three traditions, they were, I felt, nevertheless distinct. At different times and in certain contexts there were often tensions and conflicts between the different practitioners of these three traditions. What Foster and Anderson (1978) long ago described as a 'naturalistic' system of medicine relates, of course, to the cosmological traditions of Europe and Asia: Greek medicine and its development as Unani, Ayurveda and the classical tradition of Chinese medicine, as this focussed on Confucian scholars and the state. It was these traditions that became professionalized with the development of the theocratic empires.

Until recently, therapeutic systems in Africa have been essentially part of a folk tradition, but, as I have tried to show in my studies of herbalism in Malawi (1996a), this tradition is pluralistic and diverse and, as else-where, consists of several distinct systems, each with its own etiological emphasis and medical practitioners, the herbalist, diviner and spirit medium having distinct therapeutic roles and strategies. That there is a secular medical tradition with its own cultural logic, separate from both herbalism and spirit-healing, has also to be recognized. It revolves around what Richards described as 'blood, sex and fire' (1956: 30, cf. Laguerre 1987: 64–72) and is fundamentally concerned with 'balance'. In Africa 'medicine' underpins all the different folk traditions. In a sense 'herbalism', not spirit healing, is the classical, even if prosaic, therapeutic tradition of Africa. In a perceptive essay written many years ago, Douglas (1954: 7) stressed the importance of medicines in the Lele context, noting how the idiom of medicine so dominated their religious ritual that it was often hard to distinguish the two spheres of action. In Malawi the use of medicine permeates cultural life, and it is highly misleading to see it simply as an adjunct to spirit healing.

I want to focus on only one of these traditions, the herbalist tradition, and to examine specifically which mammals are used as medicine in Malawi within this empirical domain. Mammals, of course, are widely used in Malawi as medicine in other contexts, in rituals of afflictions such as *vimbuza, malombo* and *nantongwe*, and in initiation rites (*chinamwali, jando, chiputu*). They also play a crucial role in the *nyau* and *chinambande* rituals of the Chewa and Yao, respectively, when the spirits of the dead make their appearance at initiations in the form of mammals (hare, elephant, lion, hippo and various antelopes), humans essentially forming the flesh, the substance, of the *mzimu*, the horns, skins and tail of the animal structures constituting their forms. Mammals (*zirombo*) and spirits of the dead (*mizimu*) are thus intrinsically identified in these rites.

In Malawi there is a close and intimate relationship between plants and medicine, as elsewhere in Africa, where such concepts as *nguo* and *muti* are polysemic, meaning both woody plant and medicine. In Yao, *ntera* has this polysemy. But in Malawi, generally, a distinction is made between woody plants (*mtengo),* grasses (*maudzu*) and mushrooms (*bowa*) and medicine. The term for medicine is *mankhwala,* which is a cognate of the widespread term *bwanga* and is used to cover a variety of substances believed to possess an inherent potency and efficacy. In fact the term essentially refers to this vital power. It thus covers various charms, amulets and protective medicines, as well as medicines in the normal sense. Western pharmaceuticals and agricultural fertilizers are also called by the same term. It thus embraces, as White wrote with respect to the Luvale of Zambia, 'an aperient or a headache cure . . .a lucky charm or a device to injure one's neighbour (1948: 99)'. The general term for the traditional healer in Malawi, *sing'anga,* is derived from the term for medicine and essentially means 'medicine person'. The prototypical *sing'anga* is the herbalist, but the term is extended also to cover other healers such as diviners and spirit mediums. It is worth emphasizing that, although anthropologists have a strong proclivity to work with famous spirit mediums, the majority of healers to be found in Malawi are ordinary folk herbalists of both sexes (Morris, 1986a). The majority of substances used for *mankhwala* are plant materials: the roots, leaves, bark, fruit and seeds of various plant species. This seems to be a common pattern among many other African communities, for as the Kriges wrote with regard to the Lovedu, 'Fully 80 percent are of vegetable origin. There is hardly a plant in that rich lowveld vegetation that is not used in the pharmacopoeia of some herbalist or doctor' (1943: 215).

I would put this figure even higher for Malawi and suggest that the vast majority of medicines used by Malawians are of plant origin. In my studies of the medicinal plants of Malawi (1996a), I have recorded over 500 species used as medicine. Such medicines may be used for a wide variety of purposes, extending far beyond the therapeutic context, for good luck charms, for assistance in a variety of activities and concerns (hunting, friendship, employment, marriage, agriculture, court cases), as protective medicine against witches, at all important initiations (especially funerals and maturity rites), for potency and reproductive purposes, and to counter the ill effects of illicit intercourse, as well as herbal remedies for a wide variety of ailments.

In rural areas most people have a wide knowledge of herbalism, and folk herbalists and market herbalists are found throughout Malawi. The stalls of the latter contain a fascinating array of every conceivable part of any animal or plant used for medicinal purposes. Typically on the counter one may find rows of bottles containing infusions of various roots and barks, all coloured differently, owl pellets and the beaks of small birds, various animals horns, porcupine quills, pieces of hedgehog spines, pangolin scales, hyena dung, snake skins, particularly that of the python (*sato*), various tins or gourds containing resin, oil, ashes or powders, animal skins (serval is a favourite) as well as great quantities of plant material: freshly gathered leaves and fruits, seeds, pieces of bark and the roots of a wide variety of different plants. Given the esoteric impression that these stalls conjure up for many Europeans – and for some Malawians – it is, I think, worth stressing that the bulk of the saleable items on these stalls, as well as what is offered by the ordinary village herbalist, consists of plant materials which are believed to have therapeutic value. The stalls of some market herbalists consist essentially of bottles containing bark and root infusions, together with medicinal herbs, while one herbalist I knew at Migowi only had two bottles – the other commodities were roots – of which he had an enormous pile for sale. What esoteric impression these market stalls can invoke can be gleaned from Landeg White's description of one 'native doctor' selling medicines at Chimwalira. Medicines were offered to White to bring him good luck and sexual potency and to prevent thieves from ambushing him in his car. But the herbalist also had 'wrinkled pods and seeds and dried herbs for headaches, diarrhea, constipation and barrenness'. White eventually brought some good luck medicine, a lion's tooth (actually the tusk of a warthog), for K15 – almost a months wage for an agricultural worker in Malawi at that time. The herbalist lives, White writes, 'by imagination and wit and, what he sells are metaphors' (White 1987: 250–1). His metaphors seem to have worked on White! It is, however, very misleading and one-sided to see the herbalist in Malawi as simply dispensing 'metaphors', for he is crucially concerned with selling medicines – animal and plant substances that are believed to have intrinsic efficacy and power. Like Janzen, and most academics it would seem, White frequents a cultural space that is largely divorced from the material world of plants and animals, a world where language and symbol have primacy. Thus for White, like Janzen, ideas and metaphors seemingly have more reality than the plants and animals themselves. And the latter constitute part of a life-world whose essential ethos and meaning is lost if it is equated, as it usually is, simply with the economic or the pragmatic. Analogical thought, of course, permeates Malawian cultural life, and I vividly remember on one occasion asking one of my herbalist friends why the herb *Nyambata (Desmodium velutinum)* was so widely used as a medicine for friendship and love (*mankhwala achikonda*). He immediately picked a leaf from the plant, slapped it with gusto on my shirt, to which it adhered, and asked, *sagwirizana*, 'doesn't it hold?'. The homeopathic element of medicines is well known to local herbalists (cf. Evans-Pritchard 1937: 449), but this is no reason to presume, with Turner, that 'sympathetic magic' accounts for the employment of the majority of 'medicines', even in the ritual context (1967: 343). But the important symbolic dimension to life, given free play in the ritual context, and the fact that animals and plants are widely used metaphorically in Malawi should not lead us to ignore or devalue (as with Plato) the 'natural' powers that are believed to inhere in plants and animals, conceptualized by Aristotle as 'necessity'.

It is therefore important to stress that for Malawians, the plants (and even more so the animals) used as medicine are seen to have intrinsic powers and thus to have inherent curing properties. Apart from writers like Idowu (1973: 199) and Janzen (1992: 149), who seem to think that medicines only have efficacy if 'spirits' are invoked or if they become 'metaphors' through song and rite, most anthropologists writing on African cultures have stressed the widespread belief that plant medicines have intrinsic powers. Richards, for example, writes of *bwanga* (which like many early anthropologists she translates as 'magic', though 'vital power' would perhaps be more appropriate) that it is for the Bemba the force 'contained in the leaves, roots or bark of various trees and shrubs and a number of activating agencies (*fishimba*), such as parts of animals and human beings' which are used by the Nganga for a variety of purposes (1956: 29). Turner likewise, although acknowledging that the distinction between medicine as a 'drug' and as a 'ritual symbol' is not easily drawn (the distinction betrays a dualism that is quite contrary to Ndembu thought), suggests that for these people 'All things are felt to be charged with powers of various kinds and it is the job of the herbalist and ritual specialist to manipulate these for the benefit of society' (1967: 335). Writers on Zulu medicine have also stressed the powers inherent in medicinal substances (*imithi*). Ngubane notes that many medicines are believed to contain potency in themselves, independent of any ritual context (1977: 109), while Berglund in his detailed ethnographic text emphasizes that practically all the various species of vegetation, collectively known as *imithi* (medicine), are believed to contain intrinsic power (*amanda*) embedded in the material substances. The power is, he writes, 'embedded in the species itself and may be manipulated by humans for both good and evil purposes (1976: 256–7). It is equivalent to the Malawian concept of *mankhwala*, which as said is distinct from such enthnobiological categories as *nyama* (edible quadruped), *bowa* (fungi) and *mtengo* (woody plant) and which is used both as a rubric for medicinal substances and to refer to the intrinsic power that these substances contain. To interpret this vital power in theological terms as 'spirit' (in opposition to the material world) would not, I think, be appropriate, for Malawians do not make a categorical distinction between the natural and the spiritual realms (cf. Turner 1967: 302 on the Ndembu).

What is equally important, however, in the Malawian context is that an important distinction is drawn between general medicines that are used for a variety of purposes, which may or may not have symbolic import, and a special group of medicines called *chizimba*. These are seen as essentially 'activating' medicines which give additional power to the other medicines. In my paper on herbalism and divination in Malawi (Morris 1986a), I stressed that with respect to the more serious and chronic ailments that came before the diviner, the medicines have to work, as it were, on two levels. At the empirical level of symptoms, medicines are thus given with the purpose of healing (*kuchira*) the body ailment; at the level of causation, the body is protected (*kutsirika*) from further harm by medicines which ward off witches (*afiti*). As far as the diviners are concerned both kinds of substances are medicine (*mankhwala*), though their effects are different: both are considered necessary for treatment. Importantly, however, medicines used to counter sorcery or witchcraft or to influence the spirits tend also to include animal substances, whereas the purely empirical treatment of diseases or the treatment of minor ailments invariably involves only herbal remedies. The tendency to focus on the 'sorcery' or etiological aspect of therapy has led many writers to undervalue the empirical dimension of disease treatment. For this reason, to translate *mankhwala* as 'magical substances', as Marwick does (1965: 256) with reference to the Chewa of Zambia, seems to me somewhat misleading. There is nothing particularly 'magical' or 'mysterious' about the majority of medicines used in Malawi.

The recognition of a special class of medicines that have 'activating' properties has been widely reported in the literature, though, given his focus on 'spirit' healing, it is not mentioned by Janzen (1992). But his earlier seminal work on patterns of therapy among the Bakongo of Lower Zaire does indicate a similar demarcation, namely between the *nganga mbuki* (herbalist) and his therapeutic practices, and the *nganga nkisi*, whom Janzen describes as a 'magical operator'. The latter alone has 'knowledge' and uses 'consecrated' medicines (1978: 45). However, Janzen makes no mention at all of the use of animals as medicine, which is of interest, given the important role that animals play in the cultural life of the Lele. In Zambia, however, a special class of activating medicines associated with animals is recognized. Among the Bemba, as Richards records, animals are thought to have 'magical' attributes, and parts of their skin and bones 'are used as activating principles (*ifishimba*) in many charms and medicines' (1939: 343).

Among the Ndembu likewise, there is a special class of medicines (*mpelu*) that is distinct from the general medicines, the latter consisting primarily of plant material (*yitumbu*). *Mpelu* medicines, it would seem, consist essentially of parts of animals: Turner mentions antbear, wild pig, leopard, hyrax and rabid dog, as well as humans (1967: 304, 318–19). He sees this as 'symbolic' and as operating by 'contagious magic', a suggestion that presupposes that these animals embody and transmit intrinsic power. In her recent study, Edith Turner (1992) describes *mpelu* as 'vital medicine' or as 'magical substances'. Besides the *nsomu* medicine kept in a mongoose skin bag, which contains the horn of a blue duiker and the tendon of an elephant, Turner notes that the category *mpelu* also includes the famous *ihamba*, the subject not only of her own book (1992) but of Victor Turner's early studies (1967: 359–93, 1968: 156–97). *Ihamba* is a healing cult associated with hunting, the term referring to the upper incisor tooth of a dead hunter, which embeds itself in the body of the inflicted person. The tooth is therefore identified with the spirit (*mukishi*) of the dead hunter, who is said to 'bite' its/his victim for being neglected. The tooth is also an object of 'contagious magic' (*mpelu*) and has the character of a hunting charm or amulet. Turner's study is centrally concerned with her own spiritual experience and how the *ihamba* spirit was made visible. But essentially what the book portrays is the strong pantheistic ethos that pervades Ndembu culture, where, through a close pre-occupation with life processes, the spiritual (i.e. immaterial) and material aspects of being are closely identified. It is not pantheistic in Spinozian terms, involving the notion that god is identical with the world, but pantheistic in the sense that there is a close identity between spirits of the dead and the animal world, which includes humans. Mazrui (1986: 50–1) has indeed described the indigenous African world view as 'afro-pantheism'.

In his classical study of sorcery among the Chewa of eastern Zambia, Marwick writes that Chewa medicines are made from the roots, leaves and other parts of woody plants, but that, to be effective, they require the addition of 'activating agents' (*chizimba,* pl. *vizimba*) of human or animal origin. The *chizimba* gives the medicines potency, and they can then be used for a variety of 'magical' purposes (1965: 70). Given his focus on sorcery, Marwick tends to see *chizimba* as essentially activating otherwise 'inert' root concoctions (ibid.: 300), but as we have seen in Malawi and elsewhere, plants themselves have efficacy and power (as do substances used as food). What animal substances do is to give additional power (*mphamvu*) in dealing with more complex issues, concerns that have a more immaterial quality, such as success in employment or hunting, stable and fulfilling relationships, good crops and protection from the ill effects of sorcery, which itself involves the harmful use of powerful medicines. In Malawi, *chizimba* is thus often associated specifically with diviners (*asing'anga*), who are thought to possess and to have knowledge of the respective medicines, invariably the skins, bones, teeth and horns of animals or humans. As protective medicines (*ku-tsirika*) they relate to the body (*thupi*), garden (*munda*) or household (*nyumba*). The *chizimba* medicine is always only one ingredient in a remedy which contains several herbs and is seen as 'strengthening' the medicine. In contrast, ordinary herbal remedies are 'simples' given by 'empirics'. There is a contrast too in the administration of the medicines. Ordinary herbal medicines, lacking *chizimba*, are usually drunk as an infusion, taken with thin porridge (*phala*) or inhaled as a vapour. Although herbal medicine may be used as a wash, essentially it is taken internally. In contrast, medicines containing activating substances (*chizimba*) are administered externally, at the boundaries of the garden, house or the body. The medicines are thus ground and reduced to ashes (*kuocha*) and the ashes rubbed into body incisions (*ku-temerera*) or used as a wash, the medicinal waters being sprinkled by means of a medicine tail. Alternatively the ingredients, including the *chizimba*, may be put in groundnut or castor oil and the oil used to anoint the body (*ku-dzola*) after bathing. More serious ailments often entail the use of *chizimba*. The strong association between these 'activating' substances and animals has to be stressed, along with the association of animal substances (horns, skins, teeth) with the spirits of the dead. *Chizimba* is a cognate of *uzimba*, which is a general term for the communal hunt: in the past, Zimba referred to an 'ethnic' group of professional elephant hunters who made incursions into Malawi from the Zambezi region (Alpers 1975: 46–50, Mandala 1990: 89).

To give the local sense of *chizimba*, I give the words below of a Blantyre herbalist, Heronimo Kanjanga, whom I have known for more than a decade:

> *Chizimba* is a kind of medicine (*gulula mankhwala*). Its work is to strengthen (*kulimbikiza*) the medicine, so that it has power (*ndimphamvu*). Medicine without *chizimba* lacks power. It is the animal substance (*chizimba cha nyama*) that gives the medicine its power, and with it the medicine works on many ailments (*ntchito kwa mathenda onse*). For example, in the treatment of rheumatism (*nyamakazi*), we take several horns (*mitengo*) together with a scorpion (*nankalizi*) and burn them (*kuocha*) and the ashes are applied to incisions on the person (*kuntemera munthu*) to cure the ailment (*imatha*). If a person is sick with large head (*mutawaukulu*), we cut various herbs into small pieces, and these we cook (*tikaphika*), together with the blood (*magazi*) of a chicken (*nkhuku*), which is the *chizimba*. For other ailments like stomachache and *kanyera* (a wasting disease affecting men) we do not use activating substances. For epilepsy (*chifufu*) we take various woody plants (*mitengo*), and as *chizimba* we use the teeth (*mano*) of the warthog (*njiri*). Thus there is a difference between some diseases where we use activating substances and other diseases where no *chizimba* is used to protect the body (*oteteza thupi*).

Activating medicines involving animals are thus used to strengthen or 'give power' to herbal remedies, and they may be used both for positive ends (for healing, as good luck charms, for success in hunting, employment and court cases, and as a love potion) and for destructive purposes associated with sorcery (*matsenga*). Because of the latter associations, many famous spirit healers in Malawi such as Chikanga and Bwanali profess not to have any dealings with *vizimba* medicines. In the past it is evident that the teeth and claws of such animals as the crocodile, lion, leopard and other beasts of prey were widely worn around the neck as protective amulets (Maugham 1910: 367, Stannus 1922: 291). Even today these substances are frequently used as medicines. All circumcisors in the boys' initiation rites of the Yao (*jando*) and many diviners drape themselves with the skins, tails and claws of the animals that are considered to invoke power – leopard, serval, genet, crocodile, snake. The circumciser is referred to in Yao as a *mmichila*, which essentially means 'person of the tail' (*mchira*, tail), and the horns of antelope and the skins of animals such as the sun squirrel and genet are frequently used in divination rites. In a sense, by draping themselves in the skins of animals, these ritual specialists invoke the spirits of the dead, who take the form of animals (cf. the photographs in Chavunduka 1978); and the spirits get their power not simply because they are spirits, but because they are intrinsically associated with animals, which themselves express and embody the inherent powers of nature. Recent studies of the Dogon (van Beek and Banga 1992) have indicated that for these people the 'bush' is the ultimate source of power, knowledge and life energy. This is true also in Malawi, but Malawians conceive of such powers more in terms of substances, and as derived from specific plants and animals.

Table 15 indicates the medicinal uses of animals in Malawi. It is based on my own personal observations of the animal substances used as medicine by several herbalists and diviners whom I knew well. Potentially, of course, all animals may be used as an activating substance (*chizimba*), and I have no doubt that many other animals I have not recorded may be used by herbalists in Malawi for medicinal purposes. It is worth noting too that many of the larger mammal species have a restricted distribution or are confined to wildlife sanctuaries. Before discussing the main species used as medicine, however, some general observations may be made.

First, although some animals are widely used as both food and medicine – civet, serval, hyrax, giant rat – there does seem to be an almost inverse relationship between food and medicine; those animals that are important sources of medicine are thus not generally eaten. In this connection, it is worth noting the contents of the famous witches brew in Shakespeare's Macbeth. Almost every component of the brew, as Fiddes notes (1991: 18) is of animal origin – slowworm, bat, adder, lizard, frog, newt, toad and dog. What he does not mention is that none of these animals formed a part of the natural diet of people during this period; their use in the brew was 'medicinal', using this term in its Malawian sense.

It should be noted, however, that although antelopes are greatly esteemed as meat (*nyama*) by all Malawians and are generally not noted for their medicinal uses, their horns (*nyanga*) and tail (*mchira*) are crucially important as medicine. The horns, though significant in a positive sense in divination rites, in which they become the medium of the ancestral spirit, and as a protective medicine, are also widely associated with sorcery. Their horns with their associated medicines may thus be seen as having a potentially destructive (*ku-unonga*) power when holding certain

Table 15. Animals as medicine

	status as food	protection against sorcery	strengthening medicine	good luck medicine	spirit illnesses	medicine for subsistence activities	medicine for general ailments	association with witchcraft
wild dog *mbulu*	x	✓						
side-striped jackal *nkhandwe*	x	✓	✓					✓
otter *katumbu*	o	✓		✓		✓		
ratel *chiuli*	x	✓	✓		✓	✓		
zorilla *kanyimbi*	x	✓						
civet *chombwe*	✓	✓		✓		✓		
genet *mwili*	✓	✓					✓	
mongoose sp. *nyenga*	✓			✓		✓		
marsh mongoose *khakhakha*	x				✓			
banded mongoose *msulu*	x				✓			✓
spotted hyena *fisi*	x	✓	✓			✓		
leopard *nyalugwe*	x	✓	✓			✓		
lion *mkango*	x	✓	✓			✓		
serval *njuzi*	✓	✓		✓				
wild cat *bvumbwe*	x							
elephant *njobvu*	✓	✓	✓	✓		✓		
black rhino *chipembere*	✓		✓			✓		
burchell's zebra *mbidzi*	✓	✓				✓		
warthog *njiri*	✓	✓					✓	
bushpig *ngulawe*	✓	✓	✓			✓	✓	
hippopotamus *mvuu*	✓	✓				✓		✓
hartebeest *ngondo*	✓							

Table 15. Animals as medicine (*continued*)

	status as food	protection against sorcery	strengthening medicine	good luck medicine	spirit illnesses	medicine for subsistence activities	medicine for general ailments	association with witchcraft
blue duiker *kadumba*	✓					✓	✓	
grey duiker *gwapi*	✓	✓	✓		✓			
klipspringer *chinkhoma*	✓						✓	
sharpe's grysbok *kasenye*	✓						✓	
impala *nswala*	✓							
roan *chilembwe*	✓	✓						
sable *mphalapala*	✓	✓						
buffalo *njati*	✓		✓				✓	
kudu *ngoma*	✓							
nyala *boo*	✓							
bushback *mbawala*	✓				✓			
eland *ntchefu*	✓	✓						
reedbuck *mphoyo*	✓					✓		
waterbuck *nakodzwe*	✓						✓	
elephant shrew *sakhwi*	✓				✓	✓	✓	
musk shrew *sunche*	x	✓		✓	✓	✓	✓	
cane rat *nchenzi*	✓		✓			✓	✓	
mole rat *namfuko*	✓	✓					✓	
angoni vlei rat *thiri*	✓						✓	
bushveld gerbil *phanya*	✓	✓	✓		✓		✓	
giant rat *bwampini*	✓							

Table 15. Animals as medicine (*continued*)

	status as food	protection against sorcery	strengthening medicine	good luck medicine	spirit illnesses	medicine for subsistence activities	medicine for general ailments	association with witchcraft
pouched rat *jugu*	✓				✓		✓	
fat mouse *kapeta*	✓						✓	
spiny mouse nyerere	✓	✓		✓			✓	
creek rat *mende*	✓				✓		✓	
striped mouse *mphera*	✓						✓	
long-tailed forest mouse *sonthe*	✓			✓		✓	✓	
pygmy mouse *pinji*	✓							
brush furred rat *chirwa*	✓							
multimammate mouse *mpuku*	✓						✓	
red veld rat *mphakadzi*	✓						✓	
black rat *khoswe*	✗						✓	
dormouse *kadyamlamu*	✗						✓	
hedgehog *chisoni*	✗	✓		✓			✓	
fruit bat *mleme*	✗	✓	✓		✓			
insectivorous bat *nanthuthu*	✗		✓				✓	✓
bushbaby *changa*	o	✓					✓	
night ape *kamundi*	o						✓	
yellow baboon *nyani*	o		✓					
vervet money *pusi*	o		✓			✓		
blue monkey *nchima*	o	✓						

- 225 -

Table 15. Animals as medicine (*continued*)

	status as food	protection against sorcery	strengthening medicine	good luck medicine	spirit illnesses	medicine for subsistence activities	medicine for general ailments	association with witchcraft
rock hyrax *zumba*	✓				✓		✓	
yellow-spotted hyrax *mbira*	✓		✓				✓	
antbear *nsele*	✓	✓	✓			✓	✓	
pangolin *ngaka*	x			✓			✓	
sun squirrel *gologolo*	o						✓	
bush squirrel *gologolo*	o	✓					✓	
porcupine *nungu*	o			✓		✓	✓	
hare *kalulu*	✓				✓		✓	

Status as food: ✓ used widely **o** ambiguous status **x** not usually eaten medicines. Peltzer (1987: 151–8) discusses *nyanga* in relation to sorcery and to anti-witchcraft rituals in Malawi and elsewhere, without indicating the meaning of the term or discussing the close association that pertains between sorcery (*matsenga*) medicine and animals.

Secondly, and related to the above, although it is difficult to find people who will admit to using medicines for anti-social purposes, there are a number of animal substances widely recognized throughout Malawi as being used for immoral or destructive purposes. They may be referred to as *mankhwala woipa* or *akupha* ('bad or deadly medicines'). Such medicines of course belong essentially to the secret knowledge of a witch (*mfiti*) or of people with evil intent (*anthu wa chipongwe* is the usual expression, *chipongwe* meaning insolence or cheek) but they can also be acquired, it is alleged, from a medicine-person (*sing'anga*). To kill or injure someone by the use of medicines is referred to as *ku-chisa* or *kuchesa,* a verb that also, significantly, refers to cutting the meat off animal bones. Medicine for killing people is thus *ntcheso.* But although such medicine is seen as secret knowledge used by people with evil motivations, some substances are widely recognized as poisons (*ululu*). These are derived from the blue-headed agama lizard (Ch. *gunkumu,* Yao *nampopo*); the head of the *mbobo* (Yao *songo*) (the boomslang) and *phiri* (Yao *lipili*) (puff adder) snakes; the blister beetle *dzodzwe* (Yao. *ligombela*); and the gall (*ndulu*) of the crocodile (*ng'ona*) and hartebeest (*ngondo*). All these ingredients are thought to be deadly poisonous; they are usually fired, powdered and placed in the food or drink of the intended victim. Death is said to ensue fairly rapidly.

Thirdly, although a majority of mammals seem, in one context or another, to be used as medicine, the use of animals as *chizimba* tends to focus specially around a limited number of species. This becomes apparent if one examines the animal medicines that are usually sold by market herbalists. Table 16 gives details of the *chizimba* medicines offered by nine herbalists, mainly from the Zomba and Blantyre areas. Twenty-three animals were used in total, and each herbalist has, on average, six or seven *chizimba* substances available. Apart from elephant bone and the teeth of the warthog, all the other substances used consisted of the skins (*chikopa*) of the animals. Four of the animals used are of particular interest: hedgehog, porcupine, pangolin and hyena. Their use as medicine is commonly recognized throughout Malawi. Ratel, crocodile, leopard, elephant and antbear (*sele*) are also very powerful medicines, but the skins and claws of these mammals are obtained only infrequently by herbalists.

Table 16. Animal medicines sold by market herbalists

	Adoniyo Visendi	Mary Jemusi	Jafali Dzomba	Robert Mkorongo	William Pakani	Heronimo Kanjanga	Muzimu Shumba	Edwin Kamwendo	Januario Wede
shrew *sunche*	x								
hedgehog *chisoni*	x	x	x	x	x	x	x	x	x
porcupine *nungu*	x	x	x	x	x		x		x
mole rat *namfuko*									
pangolin *ngaka*	x			x	x	x	x	x	
bushbaby *changa*	x			x					
hyena *fisi*	x	x	x	x			x		
elephant *njobvu*	x							x	
lion *mkango*	x								
fruit bat *mleme*	x								
civet *chombwe*		x		x					
monitor *gondwe*		x				x			
otter *katumbu*				x					x
baboon *nyani*				x			x		x
python *nsato*				x	x				
warthog *njiri*				x					
vervet monkey *pusi*					x				
crocodile *ng'ona*					x		x	x	
serval *njuzi*					x				x
leopard *nyalugwe*					x			x	
ratel *chiuli*					x	x	x		
hippopotamus *mvuu*				x			x		x
tortoise *kamba*							x		

I can hardly discuss all the animal species that are used as medicine. I shall therefore focus on the more important species mentioned above.

The spines (*minga,* thorns) of the hedgehog are used as an activating substance in a variety of medicines that are thought to bring good luck (*mwayi*), friendship (*mankhwala achikondi*) and amiability (*achisomo*), as well as to give protection from sorcery (*matsenga*). The medicines typically used as ingredients, along with hedgehog spines, are the roots of the herb *palibekanthu* ('it does not matter') (*Dicoma anomala*), the roots of the tree *mpetu (Boscia angustifolia)* and the dried leaves of the herb *muitana* ('you call') (*Galium bussei*) and the aromatic shrub *Myrothamus flabellifolius.* This shrub is also, like the hedgehog, called *chisoni* (Yao *chanasa*), the latter term being a common exclamation and meaning essentially compassion, pity or sorrow. The dried leaves of the shrub, which is found only on rocky outcrops over 1300 metres, has the power of becoming green again and expanding on being put in water, hence its name resurrection plant. The hedgehog is said to have a sense of shame (*manyazi*) and compassion (*chisoni*) – both positive attributes for Malawians – as well as having, like the shrub, a certain tenacity towards life. The usual method of administering these protective medicines is to take the hedgehog spines along with the herbal ingredients and put them in groundnut oil for a few days, which 'absorbs' their vital power. The oil is then rubbed over the body (*ku-dzola*, to anoint oneself) to bring good luck, friendship, success in social relationships or protection from sorcery. Alternatively a few hedgehog spines may be mixed together with the herbs and sewn into a small cloth pouch or medicine bag, *chitumwa,* often decorated with beads or cowrie shells. This may be worn around the neck, attached to a piece of string, put in a pocket or placed under a pillow at night. A small bottle with the same ingredients is commonly sold on herbalist stalls in markets throughout Malawi.

The hedgehog is quite common in Malawi and is often killed on the Blantyre-Zomba road. Although, as already noted, it is widely used as a medicine, some people suggested to me that if you eat the meat of the hedgehog you would die (*kudya kufa*, 'eat die'). In 1980 hedgehogs were being sold by young boys for up to K5, which was then equivalent to two days wages as an agricultural labourer. I had a friend who always bought any hedgehogs she was offered or saw for sale, although strictly the sale of wild mammals is illegal, in order to release them in the wild. Malawian friends thought her behaviour quite unintelligible.

The quills (*minga*) of the porcupine (*nungu*) are used for a similar purpose to those of the hedgehog spine that is as a *chizimba* ingredient in medicines whose function is to bring good luck or to offer protection from sorcery. But the porcupine has more varied uses for a variety of ailments and is particularly associated with agriculture and with the protection of crops from the influences of sorcery medicine (*mfumba*). Significantly the porcupine itself is a great pest in gardens and is accredited by local people as being quite fearless, refusing to move even when harassed. I noted the porcupine, specifically the quills, being used as medicine for syphilis (*chindoko*), heart problems, backache (*msana*) and a painful tooth. For the latter remedy the burnt ashes of the quills are mixed with castor oil. Many people did not eat the meat of the porcupine, for like the bushbuck it is believed to cause the skin ailment *chiwengo*.

The scales (*liwamba*) of the pangolin (*ngaka*; in Malawi only one species is found, *Manis temminckii*) have an exactly similar function to hedgehog spines and porcupine quills: they are used in a variety of ways to give protection against sorcery and as a good luck charm, assisting in court cases, friendship, employment and family concerns. They may be used like hedgehog spines, as an ingredient in a medicine bag or bottle, or may be reduced to ashes with other herbs, the ashes then being rubbed into skin incisions (*kutemera muthupi*) in order to protect the body. The pangolin, of course, is widely used as a medicine throughout Africa and has been the subject of much anthropological discussion. Among the Lele it is the focus of a specific religious cult, the Pangolin Men, who are the leading religious experts in the village and who alone are allowed to eat its flesh. In Malawi few people eat the pangolin, though in early times its meat was considered a delicacy and could be eaten only by the chiefs (*afumu*). In her writings on the Lele, Douglas notes that the pangolin – specifically the small species, the white bellied pangolin (*'Manis tric-uspis*), which is arboreal – was ritually hunted, its meat being eaten in a communal feast by the men's cult. It was specifically associated with the spirits and with fertility (1954: 23–4, 1966: 199, 1975: 33). Douglas follows the cultural-idealist tradition in seeing folk classifications as in essence arbitrary. In a seminal and path-breaking study (1966), she interprets the food taboo and the ritual salience associated with the pangolin as being derived from their 'anomalous' classificatory status. She writes: 'Its being contradicts all the most obvious animal categories. It is scaly like a fish, but it climbs trees. It is more like an egg-laying lizard than a mammal, yet it suckles its young. And most significant of all, unlike other small mammals its young are born singly' (1966: 199). These essential characteristics of the pangolin are remarked upon by Malawians and probably by other people throughout Africa, who generally have a detailed knowledge of mammal natural history. In earlier studies (1976, 1987) I have made some critical reflections on Douglas's theory of 'taboo', questioning whether there is a simple relationship between classificatory anomaly and dietary prohibitions. In a recent paper (1991), Ioan Lewis has critically examined Douglas's thesis with respect to the Lele ethnography, highlighting the fact that the giant ground pangolin (*Manis gigantea*), which was also found in the Kasai region, was not the focus of ritual activity among the Lele. In a comparative analysis of other Congolese people – the Ba Lega, Komo and Bushong – Lewis notes the variability with which of the two pangolins are given ritual attention. He thus questions Douglas's whole theory of anomaly, suggesting that the ritual significance of the pangolin can best be understood in terms of Lele cosmology. Earlier, I had suggested something similar, proposing that the ritual significance of the pangolin among the Lele was consonant with its positioning within their system of symbolic classification, rather than to its anomalous status as a 'scaly, fish-like monster' (Morris 1987: 215). In her more recent reflections on the pangolin and animal symbolism, Douglas (1990) essentially reaffirms her earlier form of analysis, suggesting that 'anomaly' and 'metaphor' can only be understood within specific cultural contexts. Following Goodman (1972), she suggests that 'similarity' is not a quality of things in themselves but is relative, variable and culture-dependent (1990: 26), a suggestion that runs counter to common sense and which has been challenged by recent studies of folk classifications (Atran 1990, Berlin 1992), which we discussed in the last chapter.

But the important point which Douglas's rich ethnography of the Lele makes clear is that the pangolin was not the only animal that was subject to dietary restrictions or given ritual salience. It was only one of many of animal species that were associated with the spirits and the forested streams. Other species that were important in this regard included the bushbuck, crocodile, bushpig, antbear, porcupine, giant rat, monitor lizard, water chevrotain, grey duiker and it seems most carnivorous mammals, in the sense that only men belonging to the 'begetters' cult could eat the meat. Hunting among the Lele was highly ritualized, taking place mainly in the forests, and it is clear that there was a close and intimate relationship not only between spirits and animals but between spirits and fertility. Douglas writes that the 'spirit animals' (*hut a ngehe*) were 'in some contexts . . . spoken of as if they were spirits. In others they are animals, closely associated with spirits' (1975: 130). As 'the fertility of humans is thought to be controlled by the spirits inhabiting the deepest, dampest parts of the forest' (ibid.: 33), there is thus an intimate and intrinsic relationship between the forest animals, spirits and fertility. Men, as affines in this matrilineal context, are symbolically associated with this domain.

All this has resonances in the Malawian context and throughout Africa. But why is the pangolin given such prominence? Probably because the pangolin, unique among African mammals, has scales, hundreds of them. These are easily detachable and like the spirits they represent the permanency of life. A pangolin scale, like the horns and skins that once decorated many huts in Malawi, symbolize in a sense not 'eternal life', which has a Neoplatonic ring about it, but immortal life (see Arendt 1978: 34 on the Greek distinction between 'immortal' and 'eternal'). Needless to say, in Malawi a little piece of pangolin scale does wonders for fertility. And the hyena too, more so than all the mammals of Malawi, represents male fertility, or rather the fertility that comes from the affinal aspect of the ancestral spirits.

It is worth noting, finally, that among the Yao, seeing a pangolin on the path is considered a bad omen (*mpingo*), as with the blind burrowing snakes (*mbitu*), which like the pangolin also 'open' the termite mounds, *litumbula masugulu* (Stannus 1922: 310). The scales of the pangolin are also used as a hunting medicine, along with the roots of *mpetu (Boscia angustifolia)*.

The hyena, as one of my Malawian friends put it, is greatly enjoyed (*timamukonda kwambiri*) as medicine. The skin (*chikopa*), brain (*ubonga*), tail (*mchira*) and excrement (*matuzi*) are all used, and for a variety of purposes. It is particularly important as a strengthening medicine – the hyena is credited with the ability to run long distances without tiring – and as a medicine that induces dreaming (*kulota*). Throughout Malawi, parts of the hyena are thought both to offer protection against theft – whether by ordinary people or witches (*afiti*) – and to enable a person to steal without being detected. It is widely used as a protective medicine (*kusirika*) against sorcery and is used in a variety of ways, being particularly associated with the protection of goat or cattle pens (*kusirika khola la ziweto*). The hyena has a prominent place in Malawian folklore and is closely identified with the potency and fertility of the male affine among matrilineal communities in Malawi. Thus in both Chewa and Yao rituals, the surrogate male who performs the act of ritual coitus is referred to as *fisi* (Y, *litunu*). This will be discussed more fully in a companion volume. We have already noted the important toll that hyenas take of human life in Malawi and its role in Malawian folk tales. And of all the mammals found in Malawi, it is the spotted hyena that is most closely identified with witchcraft.

Two other mammals are often mentioned in discussions around medicine, one common, the other very rarely seen, though locally common in some of the game sanctuaries.

The civet cat was widely used in the past as medicine, an oily sub-stance, civette, being extracted as a secretion from its anal gland. Ethiopians are said to have considered it more valuable than gold or silver. In Malawi the skin (*chikopa*) and the excrement (*manyera*) – which is deposited in piles on conspicuous logs, stones or termite mounds – of the civet is widely used as medicine, and for a variety of purposes: for constipation, for protection against sorcery and the evil effects of *mdulo* and as a garden magic. Its excrement is planted alongside seeds not only to increase yields but to give them protection against the harmful influence of medicines (*woteteza mbewu kumunda kuti wokawa asafike*, 'to protect the seeds in the garden so that harmful medicines do not arrive', as one person expressed its uses to me).

Seen as a relative of the bushpig (*nzache nguluwe*), the ant bear is rarely seen, though in forest and game reserves it is locally common, its deep burrows often being taken over by the other mammals. Its meat is considered a delicacy (*nyama yokoma*), but parts of the animal are widely utilized as medicine, especially the skin, claws and teeth, in iron smelting and as a general protection against sorcery, as a strengthening medicine (analogically, the antbear is considered a prodigious digger) and as a remedy for backache and to assist in childbirth.

In one of his many studies of Ndembu ritual, Victor Turner stressed the need to overcome the dualism inherent in Western philosophical traditions. Echoing the thoughts of Aristotle and the pre-Socratics he wrote that African thought 'embeds itself from the outset in materiality, but demonstrates that materiality is not inert but vital' (1975: 21). But given his proclivity to emphasize a radical dichotomy between a cultural 'struc-ture' and an existential 'communitas' and to equate the latter with the 'flow of experience', reality', the 'sacred' and the 'godhead' – thus completely inverting the thoughts of Plato and Eliade – Turner ends up by 'spiritualizing' what he refers to as the *Urgrund* of social structure, the primal ground of experience, thought and social action. But the 'ground' of Malawian thought, like that of the Ndembu, is neither 'spirit-ual' nor 'mystical', nor does it entail a radical dualism between two modalities of experience, however conceptualized, but rather entails a fundamental emphasis on a 'life-world', on *moyo*, that is in a sense ontologically prior to the spirit–matter dichotomy. Malawians have essen-tially a vitalistic and pantheistic attitude towards the world, and the conception of therapy or salvation – if one wishes to use such a term – is like that of the Taoists (cf. Girardot 1983: 42): it is medicinal rather than religious or spiritual, in both intention and structure. The world that surrounds the rural Malawian is a world that is 'alive' and 'vital', and, as

Jonas (1966: 8) has perceptively written on pre-literate people more generally, life is to that extent accepted as the primary state of things. Thus the medicinal use of mammals in Malawi can only be understood if this 'panvitalism' is taken into account and medicine is not seen simply as an inert adjunct to spirit rituals. In a recent text, Dickens has advocated a dialectical way of thinking and a realist epistemology in which entities – humans, other organisms and those of inorganic nature – are envisaged as having 'latent powers or capacities' (1992: xv). This surely is Aristotle's conception of the world, suggested more than two thousand years ago. It is also the viewpoint of rural Malawians in their conception of animal medicine.

Glossary

ambuye	grandparents
banja	family, home, household
bwalo	cleared space in centre of village
bwenzi	friend, lover
chibale	kinship, friendship
chinamwali	general term for initiation rites
chiputu	girls' maturity rite among yao
chirombo	wild animal; useless or obnoxious organism
chirope	blood, ailment associated with hunting, ritual eating of meat
chisamba	dance and rituals associated with a woman's first pregnancy
chizimba	activating medicine
dambo	marsh, valley glades / grassland
dziko	country, land
jando	boys' circumcision ritual among the Yao
kachisi	small hut or shrine where sacrificial offerings are made to the spirits
litiwo	ceremony relating to a woman's first pregnancy among yao
lupanda	boys' initiation rite among Yao
makhalidwe	disposition, nature, character
maliro	funerary rites
malume	maternal uncle
manda	forested graveyard
mankhwala	medicinal substances
matsenga	sorcery, trick, mysterious happenings
matsoka	ill-luck, misfortunes
maula	divination
mbumba	matrilineal or sorority group
mdulo	disease complex related to sexual norms and hot / cold symbolism (also tsempho)
mfiti	witch
mfumu	chief or village headman

mkamwini	in-marrying male affine, son-in-law
mlamu	affine of own generation (pl. alamu)
m'michira	ritual specialist or healer (who possesses medicine tail, mchira)
mowa	beer
mudzi	village
mulungu	common name for the divinity
munthu	person
mwali	initiate
mwambo	tradition, custom, wisdom
mwayi	good fortune, luck
mwezi	moon, month, menstruation
mzimu	spirit (of the ancestors) (pl. mizimu)
mzinda	large village
namkungwi	ritual leader at initiation rites or in spirit rituals
ndiwo	relish
ngaliba	circumcision in yao boys' initiation
nsembe	offerings to the spirits of the ancestors or the divinities
nyama	wild game, meat
nyau	ritual fraternity among men, masked dancers or initiation rites
nyumba	house, home
phiri	hill, mountain
tchire	woodland, usually regenerate bush
thengo	woodland

Appendix: Some Common Malawian Proverbs

1. Carnivores

Chiwindi cha nkhandwe chalaka mwini msampha
The liver of the jackal baffled the owner of the trap
(Accept one's limitations).
Okoma atani onga fungwe
How to be nice like a civet
(never be ungrateful).
Ukapha mwiri loza mphanda
If you kill a genet, thank the branch (be grateful to those who help).
Adafa kalikongwe wa nzeru za yekha
The clever slender mongoose died by himself
(listen to others).
Chinasala chinakanika fisi
The hyena would fail to become a Muslim.
China n'china fisi alibe bwenzi
Say anything, the hyena has no friend
(People who do ill have no friends).
Fisi akagwa m'mbuna salankhula
If the hyena falls into a pit-fall trap, he does not talk
(concentrate).
Fisi akagwira sataya
A hyena who holds, does not lose
(persevere).
Fisi akakhuta salira pompwepo
A hyena who is satisfied does not cry at that place
(be grateful).
Fisi akatola pfupa sadyera pomwepo
A hyena picks up the bone but does not eat there
(show discretion).

Fisi atolapo tsoka
A hyena picks up trouble wherever it goes
(steer clear of trouble).

Fisi saopa mdima
A hyena is not afraid of the dark
(don't worry about everything).

Kupha mkango ndi kuweteka
To kill a lion, you need to be gentle (cunning).

Nkango ukasauka ukudya udzu
The troubled lion eats grass.

Kupha mkango ndi kumuweta
Kill the lion and you can tend (the domestic animals).

Maso akutari mkango ukunga nyani
Eyes far away (at a distance) the lion is like a baboon
(don't jump to conclusions).

Ukakamuka mkango kwela mwamba
If you pronounce lion, climb high (up a tree)
(Watch what you say).

Kambuku sangasinthe muwanga ake
A leopard is not able to change its spots.

Mkokoya wa wawile wanache njusi
They delayed, and the children singed the serval (skin)
(don't hang about).

Msamada bvumbwe, akudya nkhuku n'kalulu
Don't hate the wild cat, the one eating the chicken is the hare
(be careful who you accuse).

Mlamwako ndi likongwe, akalowa phanga, koma kumtsekera ndi masamba
Your sibling-in-law is the slender mongoose; if they enter the cave, close it with leaves
(be forgiving towards your affines).

Pachedwa msulu pali nyerere
Where the banded mongoose hangs about, there you will find ants.
(Be observant).

2. Ungulates

Choipa ndi mnyanga ya njobvu
Bad things are (like) the tusk of an elephant
(evil things stand out).

Mpheto mwa njobvu sapita kawiri
Between the legs of an elephant, you don't go twice.
Anonenji adapha njobvu ndi mwala
"What did he see?" – killed the elephant with a stone
(try, you never know your luck).
Nguluwe ya ana sinona
A bushpig with (many) young is not fat.
Nguluwe analire msampha utaning'a
A bushpig squealed as the spring trap broke
(persevere).
Nguruwe yikupulikira mv kukumba
The bushpig listens while digging.
Mvuu zikatha akanka bwato n'kampango
The hippo is finished, the catfish pushes the canoe
(trouble never ending).
Tiyese anapha mvuu ndi mono
We tried to kill the hippo with a fish basket
(persevere).
Anyang'wa ainsa, aona ukonde bwaguluka
Horns of the duiker (displayed), see the game net come over him
(don't be proud).
Chidule chinapetsa njati m'mbuna
The short cut led the buffalo into the game pit.
Mbawala yamantha idapota nyanga
The scared bushbuck does not grow horns.
Mbawala sikumwa madzi garu ali kambuyo
The bushbuck doesn't drink with the dog behind (him)
(get your priorities right).
Muyara wako ndi nyama, mzichi ndi mpatu
Your cousin is meat, your sister bushbuck
(bushbuck often prohibited food).

3. *Mbewa*

Nchenzi inamvu mau oyamba
The cane rat heard the first words (noise)
(listen to others carefully).
Padziwa ndi pansi mwanawa mfuko adwala
Only those underground know the mole rats' child is sick.
Kudzinga ngati ntiri, tionera mende kutha
Be quiet like the vlei rat, see the creek rat getting finished (killed).

Madooli anafera mchenga wa kuyera
The gerbil died in the light sand
(What you enjoy can lead to disaster).
Nsanjikizo zinaphetsa kunda
"More and more" killed the giant rat
(Don't be greedy).
Manyazi anapha lambe
Shyness killed the fat mouse
(Be prepared. Fat mouse's burrow does not have escape hole).
Dzenje la pinji lidziwika nkuunjika
The burrow of the pygmy mouse is known by its heap of stones
(take note of little signs).
Kapinji mayenda – yenda kasiya anzache asewera
The small pygmy mouse moves around, leaving his relatives to play
(watch out for dangers).
Khoswe akakhale pa mkhate sapheka
The black rat that sits on the clay pot is not killed.
Mbewa wa manyazi idafera ku dzenje
The shy mouse died in its burrow
(don't be too shy).
Mbewa zikachuluka zilibe mala
If too many mice, they have no nest.

4. Other animals

Kwi za changa mbawala m'mwamba
Safe and hidden is the bushbuck on high
(keep out of trouble).
Chirombo chinafera m'dambo la kamundi
The wild beast died in the marsh of the night ape
(have humility).
Anyani sakekana dzikundu
Baboons do not laugh at each other's buttocks.
Ichi n'changa chidapinditsa mchira wa nyani
"This is mine" bent the tail of the baboon
(don't be greedy).
Kulanga nyani n'kuphwanya mutu
To punish the baboon, hit the head
(go straight to the issue).

Phiri siliyendera nyani koma nyani ayendera phiri
The mountain does not come to the baboon, but the baboon goes to the
mountain (have humility).

Tisiku lofera anyani mitengo yonse iterera
The day the baboons died, all the trees were slippery
(listen to advice).

Chakoma chakoma pusi adagwa chagada
It's tasty, it's tasty, the vervet monkey fell on its back
(don't be greedy).

Zumba akoma ndi nsinjiro
The rock hyrax likes the taste of peanut oil
(don't exaggerate).

Mubvi kalasa nungu
An arrow can pierce the porcupine
(don't be too self-satisfied).

Kalulu anatuma njobvu
The hare sent the elephant
(show respect to elders).

Mau osiiza ada ombola kalulu
Words kept back redeemed (saved) the hare
(Watch what you say).

Muonere ine adanka ndi ng'ona
(The one who said) look at me went with the crocodile
(don't be too proud).

Ukaukwana ng'ona ku madzi usapitako
If you insult the crocodile, don't go near the water.

Kamba anyerera amene antola
The tortoise defecates on those who pick it up.

Tsoka likakuda kamba asanduka mwala
Dark misfortunes turn the tortoise into stone.

Kamtengo ka mwana ndiko aphera njoka
(Even) a small stick kills a snake.

Bibliography

1. Archival Material

National Archives of Malawi (MNA), Zomba.
Malawi Section, University Library, Chancellor College, University of Malawi, Zomba.
Society of Malawi Library, Limbe.
Wildlife Research Unit, Kasungu National Park, Department of National Parks and Wildlife.
Library/Archives, Wildlife Society of Malawi, Environmental Education Centre, Lilongwe Wildlife Sanctuary, Lilongwe.

2. Malawi

Abdallah, Y.B. [1919] 1973. *The Yaos* (Chiikala cha wayao), ed. M. Sanderson, London: Cass.
Alpers, E.A. 1969. 'Trade, State and Society among the Yao of the Nineteenth Century' *Journal of African History*, 10, 405–420.
—— 1975. *Ivory and Slaves in East Central Africa*, London: Heinemann.
Ansell, W.F.H. and R.J. Dowsett. 1988. *Mammals of Malawi*, St. Ives: Trendine Press.
Atkins, G. 1950. 'The Nyanja-speaking population of Nyasaland and N. Rhodesia' *Africa Studies* 9, 35–9.
Banda, J.A.K. 1991. *The Startling Revelation*, Limbe: Popular Publishers.
Bandawe, C.M. 1971. *Memoirs of a Malawian*, Blantyre: Claim.
Bennett, N.R. and M. Ylvisaker 1971. *The Central African Journal of Lovell J. Procter 1860–64*, African Studies Centre, Boston University.
Benson, C.W. 1953. *A Check List of the Birds of Nyasaland*, Blantyre: Nyasaland Society.
Berry, V. and C.Petty (ed) 1992. *The Nyasaland Survey Papers 1938–1943*, London: Academy Books.
Bertram, C.K. et al 1942. *Report of the Fish and Fisheries of Lake Nyasa*, London: Crown Agents.
Bieze, D. 1971. 'The work done by rural women in Malawi', Ministry of Agriculture and Natural Resources Agro-Economic Survey.

Bibliography

Boeder, R.B. 1984. *Alfred Sharpe of Nyasaland: Builder of Empire*, Blantyre: Society of Malawi and Pretoria: African Institute.

Boucher, C. 1976. Some interpretations of Nyau societies, SOAS: MA Dissertation.

Bradshaw, T.W. 1960. 'On Kauni', NFPS Newsletter, June pp. 6–7.

Bruwer, J.P. 1948. 'Kinship terminology among the Chewa of E.Province of N. Rhodesia', *African Studies* 7, 185–7.

—— 1950. 'Notes of Maravi origins and migration', *African Studies* 9, 32–4.

—— 1955. 'Unkhoswe: the system of guardianship in Chewa matrilineal society', *African Studies* 14, 113–22.

Buchanan, J 1885. *The Shire Highlands*, Blantyre: Printing and Publ (1982 edition)

Burgess, H.J. and E. Wheeler 1970. Lower Shire nutrition survey, Blantyre: Ministry of Health.

Campbell, W.Y. n.d. *Travellers' Records of Portuguese Nyassaland*, London: King, Sell.

Chafulumira, E.W. 1948. *Mbiri ya amang'anja*, Blantyre: Dzuka.

Chakanza, J.C. 1980. 'Annotated List of the Independent Churches in Malawi 1900–1981' Zomba: Chancellor College, Religious Studies Publ. No 10.

Chapman, J.D. 1962. *The Vegetation of Mlanje Mountains, Nyasaland*, Zomba: Govn. Press.

—— 1988. 'Mpita Nkhalango: a lowland forest relic unique to Malawi', *Nyala* 12, 3–26.

Chimombo, S. 1988. *Malawian oral tradition*, Zomba: Centre for Social Research, University of Malawi.

Chipeta, O.J. et al. 1977. *M'mbelwa Ngoni traditions I.*, Zomba: Chancellor College, Department of History, University of Malawi

Chitukuko Cha Amayi M'Malawi 1992. *Malawi's Traditional and Modern Cooking*, Lilongwe: C.C.A.M.

Clark, B. 1975. 'The Work down by Rural Women in Malawi', *European Journal of Rural Development* 8/2, 80–91.

Clark, J.D. 1972. Prehistoric Origins, in B. Pachai (ed), *The Early History of Malawi*, pp. 17–27 London: Longman.

Coudenhove, H. 1925. *My African Neighbours*, London: Cape.

Crader, D.C. 1984. *Hunters in Iron Age Malawi*, Lilongwe: Department of Antiquities. Publ. No. 21

Cromwell, E. 1992. Malawi in A.Duncan and J.Howell (ed.) *Structural Adjustment and the African Farmer*, London: James Currey.

Debenham, F 1955. *Nyasaland: the Land of the Lake*, London: HMSO.

Bibliography

Drummond, H. 1889. *Tropical Africa*, London: Hodder and Stoughton.

Duff, H. 1903. *Nyasaland under the Foreign Office*, London: Bell.

Elliot, G. 1939. *The Long Grass Whispers*, London: Routledge & Kegan Paul.

—— 1949. *Where the Leopard Passes*, London: Routledge & Kegan Paul.

—— 1951. *The Hunter's Cave*, London: Routledge & Kegan Paul.

—— 1957. *The Singing Chameleon*, London: Routledge & Kegan Paul.

Faulkner, H. 1868. *Elephant Haunts*, London: Hurst & Blackett.

Forster, P.G. 1989. *T.Cullen Young: Missionary and Anthropologist*, Hull: Hull University Press.

—— 1994. 'Culture, nationalism and the invention of tradition in Malawi', *Journal Modern African Studies* 32/3, 477–97.

Foskett, R. 1965. *The Zambesi Journal and Letters of Dr J. Kirk 1858–63*, 2 vols. Edinburgh: Oliver & Boyd.

Fraser, D. 1910. *Personal Notebook 1910–12*, Limbe: Society of Malawi Library.

—— 1915. *Livingstonia: The Story of our Mission*, Edinburgh: United Free Church of Scotland.

—— 1923. *African Idylls*, London: Seeley.

Gamitto, A.C.P. 1960. *King Kasembe and the Marave, Cheva, Bisa, Bemba, Lunda and Other Peoples of Southern Africa (Expedition 1831–32)*, 2 vols. (ed. I Cunnison) Lisbon: Estudios de Ciencias Politicas e Sociais.

Gray, E. 1939. 'Some riddles of the Nyanja people', *Bantu Studies* 13, 251–91.

—— 1944. 'Some proverbs of the Nyanja people', *African Studies* 3/3, 101–28.

Hargreaves, B.J. 1979. 'Cautious carnivorous clowns: chameleons of Malawi', *Nyala* 5, 32–9.

Hayes, G.D. 1978. *A Guide to Malawi's National Parks and Game Reserves*, Limbe: Mountford Press.

Hodgson, A.G.O. 1933. 'Notes on the Achewa and Angoni of the Dowa District', *J.Roy.Anthr.Inst.* 63, 123–65.

Isaacman, A. 1972. 'The origin, formation and early history of the Chikunda of South Central Africa', *Journal African History* 13, 443–61.

Jackson, P.B.N. 1963. *Report on the (Fish) Survey on Northern Lake Nyasa 1954–55*, Zomba: Govn.Printer.

Johnson, W.P. 1922. *Chinyanja Proverbs*, Cardiff: Smith Bros.

Kalinga,O. 1993. The Master Farmer's Scheme in Nyasaland 1950–62 *African Affairs*, 92, 367–87.

Kandawire, J.A.K. 1979. *Thangata: Forced Labour or Reciprocal Assistance*, Zomba: University of Malawi Publ.

—— 1980. 'Village segmentation and class formation in Southern Malawi', *Africa* 50/2, 125–45.

Kaphagawira, D.N. and H.F.Chidammadzi 1983. 'Chewa cultural ideas and systems of thought as determined from proverbs', Botswana *Journal African Studies* 3/2, 29–37.

Kathamalo, B.J. 1965. Khulubvi thicket – Port Herald, *Soc.Malawi J.* 1812, 53–4.

Killick, D.J. 1990. Technology in its social setting:Bloomery iron smelting at Kasungu, Malawi 1860–1940, Yale University: PhD thesis.

Kumakanga, S.L. 1975. *Nzeru za Kale*, Blantyre: Dzuka.

Kydd, J. 1984. 'Malawi in the 1970s: Development Policies and Economic Change' in *Malawi: Alternative Pattern of Development*, Edinburgh: Edinburgh University Centre of African Studies. Proc. No. 25.

Langworthy, H.W. 1975. 'Central Malawi in the 19th Century' in R.J. MacDonald (ed) *From Nyasaland to Malawi*, Nairobi: E.Afr.Publ. House.

Lawson, A. 1949. 'An outline of the relationship system of the Nyanja and Yao tribes of Southern Nyasaland', *African Studies* 8, 180–90.

Linden, I. 1974. *Catholics, Peasants and Chewa Resistance in Nyasaland 1889–1939*, London: Heinemann.

—— 1975. 'Chewa initiation rites and Nyau societies' in T.O. Ranger and J. Weller (ed.) *Themes in the Christian History of Central Africa*, London: Heinemann.

Livingstone, D. and C. 1865. *Narrative of an Expedition to the Zambezi and its Tributaries 1858–1864*, (Popular edition 1887), London: John Murray

Long, R.C. 1973. 'A List with Notes of the Mammals of Nsanje District' *Soc. Mal. J.* 26/1, 60–77.

Loveridge, A. 1954. *I drank the Zambezi*, London: Lutterworth

Lwanda, J.L. 1993. *Kamuzu Banda of Malawi*, Glasgow: Dudu Nsomba Publ.

MacDonald, D. 1882. *Africana; or the Heart of Heathen Africa* (2 vols), Edinburgh: J.Menzies.

—— 1938. 'Yao and Nyanja tales', *Bantu Studies* 12, 251–86.

MacMillan, H. 1975. 'The African Lakes Company and the Makololo 1878–1884' in R.J. MacDonald (ed.) *From Nyasaland to Malawi*, Nairobi: East Afr. Publ.House.

McShane, T.O. 1985. *Vwaza Marsh Game Reserve*, Rumphi: Wildlife Res.Inst.

Bibliography

Mair, L 1951. 'Marriage and Family in the Dedza District of Nyasaland' *J.Royal Anthr.Inst.* 81, 103–19

Mandala, E.C. 1990. *Work and Control in a Peasant Economy*, Madison: University Wisconsin Press.

Marwick, M. 1963. 'History and tradition in East Central Africa through the eyes of the N.Rhodesian Chewa' *Journal African History* 4, 375–90.

—— 1965. *Sorcery in its Social Setting*, Manchester: Manchester University Press.

Maugham, R.C.F. 1910. *Zambezia: General Description of the Valley of the Zambezi River*, London: Murray.

—— 1914. *Wild Game in Zambezia*, London: Murray

Mgomezulu, G. 1983. 'The Animal Community and Man's Changing Hunting Habits in the Linthipe Area' *Nyala* 9, 39–56.

Mikochi, J.C. 1938. Notes on African food crops, Unpublished notebook.

Mills, D.S. 1911. *What we do in Nyasaland*, London: UMCA.

Mitchell, J.C. 1956. *The Yao Village*, Manchester: Manchester University Press.

—— 1962. 'Marriage, Matriliny and social structure among the Yao of Southern Nyasaland', *Intern.J.Comp.Sociol.* 3, 29–42.

Mkandawire, T. 1983. 'Economic crisis in Malawi', in J. Carlsson (ed.), *Recession in Africa*, Uppsala: Scandinavian Institute African Studies.

Morris, B. 1970. 'Nature and origins of Brachystegia woodland' *Commonwealth Forestry Review* 49, 155–8.

—— 1980. 'Folk classifications', *Nyala* 6, 83–93.

—— 1984. 'The pragmatics of folk classifications' *Journal Ethnobiology* 41/1, 45–60.

—— 1985. 'Chewa conceptions of disease: symptoms and etiologies', *Soc.Malawi J.* 38/1, 14–43

—— 1986a. 'Herbalism and divination in Southern Malawi', *Soc.Sc. and Medicine* 23, 367–77.

—— 1987. *Common Mushrooms of Malawi*, Oslo: Fungi Flora.

—— 1990. 'Annotated checklist of the macrofungi of Malawi' *Kirkia* 13/2, 323–64.

—— 1991. 'Mwanawamphepo: children of the wind', *Nyala* 15/1, 1–17.

—— 1992. 'Mushrooms: for medicine, magic and munching', *Nyala* 16/1, 1–8.

—— 1994a. 'Bowa: Ethnomycological Notes on the Macrofungi of Malawi', in J.H. Seyani and A.C. Chikuni (ed.), *Proc. Xiii Aetfat Congress Malawi* 1, 635–47.

—— 1994b 'Animals as Meat and Meat as Food: Reflections on Meat-

Bibliography

Eating in Southern Malawi' *Food and Foodways* 6/1, 19–41.

—— 1995. 'Wildlife depredations in Malawi: the Historical Dimension', *Nyala* 18, 17–24.

—— 1996a. *Chewa medical botany: A Study of Herbalism in Southern Malawi*, Hamburg: Lit.Intern.African Institute.

—— 1996b. 'A Short History of Wildlife Conservation in Malawi', Edinburgh: Centre for African Studies, Occ.Papers No 64.

—— 1996c. 'Hunting and the Gnostic Vision', *J. Human and Environ. Sciences* 1/2, 13–39.

Morris, B and H.Patel 1994. 'Ulimbo: morphological and pragmatic aspects of plant classification in Malawi', in J.H. Seyani and A.C. Chikuni (ed.), *Proc.Xiii Aetfat Congress Malawi* 1, 103–111.

Msamba, F. and D.J.Killick 1992. Kasungu and Kaluluma oral traditions, Zomba: University Malawi, Unpubl.thesis

Murray, S.S. 1922. *A Handbook of Nyasaland*, London: Crown Agents.

Mwale, E.B. 1948. *Za Acewa*, London: MacMillan.

Nettell, S. 1995. 'African Dream', *Guardian Weekend*, April 1st pp. 42–3.

Nkondiwa, G. et al. 1977. Yao traditions III, Zomba, University Malawi.

Ntara, S.J. 1973. *The History of the Chewa*, ed. B. Heintze Weisbaden: Frans Steiner Verlag.

Nurse, G.D. 1978. *Clanship in Central Malawi*, Vienna: Acta Ethn.et Linguist. Series Africana 12.

Pachai, B. 1973. *Malawi: The History of the Nation*, London: Longman.

—— 1978. *Land and Politics in Malawi 1875–1975*, Kingston, Ontario: Limestone Press.

Peltzer, K. 1987. *Some Contributions of Traditional Healing Practices towards Psychological Health Care in Malawi*, Eschborn: Fachbuch-handling fur Psychologie.

Phiri, D.D. 1982. *From Nguni to Ngoni*, Limbe: Popular Publ.

Phiri, K.M. 1983. 'Some changes in the matrilineal family system among the Chewa of Malawi', *Journal African History* 24, 257–74.

Pike, J.G. and G.T. Rimmington 1965. *Malawi: a Geographical Study*, Oxford: Oxford University Press.

Potter, J.R. 1987. *Mizimu: Demarcated Forests and Contour ridges*, William's College, Mass.: BA Hons Thesis.

Pretorius, J.L. 1949. 'The terms of relationship of the Chewa' *Nyasaland J.* 2/1, 44–52.

Price, T. 1963. 'The meaning of Mang'anja', *Nyasaland J.* 16/1, 74–77.

Rangeley, W.H.J. 1948. 'Notes on Chewa Tribal Law', *Nyasaland J.* 1/3, 5–68.

—— 1963. 'The Ayao', *Nyasaland J.* 16/1, 7–27.

Rattray, R.S. and A.Hetherwick 1907. *Some Folklore Stories and Songs in Chinyanja*, London: SPCK.

Read, M. 1942. 'Migrant labour in Africa and its effects on tribal life', *Intern.Labour Rev.* 45, 605–31

Rita-Ferreira, A. 1968. 'The Nyau Brotherhood among Mozambique Chewa', *S.Afr.J.Science* 64, 20–24.

Robinson, K.R. 1977. *Iron-age occupation north and northeast of Mulanje Plateau*, Lilongwe: Dept. Antiquities Publ. No.17

Rogers, P.M. and H.S. Jamusana 1989. *Wildlife Pest Impacts and Wildlife Management in Malawi*, Lilongwe: FAO/DNPW Field Document No.2.

Saffroy, R. 1949. Notes on Mbewa collected at Kasina Seminary, Dedza. Unpubl. manuscript with Father C.Boucher Mua

Salaun, N. 1978. *Chichewa: Intensive Course*, Likuni: Teresianum Press.

Sanderson, G.M. 1920. 'Relationships among the Wayao', *J.Royal Anthr. Inst.* 50, 369–76.

—— 1954. *A Dictionary of the Yao Language*, Zomba: Govn.Press.

Schoffeleers, J.M. 1968. Symbolic and social aspects of spirit worship among the Mang'anja. Oxford University, PhD thesis.

—— 1971. 'The religious significance of bush fires in Malawi', *Cahiers des Religions Africaines* 10, 271–87.

—— 1976. 'The Nyau societies: our present understanding', *Soc.Malawi J.* 29/1, 59–68.

—— 1992. *River of Blood*, Madison: University Wisconsin Press

Scott, D.C. 1929. *Dictionary of the Nyanja Language*, London: Lutterworth.

Shepperson, G. 1966. 'The Jumbe of Kota Kota and Some Aspects of Islam in British Central Africa', in I.M. Lewis (ed), *Islam in Tropical Africa*, London: Hutchinson.

Shepperson, G. and T.Price 1958. *Independent African*, Edinburgh: Edinburgh University Press.

Singano, E. and A.A.Roscoe (ed.) 1980. *Tales of Old Malawi*, Limbe: Popular Publ.

Smith, A.K. 1983. 'The Indian Ocean Zone', in D.Birmingham and P.H.Martin (ed.), *History of Central Africa*, Vol.1, London: Longman.

Soka, L.D. 1953. *Mbiri Ya Alomwe*, Limbe: Malawi Publ.

Spring, A. 1990. 'Profiles of men and women smallholder farmers in Malawi' in R. Huss-Ashmore and S.H. Katz (ed.), *African Food Systems in Crisis Pt.II*, New York: Gordon and Breach.

Stannus, H.S. 1910. 'Notes on some tribes of British Central Africa', *J. Royal Anthr. Inst.* 40, 285–335.

Bibliography

—— 1922. 'The Wayao of Nyasalan', *Harvard Afr.Studies* III, 229–372.

Stewart, M.M. 1967. *Amphibians of Malawi*, Albany: State University New York Press.

Stigand, C. 1907. 'Notes on the natives of Nyasaland, N.E. Rhodesia and Portugese Zambezia, their arts, customs and modes of subsistence', *J.Royal Anthr.Inst.* 37, 119–32.

—— 1909. 'Notes on the tribes of the neighbourhood of Food Manning' *J.Royal Anthr.Inst.* 39, 35–43.

Stuart, R.G. 1974. The Chewa and Christianity: the Anglican case 1885–1950, University London, PhD thesis.

Sweeney, R.C.H. 1970. *Animal Life in Malawi*, (2 vols) Belgrade: Institute Publ. Textbooks.

—— 1971. *Snakes of Nyasaland*, Amsterdam: Asher.

Talbot, W.D.S. 1956. 'A few notes on the hippotamus hunting by the Phodzo people of Port Herald' *Nyasaland Journal* 9, 19–20.

Tew (Douglas), M. 1950. *Peoples of Lake Nyasa Region*, Oxford: Oxford University Press.

Thorold, A. 1995. Yao Muslims. University Cambridge, PhD Thesis.

Tweddle, D. and N.G. Willoughby 1979. 'An annotated checklist of the fish fauna of the River Shire south of the Kapachira Falls', *Nyala* 5/2, 75–91.

Vail, H.L. 1972. 'Religion, Language and the Tribal Myth: the Tumbuka and Chewa of Malawi', in M. Schoffeleers 1979. (ed), *Guardians of the Land*, Gwero: Mambo.

—— 1983. 'The Political Economy of East-Central Africa', in D. Birmingham and P.M. Martin (eds), *History of Central Africa*, vol.II London: Longman.

Van der Merwe, N.J. and D.H. Avery 1987. 'Science and Magic in African Technology: Traditional Iron Smelting in Malawi' *Africa* 57, 143–72.

Van Kessel, A.C. 1989. *A Collection of Chewa Proverbs*, Chipata: Missionaries Africa.

Van Velsen, J. 1959. 'Notes on the history of the Lakeside Tonga of Nyasaland', *African Studies* 18, 105–17.

Vaughan, M. 1982 'Food production and family labour in Southern Malawi', *Journal African History* 23/3, 351–64.

—— 1983. 'Which family? Problems in the reconstruction of the history of the family as an economic and cultural unit' *Journal African History* 24, 275–83.

Werner, A. 1906. *The Natives of British Central Africa*, London: Constable.

White, L. 1984, '"Tribes" and the aftermath of the Chilembe rising' *African Affairs* 83, 511–42.

—— 1987. *Magomero: Portrait of an African Village*, Cambridge: Cambridge University Press.

Williamson, J. 1941. 'Nyasaland native food' *Nyasaland Times*, pp. 1–25.

—— 1942. Nyasaland nutrition survey. Unpubl. manuscript.

—— 1943. 'The part played by legumes in the diet of the Nyasaland African' *E.Afr.Agricult.J.* 212–18.

—— 1972. 'Notes on some changes in Malawian diet over the last 30 years', *Soc.Malawi J.* 25/2, 49–54.

—— 1975. *Useful Plants of Malawi*, Zomba: Univ Malawi

Yoshida, K. 1992. 'Masks and Transformation among the Chewa of Eastern Zambia', *Senri Ethnol.Studies* 31, 203–73.

Young, E.D. 1868. *The Search after Livingstone*, London: Simpkin, Marshall.

—— 1877. *Nyassa: a Journal of Adventures*, London: John Murray.

Young, T.C. 1930. 'The religion of my fathers (Levi Mumba)', *Intern. Rev.Missions* 19, 362–76.

—— 1931. *Notes on the Customs and Folklore of the Tumbuka-Kamanga Peoples*, Livingstonia: The Mission Press

—— 1932. *Notes on the History of the Tumbuka-Kamanga Peoples*, London: Religious Tract Society.

—— 1950. 'Kinship among the Chewa of Rhodesia and Nyasaland', *African Studies* 9, 29–31

Young, T.C. and H. Banda 1946. (ed.) *Our African Way of Life*, London: United Soc.Christian Literature.

Young, W.P. 1953. 'Memories of Nyika Plateau' *Nyasaland J.* 6/1, 45–52.

Zambezi Mission 1980. *The Students' English-Chichewa Dictionary*, Blantyre: Claim.

3. General

Ackrill, J.L. 1987. (ed.) *A New Aristotle Reader*, Oxford: Clarendon Press.

Adams, C.J. 1990. *The Sexual Politics of Meat*, Cambridge: Polity Press.

Adams, J.S. and T.O. McShane 1992. *The Myth of Wild Africa*, New York: Norton.

Amadiume, I. 1987. *Male Daughters, Female Husbands*, London: Zed Books.

—— 1995. 'Gender, political systems and social movements', in M. Mamdani and E. Wamba-Dia-Wambia (ed.), *African Studies in Social Movements and Democracy*, Dakar: Codesria.

Arendt, H. 1978. *The Life of the Mind*, New York: Harcourt Brace.

Bibliography

Atran, S. 1990. *Cognitive Foundations of Natural History*, Cambridge: Cambridge University Press.

Baden-Powell, R.S.S. 1933. *Lessons from the Varsity of Life*, London: Jenkins.

Barbour, J.G. 1973. (ed.) *Western Man and Environmental Ethics Reading*, Mass.: Addison-Wesley.

Baumann, H. 1950. 'Nyama', *Paideuma* 4, 191–230.

Bell, R.H.V. 1987. 'Conservation with a Human Face', in D. Anderson and R. Grove (eds), *Conservation in Africa*, Cambridge: Cambridge University Press.

Benton, T. 1993. *Natural Relations*, London: Verso.

Berglund, A. 1976. *Zulu Thought-Patterns and Symbolism*, London: Hurst.

Berlin, B. 1978. 'Whither the savage mind?' Yonder, classifying and well, as is its nature, Unpubl. manuscript.

—— 1992. *Ethnobiological Classification*, Princeton, N.J.: Princeton University Press.

Bhaskar, R. 1989. *Reclaiming Reality*, London: Verso.

Bird-David, N. 1990. 'The giving environment: another perspective on the economic system of gatherer-hunters', *Current Anthrop.* 31, 189–96.

Bloch, M. 1992. *Prey into Hunter*, Cambridge: Cambridge University Press.

Bly, R. 1980. *News of the Universe*, San Francisco: Sierra Club Books.

—— 1990. *Iron John*, Shaftesbury: Element Books.

Boserup, E. 1970. *Women's Role in Economic Development*, New York: St Martins Press.

Brain, J.L. 1973. 'Ancestors as elders in Africa: further thoughts', *Africa* 43, 122–33.

Brown, C.H. 1974. 'Unique beginners and covert categories in folk biological taxonomies', *Amer.Anthrop.* 76, 325–7.

—— 1979. 'Folk zoological life-forms: their universality and growth', *Amer.Anthrop.* 81, 791–817.

—— 1992. 'Cognition and common sense' (Review Atran 1990), *Amer. Ethnol.* 19/2, 367–73.

Brown, J.E. 1992. *Animals of the Soul*, Rockport, Mass: Element

Bulmer, R. 1974. 'Folk biology in the New Guinea Highlands' *Soc. Sc.Inform.* 13, 9–28.

Campbell, J. 1959. *The Masks of God*, Harmondsworth: Penguin.

—— 1984. *The Way of Animal Powers*, London: Time Books.

Caplan, P. 1987. (ed.) *The Cultural Construction of Sexuality*, London: Tavistock.

Bibliography

Cartmill, M. 1993. *A View to a Death in the Morning*, Cambridge Mass.: Harvard University Press

Chavunduka, G.L. 1978. *Traditional Healers and the Shona Patient*, Gwero: Mambo Press.

Clifford, J. and G. Marcus 1986. (eds) *Writing Culture*, Berkeley: University California Press.

Collier, A. 1994. *Critical Realism*, London: Verso.

Collingwood, R.G. 1945. *The Idea of Nature*, Oxford: Oxford University Press.

Comaroff, J.1985. *Body of Power, Spirit of Resistance*, Chicago: University Chicago Press.

Connell, R.W. 1987. *Gender and Power*, Cambridge: Polity Press.

Cornwall, A. 1994. 'Gender identity and gender ambiguity among Travestites in Salvador, Brazil', in A. Cornwall & N. Lindisfarne (ed.), *Dislocating Masculinity*, London: Routledge.

Cornwall, A. and N. Lindisfarne 1994. (ed.) *Dislocating Masculinity*, London: Routledge.

Croll, E. and D. Parkin 1992. (eds) *Bush Base: Forest Farm*, London: Routledge.

De Beauvoir, S. 1973. *The Second Sex*, E.M. Parshley (trans.), New York: Vintage.

Dembeck, H. 1965. *Animals and Men*, New York: Natural History Press.

Devall, B. and G. Sessions 1985. *Deep Ecology: Living as if Nature Mattered*, Layton, Utah: Peregrine Smith.

Dickens, P. 1992. *Society and Nature*, Hemel Hempstead: Harvester Press.

Douglas, M. 1954. 'The Lele of Kasai', in D. Forde (ed.) *African Worlds*, I.A.I. Oxford University Press.

—— 1964. 'Matriliny and pawnship in Central Africa', *Africa* 34, 301–13.

—— 1966. *Purity and Danger*, Harmondsworth: Penguin.

—— 1975. *Implicit Meanings*, London: Routledge & Kegan Paul.

—— 1990. 'The Pangolin revisited: a new approach to animal symbolism', in R. Willis (ed.), *Signifying Animals*, London: Unwin Hyman.

Eliade, M. 1954. *The Myth of the Eternal Return, or Cosmos and History*, Princeton: Princeton University Press

—— 1958. *Patterns of Comparative Religion*, London: Sheed & Ward.

—— 1959. *The Sacred and the Profane*, New York: Harcourt Brace.

—— 1960. *Myths, Dreams and Mysteries*, London: Collins.

—— 1962. *The Forge and the Crucible*, Chicago: University Chicago Press.

—— 1978. *A History of Religious Ideas*, (transl. W. Trask), Chicago: University Chicago Press.

Ellen, R.F. 1993. *The Cultural Relations of Classification*, Cambridge: Cambridge University Press.

Evans-Pritchard, E.E. 1937. *Witchcraft, Oracles and Magic among the Azande*, Oxford: Clarendon Press.

Fausto-Sterling, A. 1985. *Myths of Gender*, New York: Harper Collins.

Fiddes, N. 1991. *Meat: a Natural Symbol*, London: Routledge.

Finnegan, R. 1970. *Oral Literature in Africa*, Nairobi: Oxford University Press.

Foltz, B. 1995. *Inhabiting the Earth*, New Jersey: Humanities Press.

Foran, W.R. 1958. *A Breath of the Wilds*, London: Hale.

Fortes, M. 1969. *Kinship and the Social Order*, Chicago: Aldine.

Foster, G.M. and B.G. Anderson 1978. *Medical Anthropology*, New York: Wiley.

Fox, W. 1990. *Towards a Transpersonal Ecology*, Boston: Shambala

Frazer, J.G. 1922. *The Golden Bough*, London: MacMillan.

Freeman, J.D. 1984. *Margaret Mead and Samoa*, Harmondsworth: Penguin.

Gillison, G. 1980. 'Images of nature in Gimi thought', in C. MacCormack and M. Strathern (eds.), *Nature, Culture and Gender*, Cambridge: Cambridge University Press.

Gilmore, D. 1990. *Manhood in the Making*, New Haven: Yale University Press.

Ginzburg, C. 1991. *Ecstasies*, London: Hutchinson.

Girardot, N.J. 1983. *Myth and Meaning in Early Taoism*, Berkeley: University California Press.

Glacken, C.J. 1967. *Traces on the Rhodian Shore*, Berkeley: University California Press.

Goodman, F.D. 1992. *Ecstasy, Ritual and Alternative Reality*, Bloomington: Indiana University Press.

Goodman, N. 1972. *Problems and Projects*, New York: Bobbs Merrill.

Guenther, M. 1988. 'Animals in Bushman thought, myth and art', in T. Ingold (ed.), *Hunters and Gatherers*, Vol.2 Oxford: Berg.

Gyekye, K, 1987. *An Essay in African Philosophical Thought*, Cambridge: Cambridge University Press.

Hall, M. 1987. *The Changing Past*, Cape Town: D.Philip.

Hart, A. 1994. 'Missing masculinity? prostitute's clients in Alicante, Spain', in A. Cornwall and N. Lindisfarne (eds), *Dislocating Masculinity*, London: Routledge.

Hegel, G.W.F. 1807. *Phenomenology of Spirit*, (transl. A.V. Miller 1977) Oxford: Oxford University Press.

—— 1892. *The Logic of Hegel*, (transl. W.Wallace) Oxford: Oxford University Press.

Heidegger, M. 1962. *Being and Time*, Oxford: Blackwell.

—— 1994. *Basic Questions of Philosophy*, Bloomington: Indiana University Press.

Herbert, E.W. 1993. *Iron, Gender and Power*, Bloomington: Indiana University Press.

Holm, J. 1994. (ed.) *Attitudes to Nature*, London: Pinter Publ.

Holy, L. 1986. *Strategies and Norms in a Changing Matrilineal Society*, Cambridge: Cambridge University Press.

Hountondji, P.J. 1983. *African Philosophy, Myth and Reality*, London: Hutchinson.

Howell, S. and M. Melhuus 1993. 'The study of kinship: the study of person: the study of gender?', in T. Del Valle (ed.), *Gendered Anthropology*, London: Routledge.

Hunn, E. 1982. 'The utilitarian factor in folk biological classification', *Amer.Anthrop.* 84, 830–47.

Idowu. E.B. 1973. *African Traditional Religion*, London: SCM Books.

Ingold, T. 1980. *Hunters, Pastoralists and Ranchers*, Cambridge: Cambridge University Press.

—— 1986. *The Appropriation of Nature*, Manchester: Manchester University Press.

—— 1991a. 'From trust to domination: an alternative history of human-animal relations'. Paper, Conference: Animals and Society, Royal Society, Edinburgh.

—— 1991b. 'Becoming persons: consciousness and sociality in human evolution', *Cultural Dynamics* 4, 355–78.

—— 1996. 'Hunting and gathering as ways of perceiving the environment', in R. Ellen and K. Fukui (eds), *Redefining Nature*, Oxford: Berg.

Jackson, M. 1989. *Paths Towards a Clearing*, Bloomington: Indiana University Press.

Jacobson-Widding, A. and W. van Beek 1990 (eds), *The Creative Communion*, Stockholm: Almquist and Wiksell.

James, W. 1978. 'Matrifocality and African women', in S. Ardener (ed.), *Defining Females*, London: Croom Helm.

Janzen, J.M. 1978. *The Quest for Therapy in Lower Zaire*, Berkeley: Univ,California Press.

—— 1992. *Ngoma*, Berkeley: University California Press.

Johnson, M. 1987. *The Body in the Mind*, Chicago: University Chicago Press.

—— 1993. *Moral Imagination*, Chicago: University Chicago Press

Jonas, H. 1966. *The Phenomenon of Life*, Chicago: University Chicago Press.

Junod, H.A. 1927. *The Life of a South African Tribe*, (2 vols) Neuchatel: Attinger Press.

Kagame, A. 1956. *La Philosophie Bantu-Rwandaise de l'etre*, Brussels: Academie Royal de Sciences Coloniales.

Kant, I. 1934. *Critique of Pure Reason*, London: Dent.

Katcher, A.H. and A.M. Beck 1991. 'Animal companions', in M.H. Robinson and L. Tiger (eds), *Man and Beast Revisited*, Washington: Smithsonian Inst.

Kellert, S.R. 1988. 'Human-animal interactions', in A. Rowan (ed.), *Animals and People Sharing the World*, Hanover: University Press of New England.

Kensinger, K.M. 1989. 'Hunting and male domination in Cashinahua society', in S. Kent (ed.), *Farmers as Hunters*, Cambridge: Cambridge University Press.

Kent, S. 1989. (ed.), *Farmers as Hunters*, Cambridge: Cambridge University Press

Kesby, J. 1979. 'The Rangi classification of animals and plants', in R.F. Ellen & D. Reason (eds), *Classifications in their social context*, London: Academic Press.

—— 1986. *Rangi Natural History*, New Haven,Conn: Human Relations Area Files Inst.

Kopytoff, I. 1971. 'Ancestors as elders in Africa', *Africa* 41/2, 129–42.

Krell, D.F. 1978. *Basic Writings: Martin Heidegger*, London: Routledge.

Krige, J.D. and E.J. 1943. *The Realm of a Rain Queen*, London: I.A.I. and Oxford University Press.

Kripke, S.A. 1972. *Naming and Necessity*, Cambridge, Mass.: Harvard University Press.

Kuper, A. 1982. *Wives for Cattle*, London: Routledge & Kegan Paul.

Laguerre, M. 1987. *Afro-Caribbean Folk Medicine*, S.Hadley, Mass: Bergin & Garvey.

Lakoff, G. and M. Johnson 1980. *Metaphors We Live By*, Chicago: University Chicago Press.

Lawrence, E.A. 1982. *Rodeo: An Anthropologist Looks at the Wild and the Tame*, Knoxville: University Tenessee Press.

—— 1990. 'Rodeo horses: the wild and the tame', in R. Willis (ed.), *Signifying Animals*, London: Unwin Hyman.

Leach, E. 1961. *Rethinking Anthropology*, London: Athlone.

—— 1964. 'Anthropological aspects of language: animal categories and verbal abuse', in E. Lennenberg (ed.), *New Directions in the Study of Language*, Cambridge, Mass.: M.I.T. Press.

Lee, R.B. 1979. T*he !Kung San: Men, Women and Work in a Foraging Society*, Cambridge: Cambridge University Press.

Lerner, G. 1986. *The Creation of Patriarchy*, New York: Oxford University Press.

Lévi-Strauss, C. 1966. *The Savage Mind*, London: Wiedenfeld & Nicolson.

Lewis, I.M. 1991. 'The spider and the pangolin', *Man* 26, 513–25.

Liebenberg, L. 1990. *The Art of Tracking*, Claremont: David Philip.

Linares, O.F. 1976. '"Garden hunting" in the American Tropics', *Human Ecology* 44/4, 331–49.

Loizos, P. 1994. 'A broken mirror: masculine sexuality in Greek ethnography', in A. Cornwall and N. Lindisfarne (eds), *Dislocating Masculinity*, London: Routledge.

Lovejoy, A.O. 1948. *Essays in the History of Ideas*, New York: Johns Hopkins Press.

MacCormack, C. and M.Strathern 1980. (eds), *Nature, Culture and Gender*, Cambridge: Cambridge University Press.

MacGaffey, W. 1983. 'Lineage structure: marriage and family amongst the central Bantu', *Journal African History* 24, 173–87.

MacKenzie, J.M. 1987. 'Chivalry, social Darwinism and ritualised hunting: the hunting ethos in Central Africa up to 1914', in D. Anderson & R. Grove (eds), *Conservation in Africa*, Cambridge: Cambridge University Press.

—— 1988. *The Empire of Nature*, Manchester: Manchester University Press.

Marcus, G.E. 1995. 'The redesign of ethnography after the critique of its rhetoric', in R. Goodman & W.R. Fisher (eds), *Rethinking Knowledge*, Albany: State University New York Press.

Marks, S.A. 1976. *Large Mammals and a Brave People*, Seattle: University Washington Press.

Marshall, P. 1992. *Nature's Web*, London: Simon & Schuster.

Mayr, E. 1982. *The Growth of Biological Thought*, Cambridge, Mass.: Harvard University Press.

—— 1988. *Toward a New Philosophy of Biology*, Cambridge Mass.: Harvard University Press.

Mazrui, A.A. 1986. *The Africans: a Triple Heritage*, London: BBC Publ.

Mbiti, J.S. 1969. *African Religions and Philosophy*, London: Heinemann.

Meena, R. (ed.) 1992. *Gender in Southern Africa*, Harare: Sapes Books.

Merchant, C. 1980. *The Death of Nature*, London: Wildwood House.

—— 1992. *Radical Ecology*, London: Routledge.

Bibliography

Moore, H.L. 1988. *Feminism and Anthropology*, Cambridge: Polity Press.
—— 1994. 'Understanding sex and gender', in T. Ingold (ed.), *Companion Encyclopedia of Anthropology*, London: Routledge.
Moore, S.F. 1994. *Anthropology and Africa*, Charlottesville: University Press of Virginia.
Morris, B. 1976. 'Whither the savage mind? Notes on the natural taxonomies of a hunting and gathering people', *Man* 11, 542–57.
—— 1978. 'Ecology and mysticism' *Freedom*, May pp. 9–16
—— 1979. 'Scientific myths: man the mighty hunter', *New Humanist*, Feb., pp. 129–30
—— 1979 'Symbolism and ideology: thoughts around Navaho taxonomy and symbolism, in R.F. Ellen and D. Reason (eds), *Classifications in Their Social Context*, London: Academic Press pp. 117–38.
—— 1981. 'Changing views of nature', *The Ecologist* 11, 130–37.
—— 1982. *Forest Traders*, London: Athlone Press.
—— 1983. 'The Truth about Baden-Powell and the Boy Scouts', *New Humanist* 98, 5–8.
—— 1986d. *Many Ways of Healing*, Unpublished manuscript.
—— 1987. *Anthropological Studies of Religion*, Cambridge: Cambridge University Press.
—— 1989a. 'Ayurveda and the myth of Indian spirituality', *Man & Life* 15, 103–21.
—— 1989b, 'Thoughts on Chinese medicine', *Eastern Anthropology* 42, 1–33.
—— 1991. *Western Conceptions of the Individual*, Oxford: Berg.
—— 1998. 'Matriliny and Mother Goddess religion', *J. Contemporary Religion* 13/1, 91–102.
Mudimbe, V.Y. 1988. *The Invention of Africa*, Bloomington: Indiana University Press.
Murdoch, I. 1992. *Metaphysics as a Guide to Morals*, Harmondsworth: Penguin.
Nash, R. 1967. *Wilderness and the American Mind*, New Haven: Yale University Press.
Needham, R. 1973. (ed.), *Right and Left: Essays in Dual Symbolic Classification*, Chicago: Chicago University Press.
Nelson, R. 1983. *Make Prayers to the Raven*, Chicago: Chicago University Press.
Ngubane, H. 1977. *Body and Mind in Zulu Medicine*, London: Academic Press.
Ojoade, J.O. 1990. 'Nigerian cultural attitudes to the dog', in R. Willis (ed.), *Signifying Animals*, London: Unwin Hyman.

Okely, J. and H. Callaway 1992. *Anthropology and Autobiography*, London: Routledge.

O'Neill, J. 1993. *Ecology, Policy and Politics*, London: Routledge.

Ortner, S.B. 1974. 'Is female to make as nature is to culture', in M.Z. Rosaldo and L. Lamphere (eds), *Woman, Culture and Society*, Stanford University Press.

Poewe, K. 1981. *Matrilineal Ideology*, London: Academic Press

Posey, D.A. 1984. 'Hierarchy and Utility in Folk Biological Taxonomic Systems', *Journal of Ethnobiology* 4, 123–34.

Putnam. H. 1975. 'The meaning of "Meaning"', in K. Gunderson (ed.), *Language, Mind and Knowledge*, Minneapolis: University Minnesota Press.

—— 1992. *Renewing Philosophy*, Cambridge, Mass.: Harvard University Press.

Randall, R. 1987. 'The nature of highly inclusive fold botanical categories', *Amer.Anthrop.* 89, 143–46.

Richards, A.I. 1939. *Land, Labour and Diet in Northern Rhodesia*, I.A.I. and Oxford: Oxford University Press.

—— 1950. 'Some types of family structure amongst the Central Bantu', in A.R. Radcliffe-Brown & C.D. Forde (ed.), *African Systems of Kinship and Marriage*, London: Oxford University Press.

—— 1956. *Chisungu*, London: Tavistock.

Riesman, P. 1986. 'The person and the life cycle in African social life and thought', *Afr.Stud.Review* 29/2, 71–138.

Ritvo, H. 1987. *The Animal Estate*, Harmondsworth: Penguin.

Rogers, B. 1980. *The Domestication of Women*, London: Tavistock

Rosaldo, M. and J. Atkinson 1975. 'Man the hunter and woman', in R. Willis (ed.), *The Interpretation of Symbolism*, London: Malaby Press.

Rosch, E. 1978. 'Principles of categorisation', in E. Rosch and B. Lloyd (eds), *Cognition and Categorisation*, Hillsdale, NJ: Lawrence Erlbaum.

Rowan, A.N. 1991. 'The human-animal interface', in M.H. Robinson and L. Tiger (eds), *Man and Beast Revisited*, Washington: Smithsonian Inst. Press.

Safilios-Rothschild, C. 1994. 'Agricultural policies and women producers', in A. Adepoju and C. Oppong (eds), *Gender, Work and Population in Sub-Saharan Africa*, London: James Currey.

Schneider, D.M. 1961. 'The distinctive features of matrilineal descent groups', in D.M. Schneider and K. Gough (eds), *Matrilineal Kinship*, Berkeley: University California Press.

Scudder, T. 1962. *The Ecology of the Gwembe Tonga*, Manchester: Manchester University Press.

Serpell, J. 1986. *In the Company of Animals*, Oxford: Blackwell.

Siskind, J. 1973. *To Hunt in the Morning*, New York: Oxford University Press.

Short, J.R. 1991. *Imagined Country*, London:Routledge.

Soper, K. 1995. *What is Nature?*, Oxford: Blackwell.

Spretnak, C. 1991. *States of Grace*, San Francisco: Harper.

Stefaniszyn, B. 1954. 'African Reincarnation re-examined', *African Studies* 13, 131–46.

Steinhart, E.I. 1989. 'Hunters, poachers and gamekeepers' *Journal of African History* 30, 247–64.

Stolcke, V. 1993. 'Is sex to gender as race is to ethnicity', in T. Del Valle (ed.), *Gendered Anthropology*, London: Routledge.

Strathern, M. 1980. 'No nature; no culture: the Hagen case', in C. MacCormack and M. Strathern (eds), *Nature, Culture and Gender*, Cambridge: Cambridge University Press.

—— 1988. *The Gender of the Gift*, Berkeley: University California Press

—— 1990. 'Out of context: the persuasive fictions of anthropology', in M. Manganaro (ed.), *Modernist Anthropology*, Princeton University Press.

Tambiah, S.J. 1969. 'Animals are good to think and good to prohibit', *Ethnology* 8, 424–59.

Tanner, A. 1979. *Bringing Home Animals*, London: Hurst.

Tempels, P. 1959. *Bantu Philosophy*, Paris: Presence Africaine

Turner, E. 1992. *Experiencing Ritual*, Philadelphia: University Pennsylvania Press.

Turner, V.W. 1957. *Schism and Continuity in an African Society*, Manchester: Manchester University Press.

—— 1967. *The Forest of Symbols*, Ithaca: Cornell University Press.

—— 1968. *The Drums of Affliction*, Oxford: Clarendon Press.

—— 1975. *Revelation and Divination in Ndembu Ritual*, Ithaca: Cornell University Press.

van Beek, W.E. and P.M. Banga 1992. 'The Dogon and their trees', in E. Croll and D. Parkin (eds), *Bush Base: Forest Farm*, London: Routledge.

van Den Berghe, P. 1979. *Human Family Systems*, New York: Elsevier.

van Der Breemer, J.P.M. 1992. 'Ideas and usage: environment in Aouan society, Ivory Coast', in E. Croll and D. Parkin (eds), *Bush Base: Forest Farm*, London: Routledge.

White, C.M.N. 1948. 'Witchcraft, divination and magic among the Balouale tribes', *Africa* 18, 81–104.

Walker, C. 1981. *Signs of the Wild*, Cape Town: Struik.

Weeks, J. 1986. *Sexuality*, London: Tavistock.

Weiss, F.G. 1974. *Hegel: the Essential Writings*, New York: Harper and Row.

Willis, R. 1974. *Man and Beast*, London: Paladin.

—— 1990. (ed.), *Signifying Animals*, London: Unwin Hyman.

Wiredu, K. 1981. 'Morality and religion in Akan thought', in H.O. Oruka and D.A. Masolo (eds), *Philosophy and Culture*, Nairobi: Bookwise.

Worster, D. 1985. *Nature's Economy*, Cambridge: Cambridge University Press.

Yanagisako, S.J. and J.F.Collier 1987. 'Toward a Unified Analysis of Gender and Kinship', in J.F.Collier and S.J.Yanagisako (eds), *Gender and Kinship*, Stanford: Stanford University Press.

Index

Abdallah, Y.B., 8
Adams, C., 186, 191
affinal male, 34, 73, 120
affinal relations, 34–37
African Lakes Corporation, 117
agriculture, 5, 8, 15, 17, 46, 51–54,
    58–59, 129
Alpers, E.A., 7, 65
Amadiume, I., 55–56
animals as food, 196–202
animals as medicine, 209, 218–233
Aristotle, 5, 125, 152, 168, 212–213, 217,
    233–234
arrow poison, 90–91
Atran, S. 136–138
attitudes to nature, 2, 4, 168–170

baboon, 201–2
Baden-Powell, R.S., 119
Banda clan, 19–20, 205
Banda, H.K., 11, 23
Bandawe, L., 9–10
banja, see family-household
Bemba, 63, 65, 67–68, 217, 219
Berglund, A., 15, 218
Berlin, B., 134–138
birds, 144–145
Bisa, 65, 67, 69, 115
Bloch, M., 211
Bly, R., 70–71
Boucher, C., 23
bows and arrows, 90, 103
Bradshaw, T.W., 94–95
Bruwer, J.P., 23
burial sites, 129, 197
bushbuck, 165, 197
bushpig, 233

capitalism, 17
    impact upon matriliny, 44–45
carnivores, 157–158, 237–238

chaos, 124
Chewa, 6–8, 10–11, 19, 24, 40–41, 114,
    129, 174, 219
chiefdoms, 40
Chikunda, 42–43, 114–115, 117
childbirth, 103
children 33–34
Chilembwe, J., 10
chinamwali, see initiation rites
chinjira relations, 27
Chipeta, 6–8
chirombo category, 148–150
chirope disease, 105–108
chiwengo skin disease, 207
chizimba, see medicines
Christian missionaries, 17–18
    impact on matriliny, 44
civet cat, 233
clan system, 18–21, 203–206
classification of mammals, 152–167
colour classification, 156
Comaroff, J. 126
concept of life, 140–141, 213
cooking of mice, 192
cosmology, 121, 132
Coudenhove, H., 196, 198
crop depredations, 94, 120
cross-cousin marriage, 24, 33, 36
cross-cousins, 32–33

Darwin, C., 1–2
Dedza highlands, 75–76
Department of National Parks and
    Wildlife, 95–96
Descartes, 125
Dickens, P., 234
dietary restrictions, 204–206
digging of mice, 78–79
Diop, A.C., 55
domestic animals, 149–151, 181, 193
domestic cat, 86

Index

domestic dog, 85–87
domestic slaves, 41
Dogon, 222
Douglas, M., 41, 64, 133, 214, 230–231
Drummond, H., 191
Duff, H., 173, 197

eland, 107
Eliade, M., 11, 123–124, 211–212, 233
Ellen, R., 138–40
Elliot, G., 175
essentialism, 48, 69
ethic of domination, 4–5, 74, 170, 209

family-household, 25, 28, 39, 51
father, 30
Faulkner, H., 117–118
female-headed households, 28, 51
Fiddes, N., 186, 208, 222
fieldwork, 12–14
Fipa, 172
fish, 145, 147
folk classifications, 15, 120–167
folk tales, 174–182
food, 186–188

game pits, 83
Gamitto, A., 18, 24, 203
gender, 46–50, 56–57, 69
    division of labour, 46, 53, 57, 60
giant rat, 201
Gilmore, D. 70–71
Goodman, F.D., 4
Goodman, N., 47
grandparents, 29–30

hare, 177–178, 185
Hayes, G.D., 88
hedgehog, 229
Hegel, G.W.F., 14, 133
Heidegger, M., 168–170
herbalism, 216
herbalist, 155, 215–216, 228
Herbert, E.W., 48, 69
Hill Pandaram, 3–4, 67, 134
hot/cold symbolism, 97, 102–103,
    107–108, 110
hunger season, 58, 189
hunter-gatherers, 2, 67, 74–75

hunting, 5, 15, 61–119
    commercial, 118, 170
    communal hunt, 74, 88–94
    elephant, 62, 66, 117
    hippopotamus, 83–84, 115–116
    individual, 85, 87–88
    masculinity, 69–74
    political aspects, 113–18
    procreative paradigm, 112
    ritual aspects, 97, 102–105
    skills, 87–88
    sporting, 119
    use of fire, 89, 92
hyena, 180, 209–210, 232

initiation rites, 22, 50, 59, 72, 190, 215,
    221
insects, 148, 189
iron-age, 75, 109
iron-smelting, 8–9, 109–112
ivory trade, 62, 114–118

Janzen, J., 210–212, 217
Johnson, M., 122–123, 140
Jonas, H., 142

Kandawire, J., 41, 45
Kanjanga, H., 221
Kant, I., 122, 133
kanyera disease, 103
Kaphirintiwa, 7
Kasungu National Park, 110
Kent, S., 62
Kenyatta, J., 56
Kesby, J., 146
Killick, D., 109
kinship categories, 28–36
Kololo, 43, 116–117
Kufa, J.G., 10
Kuper, A., 21

labour co-operation, 26, 54
land, 25
Lawson, A., 22, 30, 33, 37
legumes, 189
Lele, 64, 172, 230–231
Levi-Strauss, C., 134–135, 171, 204
Lewis, I.M., 231
life-form categories, 140, 148–149

Index

Linden, I., 19
lion, 179
Livingstone, D., 8, 11, 109, 115
Liwonde National Park, 97
Lomwe, 6, 9–11, 53, 202
long-distance trade, 5
Lovejoy, A., 125
Luapula, 18

MacDonald, D., 41, 56
MacKenzie, J.M., 119
Mair, L., 33, 38
Makua, 7, 9, 65
Makwawa, 13
Mandala, E.C., 22, 25, 28
Mang'anja, 6, 10
mankhwala, see medicine
manyumba rite, 130
Maravi, 6–8, 10, 18
Marks, S., 67–69
marriage, 22, 37–39
Marwick, M., 15, 18, 24, 29, 32, 219
masculinity, 69–74
matrilineal kinship, 1, 15, 17–46, 55
    social change, 40–46
Maugham, R.C., 118
Mayr, E. 137
mbalame, see birds
mbewa category, 77–79, 155–156,
    161–162, 166, 200, 239–240
Mbiti, J., 141
Mbo, 7
mbumba, see sororate group
mdulo disease, 103
Mead, M., 69
meat, 15, 94, 105, 186, 192–195
medical systems, 214
medicine, 15, 68, 104, 211, 215–129
    activating, 68, 105, 110, 217–222, 227,
        229
    destructive, 227
    hunting, 104–106
    protective, 220
Meena, R., 56
menstruation, 102–103, 111
metallurgy, 48
migrant labour, 54
Mitchell, J.C., 7, 21, 25, 33, 39, 42, 126
mizimu, see spirits of the ancestors

mkamwini, see affinal male
Moore, H., 47–48
Moslems, 203
mother, 30
mother's brother, 31, 72
mtengo, see plants
mudzi, see village community
mushrooms, 58, 110, 143, 189
muzzle-loading guns, 85, 97
Mwale clan, 205

names, 21, 36
nature/culture dualism, 125
Navaho, 139
Ndembu, 64–65, 67, 219, 233
neolithic revolution, 4
neoplatonic interpretations, 211–212, 232
Nettel, S., 27
netting of animals, 84, 92
New Guinea, 125
Ngoni, 7–8, 11, 17, 43, 52
Ngoni clan totems, 206
Ngubane, H., 218
njoka, see snakes
Nkhoma clan, 205–206
noun classes, 152–154
nsomba, see fish
Nsenga, 6
Ntara, S., 93
Ntumba, 7
Nuaula, 138
Nuer, 172
Nurse, G.D., 20, 204
nyama category, 76, 107–109, 146–148,
    222
Nyanja, 6
Nyasaland Nutrition Survey, 53–54
nyau rituals, 131

oral traditions, 15
oral literature, 173–182

pangolin, 230–231
parents, 30–31
parents-in-law, 36
pfuko, see clan system
Phiri clan, 19–20, 205
Phiri, K.M., 40, 43, 45
Phirilongwe mountain, 91

Index

Phodzo, 115–116
plants, 142–43, 215
Plato, 6, 123–125, 217, 233
poaching, 95–97
Poewe, K., 18
porcupine, 229–230
postmodernism, 12, 14
Price, T., 131
procreation, 108
procreative paradigm, 112–113
progressive farmers, 53, 55
proverbs, 182–184, 237–241
Putnam, H., 47, 122

Rangi, 146
Read, M., 45
realism, 148
relish, 188–189
Richards, A., 15, 23, 63, 65, 67–68, 217, 219
riddles, 182–184
ritual coitus, 232
rituals of affliction, 210, 215
Rogers, B., 45–46

Sanderson, M., 36
Schoffeleers, M., 23, 131–132, 146
school essays, 184–185
Scott, D.C.,195
seasons, 58–60
Serpell, J., 4
sex categories, 49
sexual relations, 47, 97, 102, 111
sexual symbolism, 112
sharing of meat, 67–68, 93
siblings, 31–32
snakes, 144–146
snaring animals, 80
sing'anga, see herbalist
sociobiology, 48
sororate group, 21–27, 57
spirits of ancestors, 23, 104, 108, 110,
        129–130, 141–142, 213
    offerings made to, 104
Spring, A., 58
spring traps, 80–81

Stannus, H., 195–196
Swahili traders, 43, 52
symbolic classifications, 121, 139,
        171–172

Tambiah, S.J., 171
Taoists, 233
territorial chief, 24–25, 113, 117–118
textualism, 13–14
Thailand, 171
Thomson, J., 57
tortoise, 178–179
trapping animals, 79–84
Tumbuka, 6
Turner, E., 219
Turner, V.W., 15, 64–65, 217, 219, 233

ungulates, 159–160, 238–239
unkhoswe insitution, see marriage
utilitarian approach to classification, 134,
        136

Vail, L., 11, 54
Vaughan, M., 25–26, 28
vegetables, 188–189
village community, 21, 26, 124, 126–128
    harmony within, 26
    head, 21–22, 91
Vwaza Marsh Game researve, 96–97

Werner, A., 174
White, L., 216–217
Williamson, J., 190–191
Willis, R., 171–172
witchcraft, 18
Wood, R.C., 89
woodland, 124, 127–130

Yao, 6, 8–9, 21, 24, 103, 222, 232
Young, E.D., 27, 115, 190
Young, T.C., 7, 11, 19
Young, W.P., 107

Zimba, 116, 221
Zimbiri clan, 205
Zulu, 218